"As a former seminarian and current pastor and evangelist, I've recently sensed a more urgent need to teach Christians theology while also noticing how difficult it is to teach anyone almost anything of true substance in our distracted, screen-addicted culture. That is why I was excited to see my friend Channing Crisler write *40 Questions About the Atonement*. This is a truly helpful book written in a format that is easy to read for the student, the scholar, and the everyday believer who only has 15 minutes to spare on their lunch break. It's conversational. It's also both biblical and practical, which I find refreshing as well as spiritually nourishing. I think this book is a gift to the church as well as the academy."

—Clayton King,
Pastor, evangelist, and author of *Reborn* and *Stronger*

"On a single page, Channing Crisler references J. I. Packer and Mark Dever, Anselm of Canterbury, Georges Florovsky, Richard Hays, and 1 Corinthians—an approach indicative of the book as a whole: saturated in Scripture, sensitive to the history of the church, ecumenical in scope but evangelical in spirit, and attuned to the breadth, depth, and nuances of this great doctrine. For those who have questions about the death and resurrection of Jesus, this is a great resource capturing the spirit of a joyful, charitable, and confident evangelicalism."

—Adam Johnson,
Associate Professor of Theology,
Torrey Honors College, Biola University

40 QUESTIONS ABOUT
The Atonement

Channing L. Crisler

Benjamin L. Merkle, Series Editor

40 Questions About the Atonement
© 2025 Channing L. Crisler

Published by Kregel Academic, an imprint of Kregel Publications, 2450 Oak Industrial Dr. NE, Grand Rapids, MI 49505-6020.

This book is a title in the 40 Questions Series edited by Benjamin L. Merkle.

ISBN 978-0-8254-4592-7

Cataloging-in-Publication Data is available from the Library of Congress

Printed in the United States of America
25 26 27 28 29 / 5 4 3 2 1

*To all those like me who sometimes still think
(wrongly) that they must atone for their owns sins.
May you find the answer in Christ.*

Contents

Part 4: The Logic of Atonement

Part 5: The Implications of Christ's Atoning Work

Abbreviations

AF	The Apostolic Fathers: Greek Texts and English Translations, 3rd ed.
BDAG	Danker, Frederick W., Walter Bauer, William F. Arndt, and F. Wilbur Gingrich. *Greek-English Lexicon of the New Testament and Other Christian Literature*, 3rd ed. Chicago: University of Chicago Press, 2000.
BrillDAG	*The Brill Dictionary of Ancient Greek*
CCC	*Catholic Catechism of the Catholic Church*, 2nd ed.
CLD	*Collins Latin Dictionary*
FC	Formula of Concord 1577
GELS	Muraoka's Greek-English Lexicon of the Septuagint
HALOT	*The Hebrew and Aramaic Lexicon of the Old Testament*
Inst.	John Calvin's *Institutes of the Christian Religion*
LC	Martin Luther's Large Catechism
LEH	Greek-English Lexicon of the Septuagint, rev. ed.
LW	*Luther's Works*, ed. Christopher Boyd Brown, 79 vols. St. Louis: Concordia, 1955–2022.
LXX	Septuagint
MT	Masoretic Text
NT	New Testament
OED	*Oxford English Dictionary*
OT	Old Testament
TAL	*The Annotated Luther*
WBC	Word Biblical Commentary
YHWH	Representation of a key Old Testament name for God

Introduction

The Christian faith as it is revealed in Scripture rises or falls on the doctrine of atonement. If we rightly understand what God has accomplished in the crucified and risen Christ, the church rises wisely, lovingly, and powerfully in its fellowship and mission. If we fail to rightly understand this atoning work, the church surely falls and stumbles in a way that hurts not only God's people but also a sinful world in desperate need of redemption. The stakes are obviously high.

Complicating matters is that the early church never articulated a definitive doctrine of atonement in the vein of its official christological and Trinitarian positions. Consequently, subsequent generations of Christian thinkers have articulated the doctrine in different ways and with different emphases. Not surprisingly, these differences have produced passionate debates and disagreements. Questions abound regarding the manner, means, and results of God's atoning work in Christ. These questions have been explored for centuries in numerous writings that represent an ongoing conversation. This book is my humble attempt to join that conversation. More importantly, this book brings the reader more firmly into that conversation by answering key questions about how God and people are reconciled to one another. Nothing is more important and rewarding than discussing Christ's atoning work. Of course, it is not merely a discussion. Nothing less than eternal life hangs in the balance, as we seek to understand the one who hung on a Roman cross for sinners like us.

I want to thank Ben Merkle for the opportunity to write this volume for the 40 Questions series. I would also like to thank my children, my church, my colleagues, and my students for the various ways they have contributed to this work.

—Channing L. Crisler
Domine memento mei

PART 1

The Need for Atonement

General Questions

What Is the Origin and Meaning of the Word "Atonement"?

> *For God was in Christ, and made agreement between the world*
> *and himself, and imputed not their sins unto them: and hath*
> *committed to us the preaching of the atonement.*[1]
> ~Tyndale Translation of 2 Corinthians 5:19

Biblical translation is a form of interpretation that can have a lasting effect on the theological vocabulary and formation of its readers. Such an effect is exemplified in the work of William Tyndale (1494–1536), a sixteenth-century English Protestant Reformer whose crowning achievement is his translation of the New Testament into English.[2] Tyndale based his translation on Desiderius Erasmus's 1516 critical edition of the Greek NT, Jerome's Latin Vulgate, and Martin Luther's 1522 German translation of the NT.[3] Tyndale's translation introduced some English terms that subsequently came to be associated with key theological concepts. One of those terms is "atonement," which stems from his translation of the Latin noun *reconciliātio* ("reconciliation") in 2 Corinthians 5:17, where Paul explains that God gave him a "ministry of reconciliation."[4] The term that stands behind Jerome's *reconciliātio* is

---

1. *Tyndale's New Testament*, ed. David Daniell, trans. William Tyndale (New Haven, CT: Yale University Press, 1989), 266.
2. Tyndale's 1526 edition of the NT began in Cologne (Germany); however, when city authorities forbade the continuation of the work, Peter Schoeffer's printing press finished it in Worms (Germany). Tyndale produced a revised translation in 1534. See David Daniell, *William Tyndale: A Biography* (New Haven, CT: Yale University Press, 1994), 134.
3. For an account of how Tyndale translated from these sources, see Daniell, *William Tyndale*, 108–51.
4. Tyndale uses the phrase "the preaching of the atonement" (*Tyndale's New Testament*, 266).

the Greek term *katallagē*. Moving from Paul to Jerome to Tyndale, we have *katallagē* → *reconciliātio* → *atonement*.

With this lexical progression in view, Tyndale's choice of the English word "atonement" must be understood in the context of the sixteenth-century English language.[5] The full meaning of the term is shaped by the adverb "at-one," which means "at one assent" or "at one accord."[6] Therefore, the full term "at-onement" bears the sense of "being at one again." Tyndale did not coin the term;[7] nevertheless, his use of "atonement" is unique in the sense that he employed it to translate a NT term that is related to God's reconciliation with sinners.

In this way, if we are to understand the meaning of the word "atonement" with its theological connotations, we must look to the biblical terms that stand behind it. We must specifically consider the terms that biblical writers employ to describe the way God reconciles himself to sinners. Three terms stand out in this regard.

Atonement Terminology in the Hebrew Bible

Kaphar in the Hebrew Bible often occurs in contexts defined by human agents who carry out divinely prescribed actions that restore a fractured relationship between God and the guilty party. The sense of *kaphar* in these contexts is often to "cover," "make amends," or "make atonement."[8] Most uses of *kaphar* occur in the Pentateuch, though not all are related to reconciliation.[9] The many uses that are related to reconciliation occasionally involve a fractured relationship between human beings, but they most often involve a fractured relationship between human beings and God. An example of the former is the rift between Jacob and Esau stemming from a stolen birthright. As Jacob makes his return to Canaan, he thinks to himself that he must offer something to Esau to make amends for the wrong done to him: "And you shall say, 'Moreover, your servant Jacob is behind us.' For he thought, 'I may *appease him* with the present that goes ahead of me, and afterward I shall see his face. Perhaps he will accept me'" (Gen. 32:20, italics added). The literal sense of *kaphar* in this verse is "cover his face" (translated "appease him"), which metaphorically refers to Jacob offering a present—in this case, hundreds of

---

5. See *OED*, s.v. "atonement."
6. *OED*, s.v. "atonement."
7. One of its earliest recorded instances in the English language occurs in Thomas More's *History of King Richard the Third*. See Thomas More, *The History of King Richard the Third: A Reading Edition* (Bloomington: Indiana University Press, 2005), 20–21. See also *OED*, s.v. "atonement."
8. See *HALOT*, s.v. "כָּפַר."
9. See the use of *kaphar* in Gen. 6:14; 32:21; Exod. 29:33, 36, 37; 30:10, 15, 16; 32:30; Lev. 1:4; 4:20, 26, 31, 35; 5:6, 10, 13, 16, 18, 26; 6:23; 7:7; 8:15, 34; 9:7; 10:17; 12:7, 8; 14:18, 19, 20, 21, 29, 31, 53; 15:15, 30; 16:6, 10, 11, 16, 17, 18, 20, 24, 27, 30, 32, 33, 34; 17:11; 19:22; 23:28; Num. 5:8; 6:11; 8:12, 19, 21; 15:25, 28; 17:11, 12; 25:13; 28:22, 30; 29:5; 31:50, 33; Deut. 21:8; 32:43.

animals (Gen 32:13–14)—that would result in Esau being favorably disposed toward him.[10]

Many Pentateuchal uses of *kaphar* involve prescribed offerings offered by appointed agents who serve in designated locations and in an approved manner that results in God's favorable disposition toward those who offer them. That is because, as John Hartley observes, the action "removes pollution" and "counteracts sin."[11] For example, priestly instructions in Leviticus 1–17 include, "Thus shall he do with the bull. As he did with the bull of the sin offering, so shall he do with this. And the priest shall *make atonement* for them, and they *shall be forgiven*" (Lev. 4:20, italics added).

Kaphar also occurs in contexts when an unexpected need for atonement arises. For example, in the aftermath of Korah's rebellion, God stands poised to consume the wilderness congregation as it continues to grumble against Moses and Aaron (Num. 16:41–50). Moses intercedes on behalf of the congregation by ordering Aaron to offer an atoning sacrifice: "And Moses said to Aaron, 'Take your censer, and put fire on it from off the altar and lay incense on it and carry it quickly to the congregation and *make atonement* for them, for wrath has gone out from the LORD; the plague has begun'" (Num. 16:46, italics added).[12]

Overall, OT writers most often use *kaphar* in contexts where a fissure between God and Israel requires action that would ultimately result in a restoration of the relationship. The action in question includes an offering prescribed by God and offered through agents appointed by him at a time, location, and in a manner approved by him. Israel needed the "cover" (*kaphar*), or protection, of a sacrifice that removed and counteracted sin. Without the restorative effect of the *kaphar*, Israel remained at enmity with God, which would ultimately lead to judgment against them.

Atonement Terminology in the LXX

Before assessing terminology related to Tyndale's use of "atonement" in the NT, let's briefly consider the Greek rendering of *kaphar* language from Israel's Scriptures. After all, the OT in its Greek form often shapes the language of NT writers.[13] In this regard, LXX translators consistently render the verb *kaphar* with *exilaskomai*. The latter term often bears the sense of "propitiate," "expiate," "make atonement," and "purge."[14] For example, in the instructions for priests in Leviticus, a form of *exilaskomai* is used to translate *kaphar*: "And he will set his hand upon the head of the burnt offering, it is a thing acceptable

---

10. *HALOT*, s.v. "כפר."
11. John E. Hartley, *Leviticus*, WBC 4 (Nashville: Thomas Nelson, 1992), 64.
12. The chapter and verse in the MT are Num. 17:11.
13. On this point, see Karen H. Jobes and Moisés Silva, *Invitation to the Septuagint* (Grand Rapids: Baker Academic, 2000), 183–205.
14. GELS, s.v. "ἐξιλάσκομαι;" LEH, s.v. "ἐξιλάσκομαι."

for him to *propitiate* (*atone*) for him" (Lev. 1:4 LXX). Based on the wider use of *exilaskomai* in ancient Greek, the verb highlights the propitiating and/or expiating effect of a sacrifice.[15] While the NT does not use *exilaskomai*, it does use the cognates *hilaskomai* and *hilasmos*:

> Therefore, he had to be made like his brothers in every respect, so that he might become a merciful and faithful high priest in the service of God, to *make propitiation* for the sins of the people. (Heb. 2:17, italics added)

> He is the *propitiation* for our sins, and not for ours only but also for the sins of the whole world. (1 John 2:2, italics added; see also 1 John 4:10)

Both examples stress that Jesus's sacrifice "wipes out," or expiates, sin, which in turn propitiates, or causes, God to be favorably disposed to sinners. As we shall see in subsequent discussions, the expiating and propitiating effect of Jesus's death stands at the heart of reconciliation, or atonement.

Atonement Terminology in the NT

When we turn our attention to the NT, as noted above, the noun *katallagē* ultimately stands behind Tyndale's use of "atonement." The noun and its verbal cognate occur ten times in the Greek New Testament.[16] All ten occurrences are found in Romans, 1 Corinthians, and 2 Corinthians.[17] Key uses of *katallagē* and/or *katallassō* include:

> For if while we were enemies we were reconciled to God by the death of his Son, much more, now that we are *reconciled*, shall we be saved by his life. More than that, we also rejoice in God through our Lord Jesus Christ, through whom we have now received *reconciliation*. (Rom. 5:10–11, italics added)

> All this is from God, who through Christ *reconciled* us to himself and gave us the ministry of *reconciliation*; that is, in Christ God was reconciling the world to himself, not counting their trespasses against them, and entrusting to us the message of *reconciliation*. Therefore, we are ambassadors

---

15. *BrillDAG*, s.v. "ἐξιλάσκομαι."
16. For Paul's uses the noun *katallagē*, see Rom. 5:11; 11:15; 2 Cor. 5:18, 19. For his use of the verb *katallassō*, see Rom. 5:10 (x2); 1 Cor. 7:11; 2 Cor. 5:18, 19, 20. See BDAG, s.v. "καταλλαγή." See BDAG, s.v. "καταλλάσσω."
17. However, the use of *katallassō* in 1 Cor. 7:11 pertains to the reconciliation of a husband and wife.

for Christ, God making his appeal through us. We implore you on behalf of Christ, be *reconciled* to God. (2 Cor. 5:18–20, italics added)

Paul's thought in these two passages implies the meaning of reconciliation, or atonement, is robust in nature, for it serves as theological shorthand for *what* God's work in Christ accomplishes and *how* God accomplishes that work in him.

The robustness of reconciliation language can be summarized in five points based on the inferences drawn from these key Pauline texts: (1) God reconciles himself to sinful human enemies through the crucified and risen Jesus; (2) the present gift of reconciliation through Christ is the assurance of eschatological salvation; (3) God's reconciliation through Jesus is cosmic in scope; (4) cosmic reconciliation is shaped by Israel's story; and (5) God entrusted the ministry of reconciliation to human agents carried out through the proclamation of a reconciling message ("the word of reconciliation," 2 Cor. 5:19).

Summary

Tyndale's use of the word "atonement" to translate *reconciliātio*, behind which stands *katallagē*, represents an attempt to capture the grandeur of God's reconciling work in Christ for sixteenth-century English speakers. The term communicated to Tyndale's readers that God's work in Christ resulted in sinners "being at one again" (at-onement) with him. The scriptural terms standing behind "atonement" primarily include *kaphar, exilaskomai* (*hilaskomai, hilasmos*), and *katallagē*. In the wider contexts of their uses, the common theme that emerges is the need for a prescribed sacrifice that solves the enmity between God and human beings, because the sacrifice removes and counteracts sin in a way that makes God well disposed toward those who sin against him. Paul's reconciliation language reworks this scriptural theme around the person and work of Jesus. Although the overall meaning of atonement within Christian theology cannot be reduced to the meanings of individual words, the contextual uses of these words clearly establish its primary focus, namely, reconciliation between God and human beings through the life and death of the risen and reigning Jesus.

REFLECTION QUESTIONS

1. What role did William Tyndale play in the origin of the word "atonement" as it relates to its use in Christian theology?

2. How is the OT word *kaphar* related to the meaning of atonement?

3. What does the word *exilaskomai* in the LXX often emphasize?

4. How is the NT word *katallagē* related to the meaning of atonement?

5. From a scriptural standpoint, what is the primary focus of "atonement"?

Why Is the Doctrine of Atonement Important for Christian Doctrine?

Keep a close watch on yourself and on the teaching. Persist in this, for by so doing you will save both yourself and your hearers.

~1 Timothy 4:16

When Paul admonishes Timothy to keep a watchful eye on his "doctrine," he of course refers to what Timothy teaches. After all, the English term "doctrine" is derived from the Latin *doctrīna*, which Jerome uses to render the Greek term *didaskalia*, or "teaching."[1] I make this obvious point because the term "doctrine" is often synonymous with official positions of Christian orthodoxy forged in the christological crises of the early church and the first seven ecumenical councils (ca. AD 325–787).[2] These positions are then taken up for defense, reflection, expansion, and supplementation in subsequent generations by various faith traditions and household names like Augustine, Aquinas, Luther, Calvin, and Wesley. Such a development in doctrine is welcome and necessary. However, at its heart, doctrine simply refers to what the early church taught, what the church has taught since then, and what it teaches today.

The early church's teaching had a robust soteriological purpose, just as Jesus modeled (see 1 Tim. 4:16; 2 Tim. 3:15). Jesus summarized the totality of his teaching along soteriological lines:

---

1. BDAG, s.v. "διδασκαλία."
2. For a helpful account of these seven councils and their subsequent impact on Christianity, see Donald Fairbairn and Ryan M. Reeves, *The Story of Creeds and Confessions: Tracing the Development of the Christian Faith* (Grand Rapids: Baker Academic, 2019).

> If anyone hears my words and does not keep them, I do not judge him; for I did not come to judge the world but to save the world. The one who rejects me and does not receive my words has a judge; the word that I have spoken will judge him on the last day. (John 12:47–48)[3]

Along the same lines, when the apostles interpret the teaching, person, and work of Jesus, their message is thoroughly saving in nature, just as Peter pleaded with his audience at the end of his Pentecost sermon: "Save yourselves from this crooked generation" (Acts 2:40).[4] NT letters are thoroughly concerned with eschatological salvation as well.[5] This concern is neither secondary nor tertiary; it is definitive for all that Jesus and the apostles did. As Peter explains, salvation is "the outcome [*telos*] of your faith" (1 Peter 1:9). Even in James, where some suppose (wrongly) that soteriological concerns are at a minimum, we find an indispensable soteriological basis and focus for Christian wisdom: "Therefore put away all filthiness and rampant wickedness and receive with meekness the implanted word, which is able to *save* your souls" (James 1:21, italics added). And, of course, the OT, which provides the theological substructure of the NT and remains its best commentary, has a clear soteriological thrust given the importance of the exodus from Egypt and the hope of a new exodus carried out by the "God of salvation" (Ps. 68:20).

If soteriology then defines the heart of what Scripture teaches, and if Scripture informs Christian doctrine, it follows that Christian doctrine is thoroughly defined by soteriological concerns. Moreover, the doctrine of the atonement organizes and informs these soteriological concerns. Therefore, how one understands atonement has far-reaching implications for how related Christian doctrines will be understood and articulated. That is the broad answer to our question, "Why is the doctrine of atonement important to Christian doctrine?" Three specific examples are offered here.

Atonement Impacts Our Perception of God's Identity

"Identity of God" is a simple way of combining three interrelated doctrines: (1) the doctrine of God; (2) the doctrine of the Trinity; and (3) the doctrine of the person of Christ. Atonement theories, mechanisms, metaphors,

---

3. See also Matt. 10:22; 24:13; Mark 8:35; Luke 8:12; 9:24; 13:23; 18:26–27; 19:10; John 10:9.
4. See also Acts 2:21, 47; 4:12; 11:14; 13:26, 47; 5:1, 11; 16:17, 30.
5. See, e.g., the explicit soteriological emphases in Rom. 1:16–17; 1 Cor. 1:18–31; 2 Cor. 5:1–21; Gal. 2:15–21; 5:1–5; Eph. 2:1–10; Phil. 3:7–11; Col. 2:11–15; 1 Thess. 1:10; 5:1–11; 2 Thess. 2:13–14; 1 Tim. 1:12–17; 2 Tim. 1:8–11; Titus 3:3–7; Heb. 2:14–18; James 1:16–21; 1 Peter 1:3–12; 2 Peter 1:3–11; 1 John 2:1–2; 4:7–11; 1 John 5:5–11; Jude 1:24–25.

and emphases directly impact the articulation of these doctrines and thereby how one understands God's identity.[6]

To begin, one's atonement theory can influence how one conceives of fundamental issues within theology proper, such as the personal nature of God and his impassibility.[7] The Christian tradition agrees that God is personal in the sense that he forges personal relationships with those whom he creates. Along these relational lines, satisfaction/substitution atonement theories (Questions 13 and 16) locate the cause of relational discord between God and humans in sin and guilt. By contrast, ransom and *Christus Victor* views (Questions 9 and 12) tend to locate this relational discord in inimical powers such as evil, sin, and Satan. Consequently, different points of emphases emerge to describe how God acts to reconcile himself to people.

With respect to divine impassibility, if God does not "feel" the misery of sinners, as Aquinas held, how are we to understand Christ's atoning suffering?[8] Does he only suffer for sinners in his human nature, thereby leaving God unaffected/unchanged by the sinners' suffering? Or can God suffer vicariously through the atoning death of Christ without changing?[9] How one understands atonement can affect how one answers such questions.

Next, how we view atonement can affect how we understand the Trinity with respect to issues such as relational unity and distinctiveness within the Godhead. Did the Father punish his Son to reconcile himself to sinners (Questions 6 and 25)? What would punishment imply about the eternal relationship between Father and Son? How are Father, Son, and Spirit involved in the work of atonement? Does favoring one view of atonement over another alter how we understand the triune nature of God (Question 32)?

---

6. Some theologians prefer the term "mechanism" to "theory." As Oliver Crisp observes in discussing the meaning of atonement, "This issue has to do with the *mechanism* by means of which Christ reconciles us to God. Put slightly differently, if the atonement is that work of Christ that removes obstacles to communion with God (particularly with respect to human sin) and somehow makes it possible to be united with God in Christ by the power of the Holy Spirit, then how is that achieved? What has to happen in order for this goal to be brought about?" (Oliver D. Crisp, *Approaching the Atonement: The Reconciling Work of Christ* [Downers Grove, IL: IVP Academic, 2020], 3). Additionally, Colin E. Gunton suggests that Christian theology has tended to treat atonement "metaphors" as full-blown theories of atonement, which Gunton argues they really are not (see Colin E. Gunton, *The Actuality of Atonement: A Study of Metaphor, Rationality, and the Christian Tradition* [Grand Rapids: Eerdmans, 1989]).

7. For a discussion of these aspects of the doctrine of God and others, see Alister E. McGrath, *Christian Theology: An Introduction*, 2nd ed. (Oxford: Blackwell, 1997), 239–91.

8. McGrath explains divine impassibility by way of the following conditions: "If God is perfect, change in any direction is an impossibility. If God changes, it is either a move away from perfection (in which God is no longer perfect), or toward perfection (in which case, God was not perfect in the past)" (*Christian Theology*, 249).

9. On this point, see Daniel Castelo, "Impassibility (Divine)," in *T&T Clark Companion to Atonement*, ed. Adam J. Johnson (London: T&T Clark, 2017), 566.

Finally, Jesus's atoning work defines his identity and thereby the identity of the one who sent him.[10] Jesus's preexistence, teachings, miracles, death, resurrection, vindication, ascension, enthronement, return, and eternal reign all coalesce around his atoning work. Moreover, all divine attributes coalesce around Jesus's atoning work. To see the atoning work of Jesus is to see Jesus and thereby to see God as he really is (Question 40). It is no coincidence in his apocalyptic vision of eternity that John consistently refers to Jesus as the "Lamb."[11] The christological title in that context reminds readers that the eternal God is eternally defined by the atoning work of the crucified and risen Jesus.

Atonement Impacts Our Perception of the Doctrine of Salvation

As noted above, the early church's doctrine was thoroughly soteriological in its nature and focus. It promoted a "wisdom for salvation" (2 Tim. 3:15). Regardless of subsequent eras and shifts in culture, the church's teaching should preserve that soteriological aim for the sake of its own identity and its ministry to the world. With that said, while various stakeholders in Christianity might agree in principle that their teaching is soteriological in nature, they might disagree on what that entails, based on how they understand the atonement.

If Jesus's atoning work is primarily a shining example of self-sacrifice and love that inspires humanity to live in righteousness and holiness, as discussed in Question 10, then the accompanying doctrine of salvation would describe "deliverance" as a rescue from the evils of self-centeredness through means of Christlike charity, giving, and selflessness. Alternatively, if Jesus's atoning work is primarily a triumph over Satan and evil, then the doctrine of salvation would focus upon Jesus as the "Victor" over that which harms human beings and separates them from God (Question 9). Or if Jesus's atoning work demonstrates what God could do to sinners, and thereby exemplifies his moral government of the universe, the church would teach about salvation in terms of civil responsibility and just interaction between one another (Question 10). Or if Jesus's atoning work is perceived as a kind of satisfaction or compensation to God on the sinner's behalf, as discussed in Question 13, then a doctrine of salvation would accentuate how the crucified and risen Jesus meets the demands of God's holy and just nature.

Other examples could be mentioned here; however, the point should be clear. There is a direct correlation between how a church understands the atoning work of Christ and the kind of salvation in Christ the church teaches. The two issues are simply inseparable.

---

10. As Wolfhart Pannenberg asserts, "The divinity of Jesus and his freeing and redeeming significance for us are related in the closest possible way" (Wolfhart Pannenberg, *Jesus, God and Man*, trans. Lewis L. Wilkins and Duane A. Priebe, 2nd ed. [Philadelphia: Westminster, 1977], 38).

11. See, e.g., Rev. 5:12, 13; 6:1, 16; 7:9, 14; 12:11; 13:8; 14:1, 4, 10; 15:3; 17:14; 19:7, 9; 21:9, 14, 22, 27; 22:1, 3.

Atonement Impacts Our Perception of the Doctrine of Human Nature

Christ's atoning work defines the identity of people in all places and times.[12] The crucifixion of the eternal Son of God diagnoses the human condition. If the rift between God and humanity requires such drastic atoning measures, then surely people are in the worst of predicaments. Scripture defines that predicament within the triad of "dead" in sins, enslaved to Satan, and under God's just wrath (see, e.g., Eph. 2:1–3; Question 5).

However, the death of Christ gauges the depth of that condition. To be dead in sin is not merely to do the wrong thing. It is the inescapable ability only to do the wrong thing. To be enslaved to Satan is not merely to be influenced by him. It is to do his will rather than God's. To be under God's wrath is not to face his temporal displeasure but eternal condemnation. Christ's atoning death then amplifies the pitiful depth of the human condition and makes its misery axiomatic.

Summary

Christ's atoning work impacts more doctrines than the ones discussed above. It, in fact, touches on every aspect of the Christian tradition, including pneumatology (Question 32), eschatology (Questions 38 and 39), and reconciliation between humans (Question 37). Therefore, atonement stands at the heart of what the church should preserve and teach, which is why we must think carefully about how we understand God's reconciliation of himself to humanity.

REFLECTION QUESTIONS

1. What is "doctrine" in the simplest sense?

2. How are the church's teaching and salvation related to one another?

3. Why does atonement matter to the doctrines of God, the Trinity, and salvation?

4. What does Jesus's atoning work say about the human condition?

5. What other doctrines are shaped by our understanding of atonement?

---

12. Despite incessant talk about "generations" from Gen X to millennials to Gen Z, people do not change as dramatically as we sometimes think. From a biblical perspective, humanity has not fundamentally changed since Eden. People are still sinful. Satan still blinds and tempts. The earth is still cursed. And God's wrath remains upon his very good creation. In fact, the unchanging nature of humanity and Christ's atoning work at the cross for all those who believe, regardless of the historical era, work hand in hand.

How Significant Was the Preaching of the Death of Jesus in the Early Church?

> *But we preach Christ crucified, a stumbling block to Jews and folly to Gentiles.*
>
> ~1 Corinthians 1:23

The NT indicates that preaching and teaching played a prominent role in the life of the early church.[1] Didactic and transformative proclamation occurred publicly in synagogues and agoras and privately in house churches scattered across the Mediterranean. With respect to its homiletical content and aim, the early church's preaching was thoroughly "Christopository."[2] "Christopository" means that early Christians preached about Christ exclusively based on apostolic testimony, early Jesus tradition, early Christian teaching, and Israel's Scriptures. "Christo-exposition," and not merely "exposition," is an exegetical and homiletical practice the early church learned from Jesus himself who, just prior to his ascension, "opened up" the apostles' minds to understand the Scriptures solely in relation to himself (Luke 23:45; see also Luke 24:27, 46–47).

---

1. For works on preaching in the early church, see, e.g., Jonathan L. Griffiths, *Preaching in the New Testament: An Exegetical and Biblical-Theological Study*, New Studies in Biblical Theology 42 (Downers Grove, IL: IVP Academic, 2017); St. Irenaeus of Lyons, *On the Apostolic Preaching*, trans. John Behr (Crestwood, NY: St. Vladimir's Press, 1997); and William D. Shiell, "Preaching, First-Century," in *Dictionary of Paul and His Letters*, eds. Scot McKnight, Lynn H. Cohick, and Nijay K. Gupta, 2nd ed. (Downers Grove, IL: IVP Academic, 2023), 845–53.

2. To my knowledge, "Christopository" is not a term currently employed in discussions on early Christian preaching or the modern field of homiletics. Adjacent phrases such as "Christocentric," "Christ-centered," "Christiconic," and "Cruciform" are part of homiletic jargon. See, e.g., Scott M. Gibson and Matthew D. Kim, eds., *Homiletics and Hermeneutics: Four Views on Preaching Today* (Grand Rapids: Baker Academic, 2018).

In preaching Christ exclusively, his death lent explanatory power to everything that was said about him. As Paul told the Corinthians, "For I decided to know nothing among you except Jesus Christ and him crucified" (1 Cor. 2:2). This does not mean that Paul announced Jesus's death and nothing more. It means that Paul, whether addressing believers or unbelievers, always preached and taught Jesus as the crucified one, with all the implications of that identity for his followers.

Paul is not alone in this emphasis, though other apostles, witnesses, and NT writers did not express it in the same way. Even in its diverse expressions, early Christian preaching shared the same essential elements. In his classic work *The Apostolic Preaching and Its Developments*, C. H. Dodd identified the essential elements of early Christian preaching.[3] Matthew Bates summarizes those elements in an eight-point outline: (1) "Jesus preexisted with the Father"; (2) "Jesus took on human flesh, fulfilling God's promises to David"; (3) "Jesus died for sins in accordance with the Scriptures"; (4) "Jesus was buried"; (5) "Jesus was raised on the third day according to the Scriptures"; (6) "Jesus appeared to many"; (7) "Jesus is seated at the right hand of God as Lord"; and (8) "Jesus will come again."[4] As I will discuss here and in Question 4, Jesus's death plays the central role in all eight elements, which in turn has implications for how early Christians understood the atoning value of that death.

The Centrality of Jesus's Death in Early Christian Preaching

That Jesus "preexisted with the Father" is an essential element of early Christian preaching, but it did not occur in a vacuum. In fact, its significance is most often explained in relation to Jesus's death. John quantifies God's love for the world by the fact that he sends his only preexistent Son to the cross (John 3:16).[5] Paul measures Jesus's obedience to God in terms of the preexistent Son not "grasping" his equality with God but humbling himself and being obedient "to the point of death, even death on a cross" (Phil. 2:6–8).

In following Dodd's outline, Jesus's incarnation fulfilled the prior promise to David that one of his descendants would reign on his throne forever (2 Sam. 7:10–14).[6] NT writers discuss the significance of that promise in relation to

---

3. C. H. Dodd, *The Apostolic Preaching and Its Developments* (New York: Harper & Row, 1964).

4. Matthew W. Bates, *Salvation by Allegiance Alone: Rethinking Faith, Works, and the Gospel of Jesus the King* (Grand Rapids: Baker Academic, 2017), 52.

5. John 3:16, as with everything that John says about Jesus, should be interpreted in relation to his Logos Christology in John 1:1–18. It is both the "gateway" to the Christology of John and the entire NT. On John 1:1–18 as a christological "gateway," see Martin Hengel, "The Prologue of the Gospel of John as the Gateway to Christological Truth," in *The Gospel of John and Christian Theology*, eds. Richard Bauckham and Carl Mosser (Grand Rapids: Eerdmans, 2008), 265–94.

6. See the explicit connection between Jesus and David in Matt. 1:1, 20; 9:27; 12:3; 15:22; 20:30, 31; 21:9, 15; 22:42, 43, 45; Mark 2:25; 10:47, 48; 11:10; 12:35, 36, 37; Luke 1:32, 69;

Jesus's death. For example, in his sermon at Antioch, Paul identifies Jesus as the anointed Son to whom God pledged the kingdom in Psalm 2, and he follows his citation with the following explanation, "And as for the fact that he raised him from the dead, no more to return to corruption, he has spoken in this way, 'I will give you the holy and sure blessings of David'" (Acts 13:34; see also Isa. 55:3). In short, God only gives an eternal reign to the one who was risen from the dead, which signals that Jesus's death and resurrection are the fulfillment of the Davidic promise.

Early Christian preaching also stressed that the purpose of Jesus's death and burial was forgiveness of sins. First Corinthians 15:3–4 abbreviates these homiletical elements, but Paul does not immediately explain them. A wider reading of his letters and the NT indicate the early church tied Jesus's death to forgiveness, which means they believed his death had an atoning value that even outpaced the Levitical/temple system. Moreover, Paul's inclusion of Jesus's burial in 1 Corinthians 15:3–4 underscored his post-crucifixion state or even his descent to hell (Question 28).

The fifth and sixth elements of early Christian preaching, that Jesus was raised on the third day and appeared to many, also find their significance in his death. His death legitimates his resurrection, and vice versa, in multiple ways. For example, Jesus's resurrection on the "third day" implies the crucified risen one settles forgiveness, salvation, judgment, and anything else associated with God's reconciliation to sinners. After all, the number three, according to Israel's Scriptures, symbolizes a divinely settled matter.[7] Additionally, as we find in the post-resurrection accounts, Jesus eats, drinks, and shows his scars to witnesses so they do not mistake him for an apparition (Luke 24:28–32, 36–43; John 20:24–29). An apparition could not atone for sin nor ascend to God's right hand as an eternal king and intercessor could.

Jesus's installation at God's right hand becomes the location from which Jesus dispenses the benefits of his death and bears witness to it. For example, it is from God's right hand that Jesus grants the forgiveness of sins secured through his death. As Peter tells the Sanhedrin, "The God of our fathers raised Jesus, whom you killed by hanging him on a tree. God exalted him at this right hand as Leader and Savior, to give repentance to Israel and forgiveness of sins" (Acts 5:30–31; see also Acts 13:37–38). Similarly, the writer of Hebrews portrays Jesus as the heavenly and eternal high priest who mediates the benefits of his earthly death in the presence of God himself on behalf of those who believe (see Heb. 4:14–5:10; 6:19–10:31). It is from God's right hand as the eternal priest that Jesus can sympathize with, intercede for, and help his people as they are tempted by sin (Heb. 4:14–16). None of that work

---

2:11; 3:31; 18:38, 39; 20:41, 42, 44; John 7:42; Acts 1:16; 2:25, 29, 34; 4:25; 7:45; 13:22, 34, 36; 15:16; Rom. 1:2–4; 2 Tim. 2:8; Heb. 4:7; 11:32; Rev. 3:7; 5:5; 22:16.

7. See, e.g., Gen. 22:4; 34:25; 40:20; Exod. 19:11; Judg. 20:30; 2 Kings 20:8; Esther 5:1; Hos. 6:2.

is efficacious, or even takes place, apart from his death. The centrality of his death should not be downplayed by the fact that the writer of Hebrews and other NT writers speak at length about other aspects of his atoning work.[8]

Finally, Jesus's death defined his *parousia* ("coming"), which the early church preached fervently. For example, Jesus's death during his first *parousia* determines what others are slated to experience during his second *parousia*. The writer of Hebrews makes this connection: "So Christ, having been offered once to bear the sins of many, will appear a second time, not to deal with sin but to save those who are eagerly waiting for him" (Heb. 9:28).

The Atoning Value of Jesus's Death in Early Christian Preaching

Although early Christian preaching contained several elements related to Jesus's person and work, all of it was bound up with his death. Jesus's death animated and informed everything preached about him. It follows that the atoning value of his death likewise proved of utmost importance. However, not everyone emphasized the same atoning value at every turn. If the variation within the NT documents is any indication, writers addressed contingent circumstances that afforded them the opportunity to express the robust but coherent value of Jesus's atoning death.[9]

For example, when we juxtapose the discussions of Jesus's death in Galatians and Hebrews, we find both overlapping and unique features. Both texts identify Jesus as crucified and risen (see Gal. 2:19–21; Heb. 1:3–4; 2:14–18; 7:23–25). Both writers indicate that Jesus's death resulted in salvation from sin and death (see Gal. 1:4; 2:19–20; Heb. 7:23–24). Both Galatians and Hebrews portray Jesus's death along substitutionary lines. Both books draw from the OT to explain the atoning value of Jesus's death.

However, there also are unique emphases in each book. For example, in Galatians Paul describes the atoning value of Jesus's death in relation to the curse of the law: "Christ redeemed us from the curse of the law by becoming a curse for us—for it is written, 'Cursed is everyone who is hanged on a tree'"

---

8. E.g., David M. Moffitt suggests, "There is no one event in the life of the incarnate Son of God that does all the work of salvation. As essential as all of these several events are for salvation, they are held together in the person of the incarnate Son—Jesus saves his people from their sins, not the death of Jesus or even the so-called Christ event" (David M. Moffitt, *Rethinking the Atonement: New Perspectives on Jesus's Death, Resurrection, and Ascension* [Grand Rapids: Baker Academic, 2022], 6). While I agree in principle that Jesus is the one who saves, nothing defines his person and other aspects of his atoning work like his crucifixion. It is why Paul said he knew to preach nothing else "except Jesus Christ and him crucified" (1 Cor. 2:2). And it is why John repeatedly refers to Jesus as the "Lamb" in his apocalypse. It is possible to give pride of place to Jesus's death without neglecting other aspects of his atoning work; however, that way is not to treat Jesus's death as merely one part of many other things that Jesus did.

9. Of course, on coherence and contingency in Paul's letters, see J. Christiaan Beker, *Paul the Apostle: The Triumph of God in Life and Thought* (Philadelphia: Fortress, 1980), 23–36.

(Gal. 3:13). By contrast, the writer of Hebrews describes the atoning value of Jesus's death in relation to the priestly system: "For if the blood of goats and bulls, and the sprinkling of defiled persons with the ashes of a heifer, sanctify for the purification of the flesh, how much more will the blood of Christ, who through the eternal Spirit offered himself without blemish to God, purify our conscience from dead works to serve the living God" (Heb. 9:13–14).

Although the contingent circumstances of NT audiences led to diverse expressions of the atoning value of Jesus's death, those expressions are not contingent in themselves. Rather, diverse circumstances helped bring out the robust, transcendent, and even eternal results inherent to Jesus's death. Nevertheless, whether NT writers overtly discuss it or assume it, the penal substitutionary effect of Jesus's death ultimately animates all other aspects of its atoning value (Questions 16 and 17). No benefit of Christ's atoning work can be enjoyed unless his atoning work definitively removes God's righteous judgment against sinners.

Summary

Nothing touches upon every aspect of Jesus's person and work quite like his death. The death of Christ is not a *part* of early Christian preaching. It is the *key* to everything said and taught about him. It follows then that reflection upon the value of his death likewise proved significant. Early Christians grounded the promise of forgiveness, righteousness, salvation, resurrection, and inheritance of an eternal kingdom in the *crucified* risen one. It is telling that even in John's apocalyptic vision of a new heaven and earth he chose to refer to Jesus as the "Lamb." Those from every tribe, tongue, and nation offer eternal praise to one who was sacrificed on a cross for them, because his death had an atoning effect.

REFLECTION QUESTIONS

1. Why does it matter if early Christian preaching found Christ's death to be significant?

2. What are some NT passages that indicate early Christian preaching found Christ's death to be significant?

3. Why do NT writers speak about Jesus's death in both overlapping and unique ways?

4. Can you outline the essential elements of early Christian preaching?

5. How is Jesus's death related to some of those essential elements of early Christian preaching?

Should the Death of Jesus Be Prominent in Preaching Today?

Preach the word; be ready in season and out of season; reprove, rebuke, and exhort, with complete patience and teaching.
~2 Timothy 4:2

Paul admonished Timothy to preach, always. The public proclamation of the sacred word has been a staple in the Christian tradition. One could say that many have heeded Paul's admonition to Timothy.[1] However, the prominence of preaching and the prominence of Jesus's death in that preaching are not one and the same. Today's preachers focus upon a variety of issues and topics that do not necessarily place Jesus's death at the center of their preaching.[2] Even proponents of expositional preaching do not necessarily accentuate Jesus's death, given the fact that most biblical texts do not speak about Jesus's death directly. Should that be the case? Should Jesus's death be prominent in preaching today? To be more specific, since I will answer in the affirmative, as I suspect many readers will, *why* should Jesus's death be prominent in

---

1. For a thorough survey of the history of preaching, see O. C. Edwards Jr., *A History of Preaching*, 2 vols. (Nashville: Abingdon, 2004).
2. The late Francis James Grimké bemoaned topical sermons that replaced careful biblical exposition, noting, "The trash that is served up to the people on Sunday mornings and Thursday evenings is deplorable. The sermons and exhortations made up largely of the gleanings of newspapers and magazines, with precious little of the word of God in them, and, even when it comes in, is handled in the most superficial manner. No church can be built up on that kind of preaching: no church can be made strong morally and spiritually unless it is fed on the word of God, line upon line, precept upon precept, here a little and there a little" (Francis James Grimké, *Meditations on Preaching* [Madison, MS: Log College Press, 2018], 42).

preaching today? As we shall see, the justification for featuring Jesus's death in preaching is grounded in this work's larger focus on atonement.

A Case for "Christopository" Preaching

There are a variety of homiletical genres.[3] One common thread in these genres is that they are tied to the biblical text in some way. Regardless of the specific genre, what I propose here is that the homilist should ultimately preach Christ from every text in any genre of preaching. A case can and should be made for what I refer to as "Christopository" preaching, which the early church practiced (Question 3).[4] Christopository preaching simply refers to preaching the person and work of Christ from every biblical text in either canon and in any homiletical setting. This is not to suggest we set aside the preaching of the word as clearly taught in Scripture (see 2 Tim. 4:2; 1 Peter 1:22–25). Rather, it is to identify the crucified and risen Jesus as the "big idea" of every passage and thereby every sermon.[5] Support for this approach to contemporary preaching rests on four points.

First, Jesus identified himself as the direct object of preaching in relation to Israel's Scriptures. For example, in response to the Jewish leaders who criticized him for healing a crippled man on the Sabbath, Jesus said, "You search the Scriptures because you think that in them you have eternal life; and it is they that bear witness about me" (John 5:39; see also Luke 24:25–27, 44–45). Similarly, in John's typical use of double meaning, Jesus assures his disciples, "And I, when I am lifted up from the earth, will draw all people to myself" (John 12:32). This is both a reference to Jesus being lifted on a cross beam at his crucifixion and the apostles "lifting him up" in their preaching.

Second, early Christian preachers regarded proclamation of the Word and Jesus as synonymous (Question 3). For example, in the speeches of Acts, references to Jesus, or the kingdom he ushered in, are often the direct object of verbal ideas related to preaching.[6] Even when a written text is involved, as in the exchange between Philip and the Ethiopian eunuch, Luke writes, "Then Philip opened his mouth, and beginning with this Scripture he told him the good news about Jesus" (Acts 8:35).

---

3. Ray Atwood identifies four genres: (1) expository preaching; (2) evangelistic preaching; (3) catechetical preaching; and (4) festal preaching. See Ray E. Atwood, *Masters of Preaching: The Most Poignant Powerful Homilists in Church History* (Lanham, MD: Hamilton, 2012), 5–6.
4. To my knowledge, this term is not currently used in academic discussions of homiletics. Multiple adjacent terms are employed such as "Christocentric" or "Christ-centered."
5. The late Haddon Robinson is responsible for the nomenclature of "big idea" preaching. Robinson explained, "Ideally each sermon is the explanation, interpretation, or application of a single dominant idea supported by other ideas, all drawn from one passage or several passages of Scripture" (Haddon W. Robinson, *Biblical Preaching: The Development and Delivery of Expository Preaching*, 2nd ed. [Grand Rapids: Baker Academic, 2001], 35).
6. See, e.g., the use of κηρύσσω in Acts 8:5; 9:20; 10:42; 19:13; 20:25; 28:31.

Third, early practitioners of Christopository preaching did not limit preaching Jesus to so-called evangelistic sermons. Several elements of early church corporate worship indicate that Christ remained its central focus, including the Lord's Supper and doxological admonitions such as, "Let the *word of Christ* dwell in you richly, teaching and admonishing one another in all wisdom, singing psalms and hymns and spiritual songs, with thankfulness in your hearts to God" (Col. 3:16, italics added; see also 1 Cor. 11:23–26). Moreover, when Paul summed up his apostleship, he described his apostolic task solely in relation to the gospel (see Rom. 1:1; 1 Cor. 9:23; 1 Tim. 2:7; 2 Tim. 1:11).

Finally, if Jesus is the full disclosure and explanation of God, then all preaching should inherently be Christopository. John's final statement in his magisterial prologue looms large here: "No one has ever seen God; the only God, who is at the Father's side, he has made him known" (John 1:18; see also 14:8–11). The writer of Hebrews makes a similar claim at the outset of his ancient homily, namely, that Jesus is God's final word (Heb. 1:1–2). Consequently, no word can or should be preached about God that is not at the same time a christological word. This holds true even in instances where Jesus is not explicitly mentioned. Only when sermons are preached in splendid isolation from what God ultimately reveals in Christ is it possible to preach a "Christless" word from Scripture.

Christopository Preaching and the Death of Christ

To take Christopository preaching a step further, and to bring it into closer contact with the focus on atonement, the death of Christ is definitive for understanding his person and work. It follows that Christopository preaching always proclaims the benefits of the crucified and risen Christ from every biblical text. This is not to suggest that other defining aspects of Jesus can be neglected. To the contrary, all aspects of Jesus are best understood in relation to his death and resurrection.

As noted in Question 3, Matthew Bates summarizes the fundamental elements of early Christian preaching in an eight-point outline: (1) "Jesus preexisted with the Father"; (2) "Jesus took on human flesh, fulfilling God's promises to David"; (3) "Jesus died for sins in accordance with the Scriptures"; (4) "Jesus was buried"; (5) "Jesus was raised on the third day according to the Scriptures"; (6) "Jesus appeared to many"; (7) "Jesus is seated at the right hand of God as Lord"; and (8) "Jesus will come again."[7] As reflected in the writings of the NT, early Christian preachers and teachers narrated these fundamental elements in both overlapping and unique ways according to the needs of their audiences. Nevertheless, even with such diversity, Christ's death informed all aspects of their proclamation.

---

7. Matthew W. Bates, *Salvation by Allegiance Alone: Rethinking Faith, Works, and the Gospel of Jesus the King* (Grand Rapids: Baker Academic, 2017), 52.

Contemporary homilists who want to be informed by early Christian practices should adopt a similar approach. While today's audiences may vary in age, location, social status, and the like, their fundamental needs are no different than those who first heard of a crucified and risen Christ. According to the biblical text, they are plagued by the anthropological tetrad of sin, death, Satan, and God's righteous judgment that places them in desperate need of reconciliation to God. God only provides that reconciliation in the person and work of Christ (Questions 5 and 6). Moreover, sermons primarily directed to believers likewise should underscore the atoning benefits of Jesus's death. This was clearly the practice of NT writers who did not downgrade the importance of Jesus's death for those who already believed in him. To the contrary, they addressed the afflictions, challenges, and expectations that defined the Christian experience through the lens of Christ's death.

The Costly Loss of Atonement-Centered Preaching

This bring us back to our overarching question and this work's wider focus on atonement. If homilists today aim for any substantive link to their homiletical ancestors, their sermons should be Christopository. A Christopository sermon has as its central focus the benefits of Jesus's death and resurrection; that is, it is atonement-centered preaching. To preach Jesus is to preach God's work of reconciliation from every biblical text to unbelievers and believers alike.

This is not to suggest that one aspect of the atonement should eclipse the historical-grammatical and biblical-canonical sense of individual books and passages of Scripture. Nor should one theory of atonement drown out all other insights that competing theories might offer. In fact, such an approach would undermine the mosaic of God's atoning work in Christ that is spread across both canons.[8] However, to deemphasize the centrality of the atonement in teaching and preaching is costly, to say the least.

The costly loss of atonement-centered preaching is threefold. First, the identity of the triune God collapses apart from the atoning work of Christ (Questions 32 and 33). The Father's love, the Son's obedience, and the Spirit's gifts are predicated on and defined by the atoning death of Christ. Without atonement-centered preaching, God cannot be worshiped in spirit and in truth (John 4:23–24). Second, sinners remain unreconciled to God apart from atonement-centered preaching. Unless unbelieving listeners are confronted with the truth that God sent Christ to die for sinners and are then urged to respond in faith, there exists no possibility for their reconciliation. After all, the apostle Paul makes it clear that people cannot call upon the Lord Jesus's name for salvation unless they hear the message of salvation from those whom God

---

8. On this point, see Joshua M. McNall, *The Mosaic of Atonement: An Integrated Approach to Christ's Work* (Grand Rapids: Zondervan Academic, 2019).

sends (Rom. 10:5–17). Third, believers lose the capacity to withstand their ongoing struggle with sin as they turn to other sources of reconciliation. Their obedience will be wrongly motivated in the sense that they will work to reconcile themselves to God.

Summary

The death of Christ should be prominent in preaching and teaching today because its absence is inconsistent with the biblical witness and too costly to believers and unbelievers alike. To preach the Word in all seasons in the way that Paul admonished Timothy is to always hold before people's eyes the atoning work of the crucified and risen Jesus. Theological formation, a Christian ethic, the church's mission, its worship, and all other dynamics of God's people depend upon how prominently Christ's death is featured in the preaching they constantly offer and hear. If preachers and teachers in the church today wish to continue in "the faith once for all delivered to the saints," their message must hold to what those saints held as most significant. As noted in Question 3, the early church found Jesus's death as most significant for their preaching, because that death defined reconciliation with God. Therefore, the contemporary church cannot afford to make anything more significant than Christ's atoning work.

REFLECTION QUESTIONS

1. Do you think Christ's death should be prominently featured in all genres of preaching?

2. What is "Christopository" preaching?

3. What is the relationship between the death of Jesus and Christopository preaching?

4. How is the significance of Jesus's death for unbelievers and believers both similar and different?

5. How does contemporary preaching sometimes minimize the importance of Jesus's death?

Questions About Reconciliation

Why Is Atonement Necessary?

And just as it is appointed for man to die once, and after that comes judgment.

~Hebrews 9:27

Among the many smash hits by the British rock band The Who, their song "Baba O'Riley" confidently asserts that one does not need to be "forgiven." While I am not sure that Pete Townshend of The Who intended to make a theological statement, the line embodies a question that demands a response. Do I really need to be forgiven? Why is forgiveness necessary? Why is reconciliation with anyone, particularly God, necessary? Along these lines, why is atonement necessary?

The writer of Hebrews provides the broadest answer, namely, that God has slated every human being for postmortem judgment before him (Heb. 9:27; see also Prov. 24:12; Matt. 12:36; 16:27; Rom. 2:6; 14:12; 2 Cor. 5:10). Unless reconciliation occurs before that moment, no living thing will stand in or survive that moment (Ps. 143:2). However, this kind of eschatological judgment assumes a certain backstory involving people and God. Consequently, we will provide three answers to the question, "Why is atonement necessary?": (1) because all humans are judged in Adam; (2) because of our fallen, sinful condition; and (3) because of God's unchanging character.

Because All Humans Are Judged in Adam

Alister McGrath summarizes the events of Genesis 3 by noting, "The image of a 'Fall' conveys the idea that creation now exists at a lower level than that intended for it by God."[1] I agree in principle with the metaphor of "fall"

---

1. Alister E. McGrath, *Christian Theology: An Introduction*, 2nd ed. (Oxford: Blackwell, 1997), 21.

to describe the human condition since Adam; however, Platonic undertones and a lack of clarity render "fallenness" language insufficient. As Philip Cary observes, such language originated from a "Platonic myth of the Fall" wherein the preexistent soul fell from a "heavenly, disembodied state" to earth, where it then took up residence in the human body.[2] Cary goes on, "We call the narrative about Adam and Eve and the forbidden fruit by the name 'The Fall' because, ironically, it invited Platonist speculations about the Fall of the soul that were entertained but eventually rejected by orthodox Christianity."[3] Even more, "fall" language neither occurs in Genesis 3 nor clearly conveys the legal framework that defines the narrative. At Eden, in the immediate aftermath of the first couple's rebellion, God passed judgment on humans then, now, and beyond in a way that makes atonement necessary. The judgment in Genesis 3 is multifaceted and its consequences reverberate throughout human history.

First, Adam and Eve exchanged their trust in God's promise of judgment for the serpent's covet-inducing assertion that eating from the prohibited Tree of Knowledge of Good and Evil would not lead to death but to divine knowledge of good and evil (Gen. 2:17; 3:5–6). Trust in the word of the serpent rather than the word of God led to sin and the penalty of death that accompanies it.

Second, the first couple's transgression brought a flood of guilt, shame, and fear in the presence of God, as indicated in the way that Adam and Eve clothed themselves and hid from the divine presence (Gen. 3:7–8).

Third, the transgression immediately fractured the relationship between Adam and Eve even as they deflected responsibility for their actions (Gen. 3:12–13). The fracture intensified in the subsequent narrative with Cain's murder of Abel, which produces the need for God to vindicate the righteous (Gen. 4:1–16; cf. Matt. 23:25; Luke 11:51; Heb. 11:4; 12:24).

Fourth, God condemned all parties involved. He condemned Satan to a life of enmity with Eve's seed, though it is embedded within the so-called *protoevangelium* (Gen. 3:15b). God condemned Eve to painful childbirth and marriage, which is synecdoche for no longer reigning as Adam's helper (Gen. 3:16; see also Gen. 1:26–30; 2:18–25; 5:1–2). God even cursed the earth and thereby condemned Adam to a life of toil, which is also synecdoche for no longer reigning with Eve as one made in the image of God.

Fifth, exile from God's presence stood as the essential judgment against Adam and Eve (Gen. 3:22–24). Without access to his presence, Adam and Eve inevitably died as God promised (Gen. 5:5). Genesis 3, then, describes more than a fall from an idyllic state. God doles out judgment against Adam and all who share in his transgression (Rom. 5:12–14).

---

2.   Philip Cary, *The Meaning of Protestant Theology: Luther, Augustine, and the Gospel That Gives Us Christ* (Grand Rapids: Baker Academic, 2019), 38.

3.   Cary, *The Meaning of Protestant Theology*, 38.

Why, though, does God apply Adam's transgression and judgment to all subsequent people? Answers can be complex; however, four brief points will move us forward. First, Adam serves as a representative for all humanity. His transgression in the garden reflects what all humans would do in the same situation, except for the "second Adam" (Rom. 5:15–21; 1 Cor. 15:47). Second, sin and death entered through Adam's transgression, which has a deleterious effect upon all Adamic descendants (Rom. 5:12–14). Sin becomes both what humans are guilty of and a deadly power they cannot escape.[4] Likewise, death is both God's enduring judgment against sin and an inescapable enemy.[5] We will return to this discussion below. Third, everyone since Adam has committed Adam-like transgressions. Consequently, the same divine judgment applies to all who sin as Adam did, that is, by mistrusting God's promise and transgressing his command. It does not matter if one transgresses a command imprinted upon the human conscience or engraved upon stones, as with the Mosaic law (Rom. 2:1–16; 5:12–14).

Because of Our Fallen, Sinful Condition

Much has transpired since God passed judgment against Adam and his descendants. From the continental drift to the dawn of the digital age, much has changed on the earth since the events of Eden. Historical writing from antiquity to the present day has often fueled the illusion of "progress" within these changes. However, as Qohelet (or the Preacher) opined long ago, ultimately "there is nothing new under the sun" (Eccl. 1:9b). The world is divinely charged with a kind of futility (Eccl. 1:2; Rom. 8:20). The cliché holds, "The more things change, the more they stay the same." That includes the human condition. Scripture insists that all people remain in the postlapsarian (i.e., post-fall) condition first experienced by Adam and Eve. As Paul declares, "in Adam all die" (1 Cor. 15:22a; see also Rom. 5:15–19).

Paul may provide the best summary of this unchanged condition in his letter to the Ephesians:

> And you were dead in trespasses and sins in which you once walked, following the course of this world, following the prince of the power of the air, the spirit that is now at work in the sons of disobedience—among whom we all once lived in the passions of our flesh, carrying out the desires of the body and the mind, and were by nature children of wrath, like the rest of mankind. (Eph. 2:1–3)

---

4. For sin as a "power," see, e.g., Rom. 3:9; 7:7–25; 1 Cor. 15:56; 1 Peter 2:11.
5. As Paul describes death in 1 Cor. 15:26, "But the last enemy destroyed is death." See also 2 Tim. 1:10 and Heb. 2:14.

We find here a triad of qualities that describe the unchanged human condition: (1) dead in sin; (2) living under the rule of Satan; and (3) under God's wrath.

To be dead in trespasses and sin but walk in that state is a paradox (Eph. 2:1–2). How can a dead person walk or live? Paul answers that human beings exist in a state of spiritual deadness that ultimately leads to eternal deadness. Separation from God's life-giving presence defines this state of existence, which results in foolishness rather than wisdom, death rather than life, condemnation rather than justification, and defeat rather than deliverance.

Simultaneous with life in deadness is life under the rule of Satan (Eph. 2:2–3). While popularized reflections on demonology might give the impression that Satanic rule is synonymous with extreme descriptions of demon-possessed figures such as the Gerasene demoniac (Mark 5:1–20), Paul broadens the scope of such rule to all human beings outside of Christ. Other NT writers confirm this broader anthropological scope, such as John who describes Satan as "the deceiver of the whole world" (Rev. 12:9; see also 2 Cor. 4:4; 11:1–4; Eph. 5:5; 6:11; 1 Tim. 2:13; 1 Peter 5:8). The outcome of this deceptive rule includes devotion to fleshly desires, brokenness, hurt, and a lifelong fear of death (see Luke 13:16; Acts 10:38; Heb. 2:14–15; 1 John 3:8).

Along with living in death and being overpowered by the rule of Satan, the unchanged human condition includes life under God's wrath (*orgē*).[6] Paul specifically describes humans as "children of wrath by nature," which means it is a condition inherited at birth and stands in contrast to Stoic contemporaries who, as Clinton Arnold explains, "emphasized the importance of living according to nature as a way of pleasing the gods" (see Eph. 2:3; cf. Ps. 51:6).[7] From Paul's perspective, the "nature" (*physis*) of humanity includes their existence under divine wrath, which means they cannot "naturally" please God. In fact, as judgment for their diverse idolatrous practices, God places Jews and Gentiles under his wrath by handing them over to the power of sin (Rom. 1:18–3:20).

Of course, as we shall see, these pieces of the unchanged tripartite human condition are interrelated. God's atoning work in Christ untangles all of them in their various machinations.

Because of God's Unchanged Character

Just as an unchanged human condition makes atonement necessary, God's unchanged character necessitates it as well. Scripture stresses that

---

6.   Cf. the use of "wrath" (*orgē*) in John 3:36; Rom. 1:24–32; Col. 3:6.
7.   Clinton E. Arnold, *Ephesians*, Zondervan Exegetical Commentary on the New Testament (Grand Rapids: Zondervan Academic, 2010), 134.

neither God's attributes nor his actions change. As YHWH announces through Malachi, "For I the LORD do not change; therefore you, O children of Jacob, are not consumed" (Mal. 3:6). Similarly, as the writer of Hebrews maintains, "Jesus Christ is the same yesterday and today and forever" (Heb. 13:8; see also 1 Sam. 15:29; Ps. 102:27; James 1:17). We should infer then that God's judgment doled out in Eden still stands, because his holy and righteous character requires that he remain in the same disposition toward sinners. Even outside of Edenic judgment, God's righteous character demonstrated in his judgment against Adam and his seed is eternal. As William Lane Craig maintains, "God's inherent righteousness, like His power or wisdom, is an essential property of God that He has objectively and independently of whether any human beings at all exist, much less have faith in Him."[8] God's righteousness, along with his love, holiness, and all indivisible attributes, are eternal, or unchangeable.

It follows that God's disposition toward sinful humanity does not change. His promise of judgment against them and his mercy for them remain intact. Such a promise from a righteous God who does not change necessitates his atoning work in Christ.

Summary

Contrary to The Who's suggestion that "I don't need to be forgiven," which assumes atonement is superfluous, Scripture clearly teaches otherwise. That teaching includes the unchanged judgment against humanity first instituted at Eden, the unchanged sinful condition of humanity, and the unchanged attributes of God, particularly his righteousness whereby his promise of judgment and mercy remain. If we ask, "Why is atonement necessary?" the answer resides in the unchanged nature of humanity and the eternal character of God. Human beings are "by nature" under God's wrath, living as those dead in sin and enslaved to Satan. Contrastively, God remains holy and righteous. In his righteousness, God obligates himself to judge sinful humanity, give mercy to them, and thereby reconcile himself to those who believe.

REFLECTION QUESTIONS

1. How does God's eschatological judgment make atonement necessary?

2. Why does Adam's transgression and subsequent judgment affect all human beings?

---

8. William Lane Craig, *Atonement and the Death of Christ: An Exegetical, Historical, and Philosophical Exploration* (Waco, TX: Baylor University Press, 2020), 54.

3. How does being "dead in sin" make atonement necessary?

4. How does misunderstanding Satan's power relate to the necessity of atonement?

5. Why is God's unchanged disposition toward humanity both a sobering reality and a reason for hope?

Why Must God Punish Sin?

I will punish the world for its evil, and the wicked for their iniquity; I will put an end to the pomp of the arrogant, and lay low the pompous pride of the ruthless.

~Isaiah 13:11

Some words in the English language make us wince. "Punishment" is one of them. It is a word that makes many people defensive, anxious, and even resentful. Such responses are compounded when one links punishment to God. The suggestion that God punishes sin can evoke its own kind of defensiveness, anxiety, and resentment. It can seem unbecoming of a God who is love (1 John 4:8).

These concerns are reflected in various discussions of the atonement. For example, some interpreters worry that underscoring the punishment of an innocent Jesus encourages women to accept abuse.[1] The oft-cited literary critic René Girard resists violence and divine punishment to the point that he encourages us to reject the belief that Christ is a sacrifice.[2] Others, while not wishing to jettison divine punishment altogether, worry that expositions of relevant biblical texts are too often more caricature than sound exegesis.[3] Such

---

1. See, e.g., Joanne Carlson Brown and Rebecca Parker, "For God So Loved the World?" in *Christianity, Patriarchy and Abuse*, eds. Joanne Carlson Brown and Rebecca Parker (New York: Pilgrim, 1989), 1–30.
2. As Girard plainly insists, "God is not violent, the truth of God has nothing to do with violence, and he speaks to us not through distant intermediaries but directly" (René Girard, *The Scapegoat*, trans. Yvonne Freccero [Baltimore: Johns Hopkins University Press, 1989], 189).
3. See, e.g., Mark D. Baker and Joel B. Green, *Recovering the Scandal of the Cross: Atonement in New Testament and Contemporary Contexts* (Downers Grove, IL: IVP Academic, 2011), 47–48.

concerns, coupled with larger worries about perceptions of a punishing God, misunderstanding about the link between God and punishment, and perhaps even wishful thinking about sidestepping culpability for sin altogether, give rise to the question "Why must God punish sin?" The answer lies in the inter-relationship between the character of God and the condition of human beings as they are described in the biblical text.

Scriptural Language of Divine "Punishment"

Scripture's language of divine punishment and its presentation of such action are not necessarily one and the same. In the previous century, C. H. Dodd famously attempted to excise the notion of divine propitiation, that is, that Jesus's death somehow satisfied God's wrath against sinners, from Paul's writings.[4] He argued that atonement terminology in the Septuagint (i.e., the Greek translation of the Hebrew OT, also known as the LXX) did not bear the sense of propitiating God's wrath; therefore, since the LXX's use of these terms influenced Paul's use of such language (Rom. 3:25), it follows the apostle did not conceive of Christ's death as a punishment that satisfied God's wrath against sinners. Although Dodd's thesis is mis-guided, it has had a lasting impact on how interpreters understand the use of language related to our concerns here.[5] It exemplifies the importance of rightly understanding and explaining the scriptural language of divine punishment.

Multiple OT terms and/or phrases are often rendered as "punish" or "punishment" in English. One of the most common verbs behind this English rendering is the Hebrew verb *paqad*, which often bears the sense of "make a careful inspection," "to look at," and "call to account."[6] In some occurrences of the verb, the divine action is linked to judgment against the disobedient; therefore, these occurrences are often and rightly rendered as "punish" or "punishment," such as "I will punish their transgression with the rod and their iniquity with stripes" (Ps. 89:32).

Of course, divine punishment can be in view regardless of a writer's word choice. In either case, the OT provides the righteous *motivation*, *means*, and *scope* of this divine action. Individual and communal rebellion against God's word *motivates* divine punishment. From Eden to Babel to Babylon and everywhere in between, whether it be elect Israel or those out-side it, the essence of human rebellion involves the transgression of divine commands, warnings, and promises. In short, rebellion against the divine

---

4. C. H. Dodd, "Ιλασκεσθαι, Its Cognates, Derivatives, and Synonyms, in the Septuagint," *Journal of Theological Studies* 32 (1931): 352–60.
5. For a recent summary and critique of Dodd's thesis, see William Lane Craig, *Atonement and the Death of Christ: An Exegetical, Historical, and Philosophical Exploration* (Waco, TX: Baylor University Press, 2020), 63–64.
6. *HALOT*, s.v. "פקד." See, e.g., Gen. 21:1; Exod. 3:16; 1 Sam. 2:21; Isa. 26:14.

word in all its forms motivates divine punishment in all its forms. As the psalmist observes in explaining the reason for Israel's exile, "For they had rebelled against the words of God, and spurned the counsel of the Most High" (Ps. 107:11).

The *means* of such punishment can include disease, drought, pestilence, invasion, exile, and death. The Torah labels this experience a "curse," as it is expressed in the Deuteronomic warning, "But if you will not obey the voice of the LORD your God or be careful to do all his commandments and his statutes that I command you today, then all these curses shall come upon you and overtake you" (Deut. 28:15).

The *scope* of the punishment described in the OT has both temporal and eternal dimensions. With respect to the former, punishment for rebellion against God's Word might include momentary disease, such as Miriam's seven-day bout with leprosy (Num. 12:9–15), a season or years of famine, death of a select group of rebels, or decades-long exile.[7] With respect to the latter, while eternal punishment is less developed in the OT as compared to the NT, we find some OT reflection on the matter. For example, Daniel's apocalyptic vision contrasts two resurrected groups: "And many of those who sleep in the dust of the earth shall awake, some to everlasting life, and some to shame and everlasting contempt" (Dan. 12:2; cf. Isa. 66:24).

OT reflection on divine punishment influences the way NT writers understand it, though, as always, they reconfigure their understanding around Christ. With respect to the NT language of divine punishment, God punishes sinners and his Son. The former involves God "handing over" idolatrous humanity to the power of sin. The latter involves the punishment of his Son on behalf of and in place of sinners while also punishing those who reject his word about the saving work of Christ (see Rom. 4:25; 8:32). The scope of such punishment is both temporal and eternal. As John remarks, "Whoever believes in the Son has eternal life; whoever does not obey the Son shall not see life, but the wrath of God remains on him" (John 3:36).

God Punishes Sin Because of the Human Condition

With this language of punishment in view, it is necessary to consider the connection between the necessity of divine punishment and the human condition, which I outlined in Question 5. Even if we grant with Paul that humans are dead in sin, beholden to Satan, and under divine wrath, why must God respond punitively to this human condition as Scripture repeatedly maintains? The answer lies largely in what knowledge emerges from divine punishment. Two salient points emerge here.

First, punishment for sin informs a proper knowledge of God. For example, Ezekiel contains several uses of the expression, "Then they will know

---

7. See also the seven-year punishment of Nebuchadnezzar in Dan. 4:13.

that I am the LORD."[8] What often precedes these expressions are warnings of impending judgment against disobedient Israel or its opponents: "And I will stretch out my hand against them and make the land desolate and waste, in all their dwelling places, from the wilderness to Riblah. Then *they will know* that I am the LORD" (Ezek. 6:14, italics added). We can infer from Ezekiel's statements, and those like them, that the sinful condition of humans requires God's punitive action if humans are to know and acknowledge that he is God.

Second, punishment for sin also informs how people acknowledge Jesus as Lord. Christ-followers must know him as the crucified one, that is, the one whom God punished for their sin: "Christ died for our sins in accordance with the Scriptures" (1 Cor. 15:3). Even those who reject him are slated to "bend the knee" in acknowledgment that Jesus is the Lord who exercised obedience to God to the point of death, or punishment, on a cross (Phil. 2:5–11; see also Isa. 45:23).

God Punishes Sin Because of His Character

Along with the human condition, God's character (Question 5) requires a specifically punitive action. He must act in his holiness and righteousness in the fullest sense, as promised, which includes punishment of the ungodly and vindication of the righteous (see Ps. 1:6). Figures in Scripture often assume that God will and must punish sin in a righteous manner. For example, while advocating for the preservation of Lot in the face of Sodom's impending destruction, Abraham exclaims, "Far be it from you to do such a thing, to put the righteous to death with the wicked, so that the righteous fare as the wicked! Far be that from you! Shall not the Judge of all the earth do what is *just?*" (Gen. 18:25, italics added; cf. Rom. 3:6). Additionally, prayers—particularly those in the psalms of lament, of which imprecatory psalms such are a subgenre—assume that God will punish the wicked in accordance with his revealed character and prior promise, as evidenced by visceral requests such as "O God, break the teeth in their mouths; tear out the fangs of the young lions, O LORD!" (Ps. 58:6; see also Pss. 3:7; 143:12). Along these lines, YHWH promises to arrive on earth for a climactic punishment of sinners, "For behold, the LORD is coming out from his place to punish the inhabitants of the earth for their iniquity, and the earth will disclose the blood shed on it, and will no more cover its slain" (Isa. 26:21). The latter promise underscores both God's character and the vindication of the righteous, which he promised them necessitates punishment of the wicked. Nothing short of punishment, even death, will do justice to his revealed character and prior promises.

Of course, God's work in Christ provides the most explanatory power for understanding the necessity of divine punishment, and it does so in at least

---

8.   See, e.g., Ezek. 6:14; 25:11, 17; 26:6; 28:23, 26; 29:9, 16, 21; 30:8, 19, 26; 32:15; 33:29; 35:15; 36:38; 38:23.

three ways. First, the barbaric form of death that is Roman crucifixion implies that God necessarily punished Jesus.[9] Although the first century provided alternative and far less painful modes of death, we can infer from a crucified Christ that God had to punish his Son if he were to atone for the sins of the world. Second, a crucified, that is, punished Son of God is necessary to indicate the depth of the depraved human condition. Third, the torturous nature of Jesus's death, both prior to and at Golgotha, assumes that reconciliation with God requires punishment.

Summary

While the term punishment might make us wince, divine punishment is well represented in the biblical text and is necessary for atonement. The necessity of punishment stems from the incongruity between the human condition and divine character. Therefore, if one asks, "Why must God punish sin?" the answer lies in who people are apart from Christ and who God is as ultimately revealed in Christ. The biblical writers did not apologize or downplay the necessity of divine punishment. They understood its necessity, as did subsequent proponents of various theories of atonement (Questions 13, 14, 16, and 17).

REFLECTION QUESTIONS

1. Why do many people find it difficult to accept that God punishes sin?

2. How do some interpreters deny the various ways that Scripture speaks about divine punishment?

3. What is it about the human condition that makes divine punishment necessary?

4. What is it about God's identity that makes punishment of sinners necessary?

5. In what sense is divine punishment a gracious act of God?

---

9. For a description of crucifixion from Greco-Roman and Second Temple perspectives, see David W. Chapman, *Ancient Jewish and Christian Perceptions of Crucifixion* (Grand Rapids: Baker Academic, 2010); and Martin Hengel, *Crucifixion in the Ancient World and the Folly of the Message of the Cross* (Philadelphia: Fortress, 1977).

How Does Christ's Atoning Work Reconcile Us to God?

How can this man give us his flesh to eat?

~John 6:52b

Answers to "how" questions are often taken for granted or ignored altogether. Many of us cannot explain how the internet works, how forecasters can predict weather patterns, how cables on a suspension bridge bear so much weight, or how machines produce food. Nevertheless, we will not hesitate to hop on the internet to see what the weather will be like today so we can safely jog across the bridge to grab a donut. We do not always stop to think about how something works even though we trust and enjoy the outcome of the work.

This oversight can apply to our understanding of atonement. Professing Christians might believe, confess, and enjoy the truth that Jesus reconciles them to God without being able to explain clearly how atonement works. Some might be able to explain certain dynamics of Christ's atoning work but still struggle to answer in a holistic way how such work ultimately reconciles them to God. At least three answers can be offered to the question "How does Christ's atoning work reconcile us to God?" First, sinners are reconciled to God by the obedient Christ's one-time death. Second, sinners are reconciled to God by Christ's ongoing intercession. Third, sinners are reconciled to God by Christ's eschatological advocacy.

The Obedient Christ's One-Time Death

Both Paul and the writer of Hebrews describe Jesus's death as "once for all" (*ephapax*; see Rom. 6:10; Heb. 7:27; 9:12; 10:10). His death is neither perpetual nor repeatable; however, its atoning effect is eternal. This effect stems from the

fact that Christ's death overwhelmingly addresses the condition of human beings in a way that is consistent with God's unchanging character (Question 5).
In Christ, a righteous and holy God gives to sinners what he demands from
them and what they need from him. Several points are in order here, though
many of them will receive fuller treatment at later points in this book.

First, Jesus's death is a sacrifice eternally planned and approved by God
that both expiates the sinner and thereby propitiates God's righteous wrath
against the sinner. Expiate simply means to "wipe out" or "cleanse" sin.
Propitiate means to satisfy God's wrath. Scripture asserts that God eternally
planned Jesus's death (see Isa. 53:1–12; John 19:28; Acts 4:28; 1 Cor. 2:7; Eph.
1:5, 11). As John remarks in describing Jesus, he was slain "before the foundation of the world" (Rev. 13:8).[1] This is a poetic way of expressing eternal
intent within the Godhead to sacrifice the Son.[2] God then demonstrates his
approval of this eternally planned sacrifice by raising Christ from the dead.
As Peter declares during his Pentecost sermon through a citation of Psalm
16:10, "For you will not abandon my soul to Hades, or let your Holy One see
corruption" (Acts 2:27). God's resurrection of Christ signals that his Son truly
is righteous (*dikaios*), as the centurion confessed (Luke 23:47); therefore, the
Father's resurrection of his Son demonstrates that he approves of the Son's
sacrificial death.

Second, this eternally planned and approved death impacts sinners in
two interrelated ways. We find this kind of death expressed in christological
descriptions such as, "He is the propitiation [*hilasmos*] for our sins, and not
for ours only but also for the sins of the whole world" (1 John 2:2). Contextual
uses of *hilasmos* in the LXX and NT, along with related terms, often bear
the sense of a two-pronged effect (cf. Lev. 25:9; Num. 5:8; Rom. 3:25; 1 John
4:10).[3] A sacrifice expiates, or removes, sin from a person and thereby propitiates, or appeases, God's righteous indignation against the sinner.[4] Only
the removal of sin through a sacrifice (expiation) satisfies God's righteous
wrath (propitiation). Simply put, without expiation there is no propitiation
and vice versa. Without removing Israel's sin through a prescribed sacrificial
system, YHWH's wrath would come upon the people. Jesus's sacrificial death

---

1. ESV and other translations link the phrase "before the foundation of the world" in Rev.
   13:8 to the writing of names within the Book of Life. However, as Grant Osborne concludes, "it is better here to respect the word order and recognize that it is God's redemptive
   plan that has been established 'from the foundation of the world'" (Grant R. Osborne,
   Revelation, Baker Exegetical Commentary on the New Testament [Grand Rapids: Baker
   Academic, 2002], 503).
2. See G. K. Beale, *The Book of Revelation*, New International Greek Testament Commentary
   (Grand Rapids: Eerdmans, 1999), 702.
3. One Hebrew term that often stands behind *hilasmos* and its cognates is *kaphar,* which
   refers to the way a sacrifice, or its blood, "covers" sin.
4. See BDAG, s.v. "ἱλασμός;" LEH, s.v. "ἱλασμός."

provides a once-for-all sacrifice whereby his shed blood, which God requires for forgiveness, both expiates and propitiates (Lev. 17:11; Heb. 9:22). As the writer of Hebrews explains in describing Jesus's incarnate work, "Therefore he had to be made like his brothers in every respect, so that he might become a merciful and faithful high priest in the service of God, to make propitiation [*hilaskesthai*] for the sins of the people" (Heb. 2:17).

The expiating and propitiating effect of Christ's one-time death has far-reaching soteriological implications. His death makes the sinner's right standing before God (justification) possible by securing forgiveness and the satisfaction of righteous wrath. Such a standing then assures and secures deliverance from the power of sin, death, evil, Satan, and eschatological-eternal judgment. As Paul assured the Romans, "Since, therefore, we have now been justified by his blood, much more shall we be saved by him from the wrath of God. For if while we were enemies we were reconciled to God by the death of his Son, much more, now that we are reconciled, shall we be saved by his life" (Rom. 5:9–10).

Third, the atoning effect of Jesus's one-time death also stems from his obedience to the Father as the God-man. Paul ties these strands together in the Philippians hymn in which he describes the preexistent Christ becoming a human servant, humbling himself, and "becoming obedient to the point of death, even death on a cross" (Phil. 2:6–8). Jesus is the obedient Son who "recapitulates" all the things that disobedient Adam and his seed got wrong with their deleterious effects (Rom. 5:15–21; Eph. 1:10). Jesus's obedience is acceptable to God because his work is perfect, as he is perfect. Jesus carries out his perfect obedience within the perfect union of his divine and human natures. Only within this hypostatic union can his work have an eternally atoning effect. As William Witt and Joel Scandrett summarize, "It is because Jesus Christ is the Second Person of the Trinity, fully God, that he is able to save humanity. Yet it is also because Jesus Christ is fully human that he is able to save humanity. The saving work of Jesus Christ in the history of salvation is thus closely related to his personal ontology."[5]

The Atoning Effect of Christ's Intercession

If we are to understand how the atonement reconciles sinners to God, we cannot separate the atoning effect of Christ's one-time death from the effect of his ongoing intercession. NT writers, influenced especially by Psalm 110:1, often described Jesus as installed at God's right hand, where he carries out his intercession.[6] The intercessory work at God's right hand has multiple links to the effect of Christ's atoning work.

---

5. William G. Witt and Joel Scandrett, *Mapping Atonement: The Doctrine of Reconciliation in Christian History and Theology* (Grand Rapids: Baker Academic, 2022), 36.
6. See Matt. 26:64; Mark 14:62; Luke 22:69; Acts 2:25, 33, 34; 5:31; 7:55, 56; Rom. 8:34; Eph. 1:20; Col. 3:1; Heb. 1:3, 13; 8:1; 10:12; 12:2; 1 Peter 3:22; Rev. 5:1.

The writer of Hebrews explains that Jesus's position at God's right hand allows him to intercede on behalf of believers in multiple ways. As both eternal priest and sacrifice, Jesus's unmatched access to the Father outpaces the "shadow" of his atoning work embedded in Israel's sacrificial system (Heb. 8:5; 9:23; 10:1). The nature of Christ's atoning work at the cross and its proximity to the Father via Christ's installment at the right hand make it eternally efficacious on behalf of those who trust in him (Heb. 1:1–14; 6:20; 7:18–19). Christ's unmatched access to God also facilitates believers' access to God, where they receive the help they need from him as those reconciled to him in Christ (Heb. 2:18; 3:6; 4:14–16; 10:19–22).

Paul also reflects on the atoning effect of Christ's intercession. In his poetic flourish that assures the Romans that nothing can separate them from God's love in Christ (Rom. 8:31–39), Paul describes Christ as "the one who died—more than that, who was raised—who is at the right hand of God, who indeed is *interceding* for us" (Rom. 8:34, italics added). He prefaces this description with a reference to unidentified agents, perhaps Satan, who might attempt to shred the reconciliation afforded to believers in Christ by bringing accusations and calls for condemnation against them.[7] These attempts fail both because God graciously handed his Son over on behalf of the accused and because that risen Son intercedes before God on their behalf in the face of accusations. In short, the Son's death and ongoing intercession have an unshakable atoning effect.

The Atoning Effect of Christ's Eschatological Advocacy

Closely related to the current atoning effect of Christ's death and intercession is its effect in the final day of judgment. How will Christ's death and intercessory work atone for the sinner on the day of judgment? We will explore this question at length later (Question 38); however, it deserves brief attention here since it is obviously integral to understanding the question before us. In short, Christ is an eschatological advocate whose work on the last day is both promised in the gospel and proleptically (i.e., a future accomplished event brought into the present) experienced.

For example, some of the speeches in Acts either imply or explicitly promise Christ's advocacy on the last day. This is most obvious in the way Luke describes Jesus as the one entrusted with eschatological judgment: "Because he has fixed a day on which he will judge the world in righteousness by a man whom he has appointed; and of this he has given assurance to all by raising him from the dead" (Acts 17:31). Similarly, as Luke describes Jesus in

---

7. Interpreters cannot agree on the punctuation of Rom. 8:34 and/or the identity of the accuser. For a discussion of these issues, see Douglas J. Moo, *The Epistle to the Romans*, New International Commentary on the New Testament, 2nd ed. (Grand Rapids: Eerdmans, 2018), 53–64.

the dialogue between Peter and Cornelius, "And he commanded us to preach to the people and to testify that he is the one appointed by God to be judge of the living and the dead" (Acts 10:42). If the apostles urged their listeners to trust in Jesus as Lord, while also identifying him as the one overseeing Final Judgment, it follows that faith in his person and work includes his advocacy for believers on the last day. Christ's work in that moment will qualify as the culmination of his atoning work that results in everlasting reconciliation with God. At least in the early church, assurance of Christ's advocacy on the last day functioned as a key dimension of the promise expressed in the gospel.

Of course, that eschatological experience is proleptically experienced. To reiterate, by "proleptically," I simply mean that Christ's future advocacy is brought into the present. Christ's advocacy on that day, though obviously not presently experienced, is brought into the present experience of believers. Once again, as Paul writes, "Since, therefore, we have now been justified by his blood, much more shall we be saved by him from the wrath of God" (Rom. 5:9; cf. 5:10). Similarly, as Paul tells the Thessalonians, "For God has not destined us for wrath, but to obtain salvation through our Lord Jesus Christ, who died for us so that whether we are awake or asleep we might live with him" (1 Thess. 5:9–10; cf. Rom. 14:4, 8–9). Therefore, Paul's assertion that there is "no condemnation for those who are in Christ Jesus" expresses the proleptic experience of what believers can expect on the last day, namely, no condemnation (Rom 8:1).

Summary

If we tie together these various strands, it follows that Christ's person and atoning work reconciles believers to God just as promised. God promises that the obedience of the God-man in his one-time death is effective for forgiveness, justification, and deliverance from the power of sin, death, Satan, and judgment. He promises that the intercessory work of the crucified and risen Christ presently and eternally preserves the believer's standing with God. God promises that the present advocacy of Christ on behalf of the believer assures the same work on the day of judgment and beyond in perpetuity.

REFLECTION QUESTIONS

1. What is the relationship between the expiating and propitiating work of Christ?

2. What are the soteriological implications of Christ's expiating and propitiating work?

3. How does Christ's intercessory work impact his atoning work?

4. Why does Christ's role as eschatological judge assure believers of reconciliation with God on the day of judgment?

5. How does Jesus's identity as the God-man and his obedience affect atonement?

How Does One Receive the Benefits of God's Atoning Work in Christ?

I am the resurrection and the life. Whoever believes in me, though he die, yet shall he live, and everyone one who lives and believes in me shall never die. Do you believe this?
~John 11:25–26

The scope and power of God's atoning work in Christ is far-reaching and ultimately mysterious (see Question 40). However, Scripture makes it clear that an individual's experience of this atoning work is not a given. Christ reconciles the ungodly to God; however, the ungodly must receive the benefits of Christ's atoning work. How, though, does one receive these benefits? The answer involves a tight connection between the saving proclamation, participatory faith, and endurance.

The Reception of Atoning Benefits in the OT

God's atoning work in Christ consists of two broad, interwoven strands: forgiveness and salvation. Forgiveness of sin requires the sacrificial death of Christ, which produces a state in which God delivers the forgiven through Christ. NT writers did not produce these atoning strands out of nothing. Rather, these strands emerged from the soil of the OT and thereby shaped how NT writers articulated these truths. This includes how ancient Israel shared in the benefits of God's atoning work for the nation, which included three interrelated experiences.

First, Israelites shared in the benefits of God's atoning work by hearing his proclamation of that work. Israel's God did not carry out any work, especially atonement, without proclaiming that work before and after the fact (see Amos 3:7). The Torah is paradigmatic in this regard. God proclaimed the deliverance of Israel from Egyptian bondage before it occurred: "Say therefore to the people of Israel, 'I am the LORD, and I will bring you out from under the burdens of the Egyptians, and I will deliver you from slavery to them, and I will redeem you with an outstretched arm and with great acts of judgment" (Exod. 6:6; cf. 6:7–8). He also instituted the annual observance of the Passover to proclaim and encourage remembrance of his saving work (Exod. 12:1–28). The sacrificial animals involved in the Passover and the display of their blood signaled the link between forgiveness, judgment, and Israel's deliverance. As YHWH instructs, "For the LORD will pass through to strike the Egyptians, and when he sees the blood on the lintel and on the two doorposts, the LORD will pass over the door and will not allow the destroyer to enter your houses to strike you" (Exod. 12:23; cf. 12:13). The sacrificial blood had an atoning effect so the Israelites did not experience the same judgment as the Egyptians. Moreover, through the judgment that Egypt experienced and Israel avoided, God delivered his people. Passover memorialized and proclaimed this atoning work in its various dimensions.

Second, Israel shared in the benefits of atoning work by hearing its proclamation and participating in what God announced. Faith was the means of their participation. Israel believed the promise of God's atoning work and expressed their faith by participating in what he prescribed. Along with participation in the Passover, participation in the sacrificial system expressed Israel's faith whereby they received the benefits of God's atoning work. The Day of Atonement especially stands out in this regard (Lev. 16:1–34). The nation annually provided two sacrificial goats to the high priest, sacrifices that represented them and stood in their place before God. The people trusted that the blood of a goat brought before the mercy seat and the sacrifice of the scapegoat would produce the forgiveness they needed to be rightly related to their God and continue sharing in the promise of his redemption.

Third, if Israel were to receive the atoning benefits of God's work, they had to endure in their faith. Rebellion and apostasy often marks Israel's storyline in the OT, including Joseph's enslavement at the hands of his brothers, Israel's initial rejection of Moses, the wilderness generation's groaning and attempted coup against the divinely appointed leadership, the trouble caused by Achan in the conquest, and the broader instances of idolatry and/or social injustice that resulted in invasion and even exile, as Moses warned beforehand.[1] What we find then is that individuals or clusters of God's people endured in their faith; however, the nation as a whole often did not. Habakkuk's lament encapsulates this dynamic as he questioned why the righteous must endure lawlessness and its accompanying wrath against the unrighteous (1:1–17). YHWH answered, "Behold, his soul is puffed up; it is not right within him, but the

---

1. See, e.g., Gen. 37:1–50:26; Exod. 2:11–25; 5:20–23; 15:22–27; Num. 11:1–15; 14:1–25; 16:1–17:28; Deut. 32:1–52; Josh. 7:1–26.

righteous shall live by his faith" (Hab. 2:4), which underscores the need for enduring faith. Nevertheless, with the righteous and unrighteous alike, it is ultimately God's mercy that endures and thereby preserves the benefit of God's atoning work for his people.

Covenant, or promise, frames this triad of proclamation, faith, and endurance. To share in the benefits of God's atoning work is to share in what he promised to Abraham, David, and Jeremiah. God's atoning work occupies the central piece in the promise of a new covenant in which Abraham's descendants have a promised king who ushers in their possession of land, glory, and the one through whom redemption reaches all nations. Therefore, to experience reconciliation with God is to share in what he promised to Abraham, David, and the prophets.

The Reception of Atoning Benefits in the New Testament

The theology of the NT indicates that Jews and Gentiles alike experience the benefit of God's atoning work in Christ in the same way that ancient Israel did, namely, the triad of proclamation, faith, and endurance (see Rom. 4:1–25; 1 Cor. 10:1–13; Gal. 3:1–29; Heb. 11:1–40). The revelation of Christ reconfigures this triad in a way that parallels the OT and fulfills what the OT prophets expected. If the incarnate Logos ultimately explains God, as John asserts, it follows that Jesus ultimately explains atonement and how one receives its benefits (John 1:18; cf. 14:1–11; Col. 1:15–20; Heb. 1:1–4).

During his earthly ministry, and just prior to his ascension, Jesus prepares his followers to proclaim his person and work (see Matt. 28:16–20; Acts 1:7–8). The content of the proclamation includes Jesus's teaching, actions, death, resurrection, place of power at God's right hand, and expected return. While all of Jesus's teaching and work has atoning value, his death animates all other atoning aspects of his identity (Questions 3 and 4). Paul's description of his preaching to the Corinthians assumes this centrality: "For I decided to know nothing among you except Jesus Christ and him crucified" (1 Cor. 2:2; cf. 1:18–32; Gal. 6:14). For Jews and Gentiles to share in the atoning benefits of a crucified and risen Jesus, they must hear about him through those whom God sends to proclaim him (Rom. 10:14–17). Such proclamations emphasize the atoning benefits of Christ's work, though NT writers narrate those benefits in different ways to meet the needs of their original recipients.

Regardless of how the NT writers narrate Christ's atoning work, faith remains the only way to share in those benefits. While faith language has various lexemes and expressions, the dominant sense in the NT is trust in the promise that God gives in Christ.[2] As in the OT, a person trusts in God's promise when

---

2. However, faith language has recently drawn the attention of NT scholars. Some now suggest that "faithfulness" to Christ, or "allegiance" to him—rather than faith, belief, or trust in him—is a more historically and contextually accurate rendering of the NT's many

there is no obvious reason to do so except for the divine word itself.[3] In fact, affliction often gives sufficient cause not to trust the divine word. Therefore, to share in the benefits of Christ's atoning work, one must live by faith in what cannot be seen and not be discouraged by the things that are seen that seem to challenge the gospel's promise. As Paul tells the Corinthians, "For we walk by faith, not by sight" (2 Cor. 5:7; cf. 4:16–18).

The source of such faith is the mysterious work of God. Paul remarks, "So faith comes from hearing, and hearing through the word of Christ" (Rom. 10:17). This statement implies that God gives faith through hearing the gospel. As Mark Seifrid observes, "He [Paul] set forth Christ as the exclusive, all-determining source of faith."[4] Faith then is God's work.[5] However, not everyone who hears the gospel believes it. This reality is in keeping with Jesus's parable of the sower where tension between "soil" (human hearts), the "seed" (the word of the gospel), and Satan's work—tribulation, the worries of the age, or deceit—result in unbelief. Therefore, while faith is a gift that Christ gives through the gospel, it does not follow that everyone who hears the gospel receives the gift and herein lies the mystery. Whether unbelief in the gospel stems from God's electing purposes, human volition, or some combination of the two remains mysterious in the NT. What is clear is that faith in the crucified and risen Christ functions as the only way to share in the benefits of his atoning work.

It is also clear, just as in the OT, that sharing in God's atoning work requires endurance. As Jesus plainly states, "But the one who endures to the end will be saved" (Matt. 24:13; cf. Mark 13:13). Similarly, Paul reminds Timothy, "If we endure, we will also reign with him; if we deny him, he also will deny us" (2 Tim. 2:12). Only the one who continually and patiently trusts in the promise of the gospel shares in the benefits of Christ's atoning work. Various afflictions related to sin, death, ungodly enemies, false teaching, the absence of love in the church, Satan, worry about divine wrath, and divine hiddenness threaten such endurance.[6] To address this concern, the NT writers sometimes

---

uses of *pistis*. See, e.g., Matthew W. Bates, *Salvation by Allegiance Alone: Rethinking Faith, Works, and the Gospel of Jesus the King* (Grand Rapids: Baker Academic, 2017); and Nijay K. Gupta, *Paul and the Language of Faith* (Grand Rapids: Eerdmans, 2020). For a more traditional understanding of faith language in the NT, see Kevin W. McFadden, *Faith in the Son of God: The Place of Christ-Oriented Faith within Pauline Theology* (Wheaton, IL: Crossway, 2021).

3.   For OT texts that inform Paul's understanding of faith in this way, see Gen. 15:1–6; Ps. 143; Hab. 2:1–4 (cf. Rom. 4:1–25; Gal. 3:1–14). See also the programmatic use of Hab. 2:4 in Heb. 10:36–11:40.

4.   Mark A. Seifrid, *Christ, Our Righteousness: Paul's Theology of Justification*, New Studies in Biblical Theology 9 (Downers Grove, IL: IVP Academic, 2000), 146.

5.   Seifrid, *Christ, Our Righteousness*, 146.

6.   See, e.g., Matt. 6:9–13; Luke 22:31–34; John 16:33; Rom. 5:1–8:39; 9:1–5; 14:15; 16:17–20; 1 Cor. 8:11–13; 2 Cor. 1:3–7; 4:7–15; Gal. 1:6–9; 3:1–5; Eph. 6:10–20; Phil. 1:12–18; 4:4–7; 1 Thess. 4:13–18; 5:1–11; 2 Tim. 1:3–18; Heb. 2:1–4, 14–18; 6:9–20; 10:32–39; 12:4.

use warnings against apostasy as a means of producing endurance while also appealing to God's work of election and predestination.[7] Paul assured the Romans that, despite afflictions that imply otherwise, God foreknew, predestined, called, justified, and glorified them so they would certainly share in the atoning benefits of Christ's work (Rom. 8:28–30; cf. Eph. 1:3–14). Such divine work is the ultimate reason that believers endure to receive these atoning benefits.

Summary

The power and scope of God's atoning work in Christ does not make the human experience of those works inconsequential. Both Testaments make clear that individuals must hear the proclamation of God's atoning work, believe that proclamation, and endure in their faith. Such endurance includes adhering to the teaching of Jesus and his apostles in the face of various afflictions. Nevertheless, mystery marks this triadic experience, especially as it relates to the interplay between belief, unbelief, God's sovereign work, and the work of Satan. Regardless of how that mystery ultimately resolves itself, a faith that participates and endures in the promise of God's atoning work remains the only way one can share in its benefits.

REFLECTION QUESTIONS

1. How does the OT provide a frame for understanding the triad of proclamation, faith, and endurance in the NT?

2. How did the NT writers reconfigure the OT's explanation of how one shares in the benefits of God's atoning work?

3. Why is faith mysterious?

4. What makes it difficult for believers to endure and trust so they share in Christ's atoning benefits?

5. What is the ultimate reason believers can share in Christ's atoning work?

---

7. For a discussion of warnings against apostasy as a way of producing endurance, see Channing L. Crisler, "Warned for Assurance in Affliction: A Baptist Reading of NT Warning Passages," in *Whom the Son Sets Free: Liberating Perspectives in the Evangelical Church*, eds. Sherelle Ducksworth and Kevaughn Mattis (Eugene, OR: Pickwick, forthcoming).

PART 2

Theories of Atonement

What Is the *Christus Victor* Theory of Atonement?

> *Whoever makes a practice of sinning is of the devil, for the devil has been sinning from the beginning. The reason the Son of God appeared was to destroy the works of the devil.*
>
> ~1 John 3:8

We now turn our attention to various theories of atonement. As Adam Johnson avers, a difference exists between "aspects" and "theories" of atonement.[1] The former refers to "mutually dependent dimensions or elements of the atoning event."[2] The latter refers to the "Church's witness to these various aspects by means of offering conceptually unified accounts of these various aspects."[3] Given this distinction, a theory of the atonement synthesizes how Jesus's person and work results in reconciliation with God according to biblical interpretation, Christian tradition, and the relationship between atonement and all other doctrines.[4]

One well-known theory is the so-called *Christus Victor* theory. Modern discussions here often begin with Gustaf Aulén's 1930 publication titled *Christus Victor*.[5] However, as Aulén himself argues, a version of this theory

---

1. Adam J. Johnson, *Atonement: A Guide for the Perplexed*, Guides for the Perplexed (London: Bloomsbury T&T Clark, 2015), 36–38.
2. Johnson, *Atonement*, 38.
3. Johnson, *Atonement*, 38.
4. Regarding the relationship between the doctrine of atonement and all other doctrines, Johnson notes, "In short, the atonement is a uniquely synthetic doctrine, for it is the point at which all Christian theology comes together" (Johnson, *Atonement*, 38).
5. Aulén originally published the work in Swedish in 1930 and then in English in 1931. The edition referenced in what follows is Gustaf Aulén, *Christus Victor: An Historical Study of*

might be present as early as the works of Irenaeus (AD 130–202). *Christus Victor*, in its basic form, attempts to synthesize the atonement around the motif of Christ's victory over sin, death, and the devil. The discussion here moves in two main parts: (1) a summary of Aulén's work and (2) a critique of Aulén's work.

A Summary of Aulén's *Christus Victor*

Aulén begins by demoting the "traditional account" of atonement—that is, what he calls the "objective" idea of deliverance from guilt related to sin—to a later development within the church largely influenced by Anselm of Canterbury's work *Cur Deus Homo* (Question 13).[6] According to Aulén, the traditional account replaced an earlier and more widely accepted view of the "classic idea of the atonement," which Aulén labels the "dramatic" idea of atonement.[7] He explains, "Its central theme is the idea of the Atonement as a Divine conflict and victory; Christ—Christus Victor—fights against and triumphs over the evil powers of the world, the 'tyrants' under which mankind is in bondage and suffering, and in Him God reconciles the world to himself."[8] The dramatic idea is "dualistic" in the sense that "God is pictured as in Christ carrying through a victorious conflict against powers of evil that are hostile to His will."[9]

Aulén marshals historical support for the dramatic idea from the entire patristic era until Anselm and then again in Martin Luther.[10] In the patristic era, he especially leans on his reading of Irenaeus,[11] from which he infers two essential features of *Christus Victor*: (1) God himself carries out the work of reconciliation through the incarnation of the Word so that incarnation and atonement "belong inseparably together"; and (2) *Christus Victor* has a "dualistic background" that consistently pits the divine will against hostile forces of evil.[12]

However, Aulén asserts that in the Middle Ages the traditional, or "Latin," theory held sway under the preliminary influence of Tertullian, Cyprian, and Gregory the Great, and then fully in Anselm of Canterbury.[13] Tertullian (AD 155–220) stressed the need for "satisfaction" whereby an individual

---

the *Three Main Types of the Idea of Atonement*, trans. A. G. Hebert (Austin, TX: Wise Path, 2016).

6. Aulén, *Christus Victor*, 1–2. See also Anselm of Canterbury, *The Major Works*, eds. Brian Davies and G. R. Evans, Oxford World's Classics (Oxford: Oxford University Press, 2008), 260–356.
7. Aulén, *Christus Victor*, 4.
8. Aulén, *Christus Victor*, 4–5.
9. Aulén, *Christus Victor*, 5.
10. Aulén, *Christus Victor*, 17–65, 108–29.
11. Aulén, *Christus Victor*, 37.
12. Aulén, *Christus Victor*, 37–38.
13. Aulén, *Christus Victor*, 87–107.

compensates God for his fault.[14] Cyprian (ca. AD 210–258) supplied the notion of transferring one person's merit to another.[15] Gregory the Great (ca. AD 540–604), while describing Christ's work in the vein of *Christus Victor*, also showed a propensity for arguing that "human guilt necessitated a sacrifice."[16] This is at least Aulén's assessment of these theologians.

According to Aulén, it is with Anselm's work *Cur Deus Homo* (i.e., *Why God Became a Man*) that the so-called Latin theory takes hold and dominates the Middle Ages. Aulén summarizes Anselm's thought as follows:

> Anselm's basic assumption is that the required satisfaction for transgression must be made by man, and the argument proceeds: Men are not able to make the necessary satisfaction, because they are all sinful. If men cannot do it, then God must do it. But, on the other hand, the satisfaction must be made by man because man is guilty. The only solution is that God becomes man; this is the answer to the question *Cur Deus homo*?[17]

What especially bothers Aulén in his reading of Anselm is a perceived downgrade of the link between incarnation and atonement as well as its "juridical scheme" wherein God receives compensation for "man's default" through Christ.[18] Such a scheme worries Aulén for numerous reasons, including the concern that "the doctrine provides for the remission of the punishment due to sins, but not for the taking away of the sin itself."[19]

With respect to Martin Luther, Aulén credits him with recovering the *Christus Victor* theory, even if interpreters have misunderstood the reformer on this point. He finds in Luther's understanding of atonement a "revival" of the classical theory from the patristic era, "but with a greater depth of treatment."[20] In Aulén's understanding of Luther, the reformer does not offer a rational solution to the relationship between divine love and divine wrath as proposed in the Latin theory. Rather, Luther insists "on the triumph of Divine Love over Divine wrath by the way of self-oblation for our sake."[21] Aulén asserts, "His [i.e., Luther's] conception of the wrath of God and the way in which it is overcome shows that there is no thought here of a satisfaction of the legal

---

14. Aulén, *Christus Victor*, 87–88.
15. Aulén, *Christus Victor*, 88.
16. Aulén, *Christus Victor*, 89.
17. Aulén, *Christus Victor*, 93.
18. Aulén, *Christus Victor*, 96.
19. Aulén, *Christus Victor*, 99.
20. Aulén, *Christus Victor*, 109.
21. Aulén, *Christus Victor*, 130.

claims of the Divine Justice; for it is God Himself, the Divine blessing, which in Christ prevails over the wrath and the curse."[22]

Aulén's exegesis focuses almost exclusively on NT texts, particularly from the Pauline corpus.[23] Aulén bristles at the assumption that Paul founded the Latin theory of atonement based on verses such Romans 3:24, which many believe reflects a satisfaction theory whereby Christ suffered "in our stead" as a sacrifice "from man's side" to God.[24] Instead, such Pauline expressions should be understood within the classical frame so that God reconciles himself to humanity and thereby frees people from the hostile forces of sin, death, the law, and Satan. He admits the OT contains texts that "could serve as a basis for the Latin type of view."[25] Nevertheless, he believes the NT writers make a "radical breach between Judaism and Christianity" at this point.[26] Aulén then highlights the OT's Divine Warrior motif as a precursor to the classical view. He ultimately concludes the NT contains "an idea or motif" of the atonement that leans toward the *Christus Victor* view, but in a largely undeveloped way.[27]

A Critique of Aulén's *Christus Victor*

Oliver Crisp has recently critiqued Aulén's view.[28] He highlights three areas of "confusion" within *Christus Victor*. First, Crisp suggests that Aulén oversimplified the church fathers' view of the atonement. Early church fathers did not hold a consensus view that later theology, such as the Anselmian approach, replaced. Moreover, Crisp reminds us that an older view is not necessarily the correct view.[29] Even if the early church fathers held the classical view that Aulén espouses, the "age of a view" does not guarantee "closer proximity to the truth of the matter."[30]

Second, Crisp suggests that Aulén popularized the mistaken notion that his classic view of atonement is the view of the early church fathers. Crisp acknowledges that some fathers, such as Gregory of Nyssa, have a *Christus Victor*–ransom motif; however, a motif does not constitute an entire doctrine of atonement.[31]

---

22. Aulén, *Christus Victor*, 126–27.
23. Aulén, *Christus Victor*, 66–86.
24. Aulén, *Christus Victor*, 67, 78.
25. Aulén, *Christus Victor*, 85.
26. Aulén, *Christus Victor*, 85–86.
27. Aulén, *Christus Victor*, 84.
28. Oliver D. Crisp, *Approaching the Atonement: The Reconciling Work of Christ* (Downers Grove, IL: IVP Academic, 2020), 31–33. See also the critique of Aulén in Colin E. Gunton, *The Actuality of Atonement: A Study of Metaphor, Rationality, and the Christian Tradition* (Grand Rapids: Eerdmans, 1989), 54–59.
29. Crisp, *Approaching the Atonement*, 31.
30. Crisp, *Approaching the Atonement*, 32.
31. Crisp, *Approaching the Atonement*, 32–33.

Third, Aulén also wrongly presented his *Christus Victor* theory as a type of ransom doctrine of atonement. Crisp explains, "The claim that Christ is victorious over the powers of evil, which is a central plank of the *Christus Victor* view of Christ's saving work, is not necessarily the same as the claim that Christ's atonement ransoms us from the powers of sin, death, and the devil."[32]

Aulén is open to criticism in other areas, such as his NT exegesis, which is beset with a historically suspect and thin discussion of relevant texts. Aulén appeals to the historically incorrect trope that a deep breach existed between Judaism and Christianity, including how the legal character of atonement in the OT influenced NT conceptions of the matter.[33] He misunderstands both the legal character of OT atonement, which he labels "legalistic," as well as its influence on NT writers.[34] Nevertheless, he appeals to the OT's Divine Warrior motif as a precursor to *Christus Victor*, though he does not mention the motif's inherent legal character that remains intact in the NT.[35]

Nevertheless, Scripture clearly describes Jesus's atoning work as a triumph over that which separates human beings from God, and the *Christus Victor* motif amplifies this description. John's atonement theology certainly includes a motif of victory in descriptions of Jesus's death. For example, Jesus declares, "Now is the judgment of this world; now will the ruler of this world be cast out. And I, when I am lifted up from the earth, will draw all people to myself" (John 12:32–33). Clearly, with John's typical penchant for double meaning, "lifted up from the earth" refers to Jesus's glorification and alludes to Jesus's crucifixion where that glorification unfolds. It is in this mode of death that Jesus is victorious over Satan, or "the ruler of this world" (see also 1 John 3:8).[36] Therefore, in principle, the *Christus Victor* view rightly accentuates the victorious nature of Jesus's death; however, such emphasis should not eclipse other contours of atonement as it often does.

Summary

Some variations of Aulén's theory have emerged in recent years, even if they do not directly engage his theory. For example, N. T. Wright often complains that, under the influence of Anselm and the Reformation, discussions

---

32. Crisp, *Approaching the Atonement*, 33.
33. Crisp, *Approaching the Atonement*, 85.
34. Crisp, *Approaching the Atonement*, 85.
35. E.g., the Divine Warrior in Hab. 3 only rescues the "righteous" who have trusted in YHWH's faithfulness (Hab. 2:4).
36. As Leon Morris observes, "And just as the cross represents the judgment of this world, so it represents the defeat of Satan. To people it appeared as his victory; it looked like the triumph of evil, but in fact it was the source of the world's greatest good. Satan was defeated in what appeared outwardly to be the very moment of his triumph" (Leon Morris, *The Gospel According to John*, rev. ed., The New International Commentary on the New Testament [Grand Rapids: Eerdmans, 1995], 531).

of atonement have too often been tied to a less biblical and more medieval concern with how sinners escape hell and get to heaven.[37] Along these lines, Wright claims, "Almost nobody in the gospels warns about 'going to hell.'"[38] He suggests that Anselm, Luther, and others have led us all astray, especially in the West, from the true significance of Jesus's death, which is not the satisfaction of divine wrath.[39] Rather, in the vein of Aulén, though based on different arguments and seeking different aims, Wright stridently dismisses all conclusions about Christ's atoning work except what he himself holds to:

> Forget the "works contract," with its angry, legalistic divinity. Forget the false either/or that plays different "theories of atonement" against one another. Embrace the "covenant of vocation" or, rather, be embraced by it as the Creator calls you to a genuine humanness at last, calls and equips you to bear and reflect his image. Celebrate the revolution that happened once and for all when the power of love overcame the love of power. And, in the power of that same love, join in the revolution here and now.[40]

Wright caricatures all prior theories of atonement and implies that only his "revolution" view, which resembles *Christus Victor*, weighs the biblical evidence carefully and correctly. But of course, those who preceded and followed Wright, just as those who preceded and followed Aulén, were reading the Bible too. One cannot simply claim to have the exegetical (Wright) or historical (Aulén) high ground and then summarily dismiss all other articulations of atonement.

These criticisms aside, *Christus Victor* amplifies the triumph that emerges from God's work in the crucified, risen, and enthroned Jesus. God brings victory out of death. He brings light out of darkness. He demonstrates his saving power in weakness. As Paul explains to the Colossians, "He disarmed the rulers and authorities and put them to open shame, by triumphing over them in him" (Col. 2:15).

---

37. E.g., Wright complains, "To put it crudely, the Eastern Orthodox churches never had 'an Anselm.' That alone should alert us to the possibility that some of our great controversies may have more to do with fresh interpretative schemes introduced at a later date than with the original meaning of the Bible" (N. T. Wright, *The Day the Revolution Began: Considering the Meaning of Jesus's Crucifixion* [New York: HarperOne, 2016], 26).
38. Wright, *The Day the Revolution Began*, 196.
39. Wright, *The Day the Revolution Began*, 19–49.
40. Wright, *The Day the Revolution Began*, 416.

REFLECTION QUESTIONS

1. How would you describe Gustaf Aulén's *Christus Victor* theory of atonement?

2. How does Aulén distinguish the classical view of atonement from the Latin view?

3. What roles do Irenaeus and Luther play in Aulén's theory?

4. In what ways is Aulén's theory, and theories like his, open to criticism?

5. What might be some helpful elements of the *Christus Victor* theory?

What Is the Moral Exemplar Theory of Atonement?

For I have given you an example, that you also should do just as I have done to you.

~John 13:15

Humans have an innate tendency to imitate one another. Attempts are often made to mimic figures who are deemed worthy of imitation based on their accomplishments, their moral virtue, or the heroism they showed in difficult circumstances. Following worthy exemplars was a pillar of the classical world. Greco-Roman writers encouraged the practice of *mimesis*, the "act of imitating."[1] Likewise, NT writers encouraged the imitation of those worthy of it: "Remember your leaders, those who spoke to you the word of God. Consider the outcome of their way of life, and imitate [*mimeisthe*] their faith" (Heb. 13:7; cf. 2 Thess. 3:7, 9; 3 John 11). Of course, above all, the NT writers urged their recipients to imitate Christ: "Be imitators [*mimetai*] of me, as I am of Christ" (1 Cor. 11:1; cf. 1 Cor. 4:16; Eph. 5:1; 1 Thess. 1:6; 2:14; Heb. 6:12). Following Christ's example is a key element of the Christian experience that aligns with the human propensity for imitation and biblical admonitions.

For some, however, imitation also provides the key to understanding the atoning work of Christ. The moral exemplar theory asserts that Christ's work is mainly an example to be followed that in turn has a transformative and even salvific effect.[2] One of the difficulties in discussing this theory is that many theologians and interpreters use exemplar language to describe God's work

---

1. *BrillDAG*, s.v. "μίμησις."
2. For definitions of the moral exemplar theory, see Oliver D. Crisp, *Approaching the Atonement: The Reconciling Work of Christ* (Downers Grove, IL: IVP Academic, 2020),

in Christ; however, it does not follow that they embrace a purely moral exemplar theory of atonement. For example, in his letter to the Romans, Ignatius requests of his recipients, "Permit me to be an imitator [*mimeten*] of the suffering of my God" (Ign. Rom. 6:3a). Ignatius wishes to imitate Jesus's death as a means of reaching Christ (see Ign. Rom. 5:3). However, other reflections in the letter indicate that imitation does not exhaust Ignatius's understanding of Jesus's death, such as his description of Jesus as one who "died for us" (Ign. Rom. 6:1; cf. Ign. Trall. 2:1).

Given this kind of difficulty, we will primarily focus on those who treat Jesus's atoning work as purely a moral example, or, in some instances, those who are thought to hold a purist position.

Moral Exemplarism in Peter Abelard

Discussions of the moral exemplar theory often begin with Peter Abelard (AD 1079–1142), a medieval French philosopher and theologian.[3] Abelard's comments on Romans 3:26 in his commentary on the letter is the reason some have inferred he held to an exemplary view.[4] In typical medieval style, while answering his own slate of questions related to the verse, Abelard writes:

> Nevertheless, it seems to us that in this we are justified in the blood of Christ and reconciled to God, that it was through this matchless grace shown to us that his Son received our nature, and in that nature, teaching us both by word and by example, preserved to the death and bound us to himself even more through love, so that when we have been kindled by so great a benefit of divine grace, true charity might fear to endure nothing for his sake.[5]

Taken in isolation from the rest of Abelard's commentary and wider works, it appears he regards Jesus's death as example of divine grace and love that in turn produces "true charity" toward God and others, regardless of the cost. Reconciliation with God becomes a matter of being inspired by Christ's example and following it. However, as Steven Cartwright observes, "Abelard does not present an entirely consistent theology of redemption in his Romans commentary. At some points he presents what seems to be a strictly

---

78; Alister E. McGrath, *Christian Theology: An Introduction*, 2nd ed. (Oxford: Blackwell, 1997), 407–12.

3. Don Schweitzer, *Contemporary Christologies: A Fortress Introduction* (Minneapolis: Fortress, 2010), 33–54.

4. Steven R. Cartwright, "Introduction to The Fathers of the Church Medieval Continuation," in Peter Abelard, *Commentary on the Epistle to the Romans*, trans. Steven R. Cartwright (Washington, DC: Catholic University of America Press, 2011), 46.

5. Abelard, *Commentary on the Epistle to the Romans*, 167–68.

exemplarist view of redemption; at still others he seems to mix them."[6] Such lack of consistency, along with the way Abelard attacked "the morality of the ransom theory," likely fueled his contemporary critics, such as William of St. Thierry and Bernard of Clairvaux.[7] Modern voices are divided on the issue.[8]

It follows that, in the spirit of fairness, one should not assume Abelard held to an "exclusively or even dominantly exemplarist" view of atonement.[9] Instead, we should examine Abelard's exemplarist reflections that contributed to the later development of the moral exemplar theory, with the understanding that he himself did not necessarily hold to an exclusively exemplarist view.[10]

With this qualification in place, Alister McGrath suggests that Abelard's main influence on the moral exemplar theory is his "emphasis upon the subjective impact of the cross."[11] Abelard finds in the cross the quintessential demonstration of God's love that in turn propels people to love him. That God's demonstration of love in the cross propels love in others may not be adequately accounted for in Abelard's predecessors, particularly Anselm of Canterbury.[12]

Moral Exemplarism in the Enlightenment

While Abelard's impact on the matter is clear, articulations of exemplarism begin in earnest with the Enlightenment. McGrath's assessment of the developments in this era are helpful.[13] He insists that many Enlightenment thinkers could not countenance the belief that Christ's death was a transcendent sacrifice for humanity that provided payment for a penalty. Nor did they hold to a resurrected Christ who had both a divine and human nature, an orthodox position established since Chalcedon (AD 451).[14]

---

6. Cartwright, "Introduction," 44.
7. Cartwright, "Introduction," 43–51.
8. Cartwright, "Introduction," 44–45. As Stephen Westerholm recently noted, "Since no one would deny [what Abelard affirms] that Christ's love is exemplary, and since he, too, can speak of Christ paying the penalty for human sin, perhaps Abelard differs from others only in what he chooses to emphasize? Perhaps. Still, it seems reasonable to assume that Abelard emphasizes what he deems most important, and it is surely significant that he associates justification with the evoking of human love by divine love" (Stephen Westerholm, *Romans: Text, Readers, and the History of Interpretation* [Grand Rapids: Eerdmans, 2022], 139).
9. Adam J. Johnson, "Peter Abelard," in *T&T Clark Companion to Atonement*, ed. Adam J. Johnson (London: Bloomsbury T&T Clark, 2017), 359.
10. Johnson explains that the term "exemplarism" did not emerge until the Enlightenment with respect to the doctrine of the atonement (Johnson, "Peter Abelard," 359).
11. Alister E. McGrath, *Christian Theology: An Introduction*, 2nd ed. (Oxford: Blackwell, 1997), 407.
12. McGrath, *Christian Theology*, 408.
13. McGrath, *Christian Theology*, 408–10.
14. See Donald Fairbairn and Ryan M. Reeves, *The Story of Creeds and Confessions: Tracing the Development of the Christian Faith* (Grand Rapids: Baker Academic, 2019), 80–108.

When Enlightenment thinkers brought this truncated view of Jesus to bear upon atonement theory, a "consistent pattern" marked by three traits developed, as McGrath maintains: (1) Jesus's cross does not represent a transcendent sacrifice for sin but only a relinquishment of his life; (2) Jesus was only a human being; therefore, the impact of his death is only on human beings, not God, in the form of setting an example for others that inspires them; and (3) the primary aspect of the cross is that it "demonstrates the love of God towards us."[15]

The emergence of this moral theory swept "rationalist circles" in nineteenth-century Europe.[16] Like Enlightenment Christology, it rationalized Jesus's death. Rationalists did not have to see Jesus as the eternal Son of God whose sacrificial death reconciled sinners from all historical eras to their God. Rather, they could see him as a model for the "moral improvement of humanity."[17]

Moral Exemplarism in Friedrich Schleiermacher

Given his connection to exemplarism and his influence on the matter, we must also consider Friedrich Schleiermacher (1768–1834), a German theologian, philosopher, and pastor who challenged the rationalist reduction of Jesus's death to a moral example but whose thoughts are still adjacent to the position. He found in Jesus not a "human moral example" but the "one ideal example of a perfect human consciousness of God."[18] Nevertheless, like the rationalists whom he opposed, Schleiermacher rejected substitutionary atonement, noting in a letter to his father, "I cannot believe that [Christ's] death was a substitutionary atonement because he never expressly said so, and because I cannot believe that it was necessary. For it would be impossible for God to desire the eternal punishment of those whom he had obviously not created perfect, but for the pursuit of perfection, since they are not [yet] perfect."[19] This remark and Schleiermacher's lifelong theological reflections indicate an emphasis on humanity's perfection, particularly human consciousness, rather than its punishment, as Justin Stratis observes.[20]

In his philosophical effort to relate "God (*theos*), the world, (*cosmos*), and the self (*ego*)" through the "Christian self-consciousness of sin and grace," Schleiermacher leans into the idea that people can experience absolute dependence on God in the perfect way that Jesus did, though he did not believe that the divine literally entered the world through Jesus.[21] For Schleiermacher,

15. McGrath, *An Introduction*, 408–9.
16. McGrath, *An Introduction*, 409.
17. McGrath, *An Introduction*, 409.
18. McGrath, *An Introduction*, 410.
19. Justin Stratis, "Friedrich Schleiermacher," in Johnson, *T&T Clark Companion to Atonement*, 739.
20. Stratis, "Friedrich Schleiermacher," 739.
21. Stratis, "Friedrich Schleiermacher," 740.

the essence of humanity's sin is its failure to act with a consciousness of God. Jesus both models and evokes the ideal of such consciousness, particularly in his crucifixion, where it remains "radically imperturbable."[22] In this way, atonement becomes being inspired by and following the example of Jesus's God-consciousness even in the face of death.

Moral Exemplarism Today

The twentieth and twenty-first centuries have witnessed a sharpened and unapologetic moral exemplar theory of atonement in different parts of the world and with various nuances. McGrath points to the English modernist Hastings Rashdall and his 1915 Bampton Lectures as a starting point. Rashdall suggested a radical reworking of the traditional theories of atonement:

> Translated into still modern language the meaning of the Church's early creed "There is none other name given among men by which we may be saved" will be something of this kind: "There is none other ideal given among men by which we may be saved, except the moral ideal which Christ taught us by his words, and illustrated by his life and death of love: and there is no other help so great in the attainment of that ideal as the belief in God as He has been supremely revealed in Him who so taught and lived and died. So understood, the self-sacrificing life which was consummated by the death upon the Cross has indeed power to take away the sins of the whole world."[23]

Rashnall's suggestion reflects the spirit of his age. As McGrath explains, "In an age which had discovered both Darwinianism and biblical criticism, there was no longer any place for any understanding of Christ's death which was based upon an objective notion of sin or divine punishment."[24]

Others have opted for a moral exemplar theory as part of larger religious projects, including pluralists, such as the late John Hick, who ultimately defined the meaning of the cross as "the inspirational power of Christ's self-sacrifice."[25] However, as Crisp assessed Hick's exemplarism, "it is not atoning in the narrow sense of the term; there is no mechanism in Christ's crucifixion by means of which human beings are reconciled to God."[26]

---

22. Stratis, "Friedrich Schleiermacher," 741.
23. Hastings Rashdall, *The Idea of Atonement in Christian Theology: Being the Bampton Lectures for 1915* (London: MacMillan and Co., 1920), 463.
24. McGrath, *Introduction*, 411.
25. Crisp, *Approaching the New Testament*, 84.
26. Crisp, *Approaching the New Testament*, 84.

Summary

Multiple salient points emerge from this discussion of the moral exemplar theory of atonement. First, the NT writers encouraged their readers to imitate Jesus; however, in doing so, they did not jettison the historicity of his person, his human and divine nature, the understanding of sin as unbelief in God's word that warrants his righteous judgment, the atoning benefits of his work, and other related matters. Second, the exhortation to imitate Jesus needs to be given in the context of a wider and clearer doctrine of atonement, unlike what Peter Abelard offered. Third, rational progress in the wider culture, such as developments often associated with the Enlightenment and its modern successors, often fuels the reduction of Jesus's death to an inspiring act that can be imitated and thereby contribute to humanity's "progress."

To be fair, the moral exemplar theory reminds us that Christ's atoning work possesses an inherently robust ethic. We should not live as though the old hymn "Jesus Paid It All" allows believers to "Do It All," that is, to do whatever they sinfully please. Rather, believers should see themselves as dead to sin through their participation in Christ's death (Rom. 6:1–11). Moreover, believers should imitate the crucified Christ. But that imitation must reflect an awareness that God ultimately gives the morality that he demands. At the heart of that gift is the indwelling presence of Christ, who produces the kind of moral exemplarism worthy of his name (John 15:1–8).

REFLECTION QUESTIONS

1. How does the NT encourage its readers to imitate Jesus?

2. Why is the imitation of Jesus insufficient for reconciliation with God?

3. How did Peter Abelard contribute to the moral exemplar theory?

4. What are some examples of modern exemplar theory in Christianity today?

5. How would you respond to someone who saw the death of Christ as an inspirational example to live by but nothing more?

What Is the Socinian Theory of Atonement?

Christ takes away sins because by the example of his most inno-
cent life, he very readily draws all, who have not lost hope, to leave
their sins and zealously to embrace righteousness and holiness.
~Faustus Socinus

Faustus Socinus (1539–1604), who led the "so-called Minor Reformed Church" in sixteenth- and seventeenth-century Europe, reduced Jesus's atoning work to a kind of moral exemplarism (Question 10).[1] To be sure, Socinus believed that God revealed the way to eternal life through Jesus; however, obtainment of that life had nothing to do with faith in Jesus's atoning work that somehow satisfied a penalty before God.[2] Jesus simply delivered people from sin through his example, which inspired them to turn to a life of holiness and righteousness.[3] As Socinus avers, "Christ takes away sins because by the example of his most innocent life, he very readily draws all, who have not lost hope, to leave their sins and zealously to embrace righteousness and holiness."[4] Consequently, Socinus and his followers railed against the satisfaction theory of atonement espoused by their sixteenth- and seventeenth-century orthodox Protestant opponents.[5]

---

1. Alan W. Gomes, "Socinus," in *T&T Clark Companion to Atonement*, ed. Adam J. Johnson (London: Bloomsbury T&T Clark, 2017), 753–54.
2. Gomes, "Socinus," 754.
3. See Oliver D. Crisp, *Approaching the Atonement: The Reconciling Work of Christ* (Downers Grove, IL: IVP Academic, 2020), 78–95.
4. See citation in L. W. Grensted, *A Short History of the Doctrine of the Atonement* (Manchester: Manchester University Press, 1920), 287.
5. Alan W. Gomes, "*De Jesu Christo Servatore*: Faustus Socinus on the Satisfaction of Christ," *Westminster Theological Journal* 55 (1993): 209.

The influence of Socinus's challenge to the satisfaction theory through his own exemplar theory has long outlived him. Socinus obviously has a link with his namesake, the Socinians.[6] Socinians is generally a label applied to people who adhered to and expanded on the teachings of Faustus Socinus, some of which are described here. Additionally, although the precise link between them remains disputed, Socinians influenced the emergence of Unitarians (i.e., a non-Trinitarian branch of Christianity that adheres to the salvation of all regardless of faith in Christ).[7] Most important for our purposes here, as Oliver Crisp observes, Socinus is "the fount of much subsequent moral exemplarism in theology."[8] Given its importance to multiple theories of atonement, including moral exemplarism (Question 10) and the governmental theory of atonement (Question 14), it is necessary to understand the inner workings of Socinus's theory. As indicated in his work *De Jesu Christo Servatore* (*Concerning Jesus Christ the Savior*), Socinus's understanding of atonement is animated by an ultra-rationalistic interpretation of Scripture, an anti-Trinitarian theology in which God is free to not punish sin, and a belief in the moral neutrality of the human condition.[9] Each of these will receive brief treatment in what follows.

A Summary of *De Jesu Christo Servatore*

Socinus's 1578 treatise *Concerning Jesus Christ the Savior* is the main source for his understanding of the atonement. Unfortunately, no complete English translation of this work currently exists. Therefore, we will rely largely on Alan Gomes's analysis.[10] The treatise emerged from an ongoing debate with Jacques Couet, a French Reformed minister who met Socinus in Basel. The loosely structured work addresses several issues related to Christ's atoning work.

First, Socinus argues *against* "an immanent justice in God that demands punishment for sins" and *for* the salvation provided by Christ that is obtained through imitating him.[11] Second, Socinus addresses the kind of "scriptural evidence" that those such as Couet relied upon.[12] Third, he sets out to logically and morally disprove the arguments that undergird a satisfaction theory of atonement. Gomes summarizes Socinus's arguments at this point, noting:

---

6. However, Gomes observes it was Socinus's opponents who first applied this label to his adherents (see Gomes, "Socinus," 753).
7. Sarah Motimer suggests that similarities between Socinians and modern Unitarians have been "exaggerated." See Sarah Mortimer, *Reason and Religion in the English Revolution: The Challenge of Socialism* (Cambridge: Cambridge University Press, 2010), 4.
8. Crisp, *Approaching the Atonement*, 80.
9. As Charles Beard explains, this work is "a book in which is to be found every rational and moral argument since directed against the theory of satisfaction" (Gomes, "Socinus," 753).
10. Gomes, "*De Jesu Christo Servatore*," 209–31.
11. Gomes, "*De Jesu Christo Servatore*," 213.
12. Gomes, "*De Jesu Christo Servatore*," 213.

He [i.e., Socinus] begins (chap. 1) by arguing that God could forgive sins without satisfaction; such an action would not be contrary to his nature or justice. Next, he attempts to establish that God "was in fact willing" to do so (chap. 2). In chaps. 3–6, Socinus seeks to prove that even if one grants the necessity of satisfaction, Christ would not in any way offer the kind of satisfaction required to satisfy the demands of the punitive justice postulated by the orthodox theory. He could not satisfy justice either through his passive obedience (chap. 4) or through his active obedience (chap. 5).[13]

Socinus also denies that death is the punishment for sin, along with its christological inference, namely, that a sinless Christ means God punished him for the sins of others.[14]

Finally, Gomes maintains, Socinus's work is replete with a denial that Christ's righteousness is imputed to others through faith. Socinus argues, "Our righteousness must be genuine rather than a legal fiction; we must evidence our righteousness by a holy life-style."[15]

Socinus's Biblical Hermeneutic

Despite popular belief, Socinus is as much a "biblicist" as he is a "rationalist."[16] He finds in certain texts an indication that God can freely forgive sins without satisfaction or payment of a debt. Examples include Cain and the parable in Matthew 18:23–35.[17] With respect to the former, Socinus stresses that in Genesis 4:1–16 God "makes absolutely no mention of literal satisfaction he is going to receive for Cain's sins."[18] In fact, for Socinus, the conditional clause "if you do well" in Genesis 4:7 implies that "nature itself teaches that God freely forgives the penitent."[19] Similarly, in his reading of Matthew 18:23–35, the so-called parable of the unforgiving servant, Socinus highlights that the master forgives the debt of his servants without payment of a penalty.[20] In short, Socinus's reading of these texts and others supports two pillars of his atonement view: (1) God freely forgives without satisfaction; and (2) right conduct secures a right standing with God. Socinus concludes that a right standing with God

---

13. Gomes, "*De Jesu Christo Servatore*," 213.
14. Gomes, "*De Jesu Christo Servatore*," 214.
15. Gomes, "*De Jesu Christo Servatore*," 214.
16. Crisp, *Approaching the Atonement*, 81.
17. Gomes, "*De Jesu Christo Servatore*," 222.
18. Gomes, "*De Jesu Christo Servatore*," 223.
19. Gomes, "*De Jesu Christo Servatore*," 223.
20. Crisp, *Approaching the Atonement*, 81. For a thorough discussion of this parable, see Klyne R. Snodgrass, *Stories with Intent: A Comprehensive Guide to the Parables*, 2nd ed. (Grand Rapids: Eerdmans, 2018), 61–77.

does not stem from a belief "that God would at some point make satisfaction for our sins by Christ, or that such satisfaction has already been made."[21]

How then does Socinus treat texts that indicate God redeemed people from sin through the death of Christ?[22] He simply reads such texts metaphorically. Crisp explains, "But these passages Socinus understands to be metaphorical in nature, pointing to the way in which God's action liberates us from the debt of sin by forgiving us, not literally requiring some satisfaction for the sin we have committed."[23] Gomes maintains that Socinus recognizes many links between a literal redemption and Christ's work; however, Socinus ultimately regards redemption as a metaphor since no one actually receives the price of redemption that Christ pays.[24] He thereby urges biblical readers to regard redemption language in the general and metaphorical sense of "liberation."[25]

A Brief Critique of Socinus's Hermeneutic

Overall, Socinus's hermeneutic reflects at least three missteps. First, he tends to privilege narrative and parabolic material over propositional statements, which allows him to fill such material with meaning that makes logical sense to him. Second, he implies that either the NT writers did not, or should not, use atonement metaphors to make literal statements about Christ's redemptive work. Of course, such metaphors are clearly present in the NT. Moreover, who is Socinus to dictate what NT writers should or should not have done? Third, as Gomes observes, Socinus treats key atonement prepositions such as *anti* and *hyper*, both rendered in Latin as *pro*, exclusively as "for the benefit or welfare of another" and never as "in the place of."[26] Consequently, he removes from these prepositions any notion of substitution and/or satisfaction that they convey contextually and historically.[27]

Socinus's Theology Proper

Two aspects of Socinus's anti-Trinitarian doctrine of God directly influence his view of atonement: (1) divine freedom and (2) divine justice.[28]

21. Gomes, "*De Jesu Christo Servatore*," 223.
22. See, e.g., Matt. 20:28; Mark 10:45; Rom. 5:6–10; 1 Cor. 15:3–4; 2 Cor. 5:20–21; Gal. 3:10–14; Col. 2:11–15; Rev. 1:5.
23. Crisp, *Approaching the Atonement*, 82.
24. Gomes adds, "Socinus singles out the patristic theory, held by Augustine, Ambrose, and others, of a ransom paid to Satan as 'utterly absurd'" (Gomes, "*De Jesu Christo Servatore*," 221).
25. Gomes, "*De Jesu Christo Servatore*," 221.
26. Gomes, "*De Jesu Christo Servatore*," 222.
27. On the contextual use of these prepositions in a substitutionary sense, see Murray J. Harris, *Prepositions and Theology in the Greek New Testament: An Essential Reference Resource for Exegesis* (Grand Rapids: Zondervan Academic, 2012), 50–51, 211–16.
28. On the anti-Trinitarian nature of Socinus's doctrine of God, see Mortimer, *Reason and Religion in the English Revolution*, 33–38, 177–204.

Socinus argues that nothing within God compels him to forgive, not even a sacrificial death. Rather, God can forgive without any payment of a debt.[29] In fact, as Crisp explains, Socinus saw a logical incongruity between forgiveness of sin and satisfaction for sin.[30] The former could not entail the latter. God could not forgive the debt and require payment for the debt. A forgiveness that requires satisfaction is not forgiveness at all.

Similarly, with respect to divine justice, Socinus argues that "punitive justice" is not one of the "real attributes of God."[31] He associates punitive justice with references to God's wrath but does not regard it as justice in the pure sense. Rather, as Gomes explains Socinus's position, "It is simply God's decision to punish sin."[32] Socinus does not believe God always exercises punitive justice, because that would mean he never forgives.[33] Therefore, if God does not always exercise punitive justice, it is not a divine attribute. Moreover, if punitive justice is not a divine attribute, it follows that God can forgive sin without satisfaction.[34]

Socinus's Anthropology

Unlike the position of his Protestant opponents, or the clear scriptural descriptions on the matter (Question 5), Socinus does not believe that human beings are dead in their sins or helplessly impacted by the events at Eden.[35] Like Adam before them, people are endowed with reason and the freedom to respond to divine revelation or to follow their "appetite."[36] For Socinus, true religion had to be a free choice. The best choice is a response to what God revealed through the example of Christ that could inspire others to live in righteousness and holiness if they chose to do so.

Summary

Socinus's contemporary critics acknowledged the logical strength of his exemplar theory. Subsequent interpreters have noted that modern denials of a satisfaction theory of atonement, even if unaware of Socinus himself, do not move far beyond his arguments.[37] As Craig insists, "Indeed, I should

---

29. Gomes, "Socinus," 755.
30. Crisp, *Approaching the Atonement*, 82.
31. Gomes, "*De Jesu Christo Servatore*," 219.
32. Gomes, "*De Jesu Christo Servatore*," 219.
33. Gomes, "*De Jesu Christo Servatore*," 220.
34. Socinus couples this view of divine justice with divine mercy so that neither the former nor the latter are divine attributes. Rather, his punitive justice and mercy are decisions he makes within his own free and loving will. On this point, see William Lane Craig, *Atonement and the Death of Christ: An Exegetical, Historical, and Philosophical Exploration* (Waco, TX: Baylor University Press, 2020), 129.
35. Mortimer, *Reason and Religion in the English Revolution*, 15–18.
36. Mortimer, *Reason and Religion in the English Revolution*, 16–17.
37. Craig, *Atonement and the Death of Christ*, 128.

say that Socinus' critique of penal substitution remains today unsurpassed in terms of its depth and breadth."[38] A formal response to Socinus is embedded in the governmental theory of atonement (Question 14). Indirect responses are also offered in discussions of the satisfaction and penal substitution theories of atonement (Questions 13, 16, and 17). At the heart of these critiques is Socinus's flawed hermeneutic, his misunderstanding of the interrelationship of divine attributes, and an extremely deficient view of the human condition.

REFLECTION QUESTIONS

1. According to Socinus, how does Christ save people from their sin?

2. What biblical texts challenge Socinus's view of the human condition?

3. How does Socinus treat the Bible's propositional statements about redemption?

4. How does Socinus's theology proper contribute to his moral theory of atonement?

5. What are some of Socinus's hermeneutical flaws that shape his theory?

---

38. Craig, *Atonement and the Death of Christ*, 128.

What Is the Ransom Theory of Atonement?

For even the Son of Man came not to be served but to serve,
and to give his life as a ransom for many.

~Mark 10:45

In perhaps the most theologically robust verse of the gospel of Mark, Jesus uses one word to summarize the purpose of his arrival: *lutron* (Mark 10:45). English translators often render the latter noun as "ransom." NT scholars tell us that, in its historical context, *lutron* referred to the "ransom money for the manumission of slaves."[1] "Manumission" refers to a release from slavery that slaves could obtain in multiple ways during antiquity.[2] Mark obviously reconfigures this common historical usage to describe the purpose of Jesus's death, which was to pay the ransom price required for the freedom of those enslaved to sin, death, and Satan, and thereby slated for divine wrath. Mark's use of ransom language at this point seems straightforward enough.

However, in the subsequent history of interpretation, Mark 10:45 and scriptural statements like it became one of the catalysts for the so-called ransom theory of atonement.[3] As noted previously, Gustaf Aulén's twentieth-century work *Christus Victor* (Question 9) brought renewed attention to this theory, which some consider the "normative account of redemption in the mainstream

---

1. BDAG, s.v. "λύτρον." See also the classic work Leon Morris, *The Apostolic Preaching of the Cross*, 3rd ed. (Grand Rapids: Eerdmans, 1965), 29–53.
2. For a discussion of manumission as it relates to literal slavery in antiquity, see Jennifer A. Glancy, *Slavery in Early Christianity* (Minneapolis: Fortress, 2006), 92–96.
3. See also Matt. 20:28; Luke 1:68; 2:38; 21:28; 24:21; Rom. 3:24; 8:23; 1 Cor. 1:30; Eph. 1:7, 14; 4:30; Col. 1:14; 1 Tim. 2:6; Titus 2:14; Heb. 9:12, 15; 11:35; 1 Peter 1:18.

Christian tradition."[4] However, as Oliver Crisp suggests, *Christus Victor* and the ransom motif are not one and the same.[5] The former tends to stress Jesus's death as a victory over various forces that plague human beings, but the latter normally stresses that his death provides a payment whereby sinners are set free. It seems then that Aulén helped popularize the *Christus Victor* approach that some have subsequently and wrongly associated with the ransom theory. Therefore, we need to answer the specific question, "What is the ransom theory of atonement?"

Basic Elements and Questions of the Ransom Theory

Crisp defines the ransom motif as "The picture of Christ's work of reconciliation by means of which he buys back the lives of fallen human beings subject to sin, and death, and afflicted by the devil—in a way similar to a ransom price that is paid out in order that some number or fallen humanity may be redeemed from destruction, and brought to salvation."[6] All of the basic elements of a ransom approach are present in this definition and enjoy scriptural support. Satan, sin, and death have enslaved human beings (see Luke 13:16; Acts 26:18; Eph. 2:2). Jesus's death provides the release of those who are enslaved, which some NT writers liken to a manumission payment (see Matt. 20:28; Mark 10:45; Luke 24:21; Titus 2:14; 1 Peter 1:18). Jesus's death, or payment, results in the release from death, sin, and Satan while also securing eternal salvation.

However, the basic elements of the ransom theory raise questions that have occupied Christian thinkers for centuries. First, to whom does Jesus pay the ransom? Or is such a question entirely ill-conceived and stretching a biblical metaphor well beyond its conceptual boundaries and/or authors' intent? Second, what role, if any, does substitution/satisfaction play in a ransom theory? Third, is the ransom view of atonement less than a full-fledged theory? Is it perhaps better taken as a motif? These questions have received various answers that have produced various explanations of the theory.

Patristic Versions of the Ransom Theory

The starting point here is the patristic era (AD 100–451) in which the christological controversies and Trinitarian articulations that ensued tended to occupy the attention of both Greek and Latin writers. This tendency, as L. W. Grensted suggested some time ago, likely contributed to the fact that no thorough theory of the atonement emerged until the work of Anselm of Canterbury (AD 1033–1109).[7] Nevertheless, the works of this era note var-

---

4. Adam Kotsko, "The Persistence of the Ransom Theory of the Atonement," in *T&T Clark Companion to Atonement*, ed. Adam J. Johnson (London: Bloomsbury T&T Clark, 2017), 279.
5. Oliver D. Crisp, *Approaching the Atonement: The Reconciling Work of Christ* (Downers Grove, IL: IVP Academic, 2020), 51–53.
6. Crisp, *Approaching the Atonement*, 54–55.
7. L. W. Grensted, *A Short History of the Doctrine of the Atonement* (Manchester: Manchester University Press, 1920), 31–33.

ious reflections on the atonement. Craig summarizes these patristic works by noting, "All the NT motifs concerning atonement—sacrifice, substitutionary punishment, ransom, satisfaction, and so on—may be found in their pages."[8]

Until Anselm, one unofficial theory, or explanation, regarding Christ's death was that it involved "the idea of a transaction between God and the devil."[9] An early version of the "transaction" idea occurs in Origen of Alexandria's (AD 185–253) commentary on Romans in an excursus on circumcision:

> If then we have been bought at a price, as Paul also confirms, undoubtedly we were bought from someone whose slaves we were, who also demanded the price he wanted so that he might release from his authority those whom he was holding. Now it was the devil who was holding us, to whom we had been dragged off by our sins. Therefore he demanded the blood of Christ as the price for us.[10]

Origen does not expand much beyond this kind of comment, which hardly constitutes an entire theory; therefore, his ransom view is incomplete, as some have noted.[11] Nevertheless, Craig regards him as "one of the most influential and seminal atonement theorists."[12] Such praise partly stems from the fact that Origen's collective works indicate he considered atonement from angles besides the idea of ransom, namely, penal substitution and expiation, and he did so by reading NT atonement language through an OT lens.[13] However, Origen provides no integration of these motifs.[14] Moreover, our interest here lies in understanding Origen's ransom idea, which is shaped by Irenaeus's suggestion "that Satan had certain legal rights over man in virtue of his sinning that God, as perfectly just, had to respect."[15] God, though able to extract humans from Satan by force, used "rational persuasion" in offering Christ as an exchange.[16]

---

8. William Lane Craig, *Atonement and the Death of Christ: An Exegetical, Historical, and Philosophical Exploration* (Waco, TX: Baylor University Press, 2020), 92.

9. Craig, *Atonement and the Death of Christ*, 33–34.

10. Origen, *Commentary on the Epistle to the Romans, Books 1–5*, trans. Thomas P. Scheck, The Fathers of the Church, vol. 103 (Washington, DC: Catholic University of America Press, 2001), 161.

11. See, e.g., Thomas P. Scheck, *Origen and the History of Justification: The Legacy of Origen's Commentary on Romans* (Notre Dame, IN: University of Notre Dame Press, 2008), 40.

12. Craig, *Atonement and the Death of Christ*, 94.

13. Craig, *Atonement and the Death of Christ*, 94.

14. Craig, *Atonement and the Death of Christ*, 99.

15. Craig, *Atonement and the Death of Christ*, 100.

16. Craig, *Atonement and the Death of Christ*, 100.

Gregory of Nyssa (AD 330–395), one of the three Cappadocian fathers, develops the ransom motif beyond Origen's unintegrated reflection. Gregory imagines what Satan "our overlord" would accept in exchange for enslaved human beings.[17] In reflecting on the allure of Christ's miracles to Satan, Gregory suggests:

> When the enemy saw such power, he recognized in Christ a bargain which offered more than he held. For this reason he chose him as the *ransom* (emphasis mine) for those he had shut up in death's prison. Since, however, he could not look upon the direct vision of God, he had to see him clothed in some part of that flesh which he already held captive through sin. Consequently the Deity was veiled in flesh, so that the enemy, by seeing something familiar and natural to him, might not be terrified at the approach of transcendent power. So when he saw this power softly reflected more and more through the miracles, he reckoned that what he saw was to be desired rather than feared.[18]

In this development, as Adam Kotsko explains, Gregory "primarily relies on political and economic imagery" to explain the slavery metaphor as it relates to Christ's atoning work.[19] Gregory surmises that human beings permitted the devil to mislead them and thereby sold themselves into satanic bondage. Consequently, since God could not simply seize humanity through violence, since it would be contrary to his nature, as Gregory's fellow patristic writers agreed, the transaction required an appropriate payment. Gregory ties that payment to his belief that God had given the "government of the earth" to the devil; however, the devil resented the exalted status of humanity.[20] Therefore, he "devised the plan to lead humanity astray and assumed lordship over them."[21] If God were to ransom captive humans, he would have to offer Satan something more valuable, namely, Christ. As Gregory asks, "What, then, would he exchange for the one in his power, if not something clearly superior and better?"[22]

Satan then agrees to release his captives in exchange for Christ; however, since Christ is God, it is not possible for Satan to rule over him. As Kotsko asserts, "The devil naturally would never agree to this, and so Christ must appear as a mere human being to prevent the devil from knowing he's getting

---

17. Gregory of Nysa, "An Address on Religious Instruction," ed. Edward Richie Hardy, *Christology of the Later Fathers*, Vol. 3 (Philadelphia: Westminster, 1954), 299.
18. Gregory of Nysa, "Address on Religion Instruction," 300)
19. Kotsko, "The Persistence of the Ransom Theory of Atonement," 283–84.
20. Kotsko, "The Persistence of the Ransom Theory of Atonement," 284.
21. Kotsko, "The Persistence of the Ransom Theory of Atonement," 284.
22. Kotsko, "The Persistence of the Ransom Theory of Atonement," 284.

more (and therefore less) than he bargained for."[23] Gregory expresses this kind of divine trickery through his well-known fishing analogy: "As it is with greedy fish, [the devil] swallowed the Godhead like a fishhook along with the flesh, which was the bait."[24] However, Gregory takes matters a step further by suggesting that Christ both "freed humanity from evil, and healed the very author of evil himself."[25] In other words, the divine trickery in Christ saved both enslaved humanity and the devil who enslaved it.

Not surprisingly, Gregory's ransom motif drew criticism for different reasons. For example, some subsequent patristic writers found Gregory's suggestion that Satan held a power in the cosmos seemingly equal to God's to be problematic (cf. Luke 4:6; John 12:31; 2 Cor. 4:4). Moreover, Gregory takes great liberties with the limited references to Satan in the biblical text. It is only theological conjecture to suggest that God tricked Satan into releasing his captives or that, by doing so, he redeemed Satan himself. Nothing in the biblical canon supports such conjecture.

A Viable Theory?

If a theory of atonement explains how God reconciles himself to sinners, the ransom theory does not necessarily qualify as a theory at all. Crisp suggests that ransom is more of a motif than a theory because it does not explain the means, or mechanism, by which God reconciles himself to sinners.[26] Despite its popularity as the definitive statement of God's atoning work, it cannot account for how God forgives and thereby reconciles himself to sinners. These are definitive issues in Scripture that cannot simply be glossed over, which is sometimes a weakness of those who are so enthusiastic about accentuating Jesus's death as a ransom from Satan, evil, or the "power of sin," to the neglect of the sinner's personal guilt before God, which Scripture discusses at length (see Rom. 14:10–12; 2 Cor. 5:10).[27]

Perhaps as a motif, rather than a theory, ransom can serve as a key aspect of a larger and primary theory of atonement (Question 17). To describe Jesus's atoning work as a ransom is to abbreviate or take for granted an entire nexus

---

23. Kotsko, "The Persistence of the Ransom Theory of Atonement," 284.
24. Kotsko, "The Persistence of the Ransom Theory of Atonement," 284–85.
25. Kotsko, "The Persistence of the Ransom Theory of Atonement," 285.
26. In describing the meaning of atonement, Crisp identifies the "mechanism" of atonement as the central issue. He explains, "This issue has to do with the mechanism by means of which Christ reconciles us to God. Put slightly differently, if the atonement is that work of Christ that removes obstacles to communion with God (particularly with respect to human sin) and somehow makes it possible to be united with God in Christ by the power of the Holy Spirit, then how is that achieved? What has to happen in order for this goal to be brought about?" (Oliver D. Crisp, *Approaching the Atonement: The Reconciling Work of Christ* [Downers Grove, IL: IVP Academic, 2020], 3).
27. Some of Paul's eschatological reflections about judgment day suggest the gravity of one's responsibility before God.

of ideas related to atonement. God does more in Christ than rescue believers from the power of sin, death, and Satan. To rework a theological flourish from Paul, those whom God ransoms in Christ, he also cleanses from sin (see Rom. 8:28–30). Those whom he cleanses from sin are no longer under his wrath. Those who are no longer under his wrath are forgiven, justified, and glorified in Christ. Simply put, as a stand-alone theory, ransom cannot adequately account for other elements that are required for God to reconcile himself to sinners.

Summary

To be sure, the NT writers sometimes describe Jesus's work on behalf of sinners as a ransom. The death of Christ provides the payment required for freeing sinners. This truth highlights one of the positive contributions of the ransom theory of atonement. However, we should not stretch the soterio-logical metaphor too far so that we try to determine to whom God made such a payment. Additionally, while ransom may overlap with *Christus Victor*, they are not one and the same. Even more, ransom functions better as a part of a larger theory of atonement than a stand-alone theory, because it does not contain a mechanism whereby God reconciles himself to sinners.

REFLECTION QUESTIONS

1. What is the difference between ransom and *Christus Victor*?

2. What does Christ ransom people from?

3. How did patristic writers understand God's ransom in Christ?

4. What must happen for sinners to be reconciled to God?

5. Does a ransom theory account for everything that must happen for reconciliation?

What Is the Satisfaction Theory of Atonement?

Necessarily, then, when God's honor is taken away, either it is paid back or else punishment follows.

~Anselm of Canterbury

In the medieval era, the Latin noun *satisfactio* often bore the sense of "amends, reparation, apology."[1] A guilty party made amends of some kind, or *satisfactio*, to an offended party. Obviously, the English term "satisfaction" is derived from this Latin noun. This Latin-English link also informs the basic definition of the satisfaction theory of atonement. Simply put, Christ's death satisfies, makes amends, or provides "compensation" to God on behalf of sinners.[2]

Many interpreters and theologians primarily associate this theory with Anselm of Canterbury (AD 1033–1109). Critics often suggest that satisfaction theories originate from sources other than a correct interpretation of Scripture or a proper understanding of God's character. Some assert that Anselm's satisfaction theory stems from Germanic law, wherein "an offense had to be purged through an appropriate payment."[3] Others locate the source in Roman law, which distinguished between "compensation and punishment," as Anselm did.[4] Still others point to the influence of the penitential

---

1. *CLD*, s.v. "satisfactio."
2. William Lane Craig summarizes Anselm's satisfaction theory of atonement: "Anselm's theory ought therefore properly to be called the compensation theory of the atonement" (William Lane Craig, *Atonement and the Death of Christ: An Exegetical, Historical, and Philosophical Exploration* [Waco, TX: Baylor University Press, 2020], 117).
3. Alister E. McGrath, *Christian Theology: An Introduction*, 2nd ed. (Oxford: Blackwell, 1994), 401.
4. Craig, *Atonement and the Death of Christ*, 116.

system within the medieval European church wherein reconciliation required an expression of compensation.

Given these criticisms, it is necessary to clearly define the satisfaction theory of atonement from two perspectives: (1) the scriptural support for satisfaction and (2) a summary of Anselm's theory.

Scriptural Support for Satisfaction

Does Scripture support the two pillars of the satisfaction theory, namely, that God both requires and provides compensation for sin? To put it another way, does God require humans to make amends for their sins and, if he does, what form does that compensation take?

The OT preserves both acute crises and instructions that reflect the need and provision of satisfaction before God (Question 24). Both the primeval narrative (Gen. 1–11) and the rest of the OT feature many instances in which people sin against God so that his judgment remains upon them until the prescribed compensation is carried out. For example, immediately after the flood, the narrator explains that Noah built an altar upon which he offered sacrifices to God:

> Then Noah built an altar to the LORD and took some of every clean animal and some of every clean bird and offered burnt offerings on the altar. And when the LORD smelled the pleasing aroma, the LORD said in his heart, "I will never again curse the ground because of man, for the intention of man's heart is evil from his youth. Neither will I ever again strike down every living creature as I have done." (Gen. 8:20–21)

God's response assumes his prior wrath against humanity, which the narrator expresses at the outset of this section (Gen. 6:13). The divine response also points to an awareness that amends are required to remove wrath.

The means of compensation involves sacrificial death. Several acute crises within ancient Israel reflect the same pattern of *human sin→divine wrath→compensatory sacrifice→deliverance from wrath*. However, the compensatory sacrifice sometimes involves an intercessor's willingness to die rather than an actual death, such as with Moses in the golden calf incident (Exod. 32:32). Of course, Israel's seminal experience of deliverance in the Exodus reflects aspects of this pattern which is enshrined in the Passover, though Israel is not guilty of sin in this scenario and divine wrath is levelled against Pharoah and the gods of Egypt (Exod. 12:1–13:22).[5] With that said,

---

5. For the same pattern in other moments of Israel's history, see, e.g., Exod. 4:24–26; Num. 12:1–16; Josh. 7:1–8:35.

the wrath poured on Egypt became a warning for subsequent generations of Israel.

The sacrificial system assumes the same pattern, which unfolds as follows: *human sin→divine wrath→compensatory sacrifice→deliverance from wrath*. Leviticus underscores the need for holiness in Israel; however, it does so in close association with the nation's need for forgiveness, as often indicated by sacrificial offerings.[6] While OT scholars acknowledge that Leviticus leaves much about the sacrificial system unexplained, it is clear that "the first priority of the sacrificial system is the need for sin to be forgiven."[7] As William Dumbrell observes, "When the worshiper drew near to the sanctuary, killed his own beast, and laid his hand on its head as an indication of its substitution for him, he underscored the personal recognition that a breach in relationships had occurred."[8] Without this identification with a prescribed sacrifice, one could not secure forgiveness, and without forgiveness one would face wrath for offending God's holiness.

The NT likewise reflects the pattern *human sin→divine wrath→compensatory sacrifice→deliverance from wrath* (see John 1:29; 3:36; 1 John 2:1–2). The NT writers sometimes describe Jesus as a compensatory sacrifice whose death secures forgiveness and removes divine wrath leveraged against the guilty. For example, the writer of Hebrews works under the scripturally informed assumption that God requires a compensatory sacrifice as indicated in assertions such as "without the shedding of blood there is no forgiveness [*aphesis*]" (Heb. 9:22). Jesus's blood provides such forgiveness (Heb. 9:28). However, in keeping with the pattern, without participation in Christ's compensatory sacrifice, divine wrath remains, which the writer summarizes in the warning, "It is a fearful thing to fall into the hands of the living God" (Heb. 10:31; cf. 10:26–30).

Scripture then reflects a pattern of satisfaction that finds its ultimate expression in Jesus's death. However, while Scripture assumes satisfaction, it does not offer a purely propositional explanation of how Jesus's death makes amends for sinners. Later writers, such as Anselm and Aquinas, come closer to providing such an explanation.[9]

Anselm's Satisfaction Theory

In his *Cur Deus Homo* (*Why God Became a Man*), Anselm of Canterbury does not offer an exhaustive account of Christ's work.[10] He explains the

---

6. On this point, see William J. Dumbrell, *The Faith of Israel: A Theological Survey of the Old Testament*, 2nd ed. (Grand Rapids: Baker, 2002), 42.

7. Dumbrell, *The Faith of Israel*, 43.

8. Dumbrell, *The Faith of Israel*, 43.

9. Of course, one can assume the NT writers had a fuller understanding of Christ's work than the occasional nature of their works sometimes allows to be expressed.

10. On this point, see Anthony N. S. Lane, *Bernard of Clairvaux: Theologian of the Cross* (Collegeville, MN: Liturgical Press, 2013), 25.

necessity of Jesus's incarnation and death.[11] Anselm crafts his explanation in the form of a dialogue between himself and Boso, a monk at the Bec Abbey in France where Anselm served as abbot. Boso plays the role of an unbeliever. In *Cur Deus Homo*, Anselm presents interrelated questions and answers to address concerns raised by unbelievers about the fittingness of the incarnation and the necessity of Jesus's crucifixion.[12]

In laying out the "logic of our beliefs," Anselm appeals sparingly to Scripture, though his reasoning assumes it and he aims not to contradict it.[13] Several themes emerge from this logical oscillation between Anselm and Boso that define Anselm's satisfaction theory.[14] It consists altogether of forty-seven points; therefore, we can only highlight some of the main features.[15]

First, in contrast to the *Christus Victor* theory (Question 9), humanity's salvation involves more than deliverance from Satan.[16] Second, Anselm responds to various objections about the manner, means, and logical necessity of God's reconciling work in the incarnate Christ.[17] For example, death entered humanity through a disobedient man born of a woman; therefore, salvation must enter through an obedient man born of woman, which necessitates the incarnation.[18] By the same token, God could not deliver humanity from sin through a "non-divine person," because people are a "bondslave" of the one who frees them.[19] If people are to be servants of the one who delivers them, then God must deliver them, which also necessitates the incarnation. Only a perfect man and God can offer the necessary recompense.[20]

---

11. See Anselm of Canterbury, "Why God Became Man," in Anselm of Canterbury, *The Major Works*, eds. Brian Davies and G. R. Evans (Oxford: Oxford University Press, 2008), 261–62.
12. On this point, see Lane, *Bernard of Clairvaux*, 22–23.
13. Anselm, "Why God Became Man," 261, 298.
14. William Lane Craig, *Atonement and the Death of Christ: An Exegetical, Historical, and Philosophical Exploration* (Waco, TX: Baylor University Press, 2020), 114.
15. Book 1 contains twenty-five "chapters," or points. Book 2 contains twenty-two. See Anselm, "Why God Became Man," 262–65.
16. That is not to say that Anselm ignores the issue of humanity's enslavement to the devil. He in fact addresses objections that unbelievers raise regarding the supposed illogicality of the devil's "jurisdiction" over humanity (see Anselm, "Why God Became Man," 272).
17. Boso summarizes these objections, noting, "Unbelievers, deriding us for our simplicity, object that we are inflicting injury and insult on God when we assert that he descended into a woman's womb; was born of a woman; grew up nurtured on milk and human food and—to say nothing of other things which do not seem suitable for God—was subject to weariness, hunger, thirst, scourging, crucifixion between thieves, and death" (Anselm, "Why God Became Man," 268).
18. Anselm, "Why God Became Man," 268–69.
19. Anselm, "Why God Became Man," 270.
20. As Anselm concludes, "In order, therefore, that a God-Man should bring about what is necessary, it is essential that the same one person who will make the recompense should be perfect God and perfect man. For he cannot do this if he is not true God, and he has no obligation to do so if he is not a true man" (Anselm, "Why God Became Man," 321).

Third, woven throughout the entire work is a concern with the proper satisfaction of divine justice. Anselm's critics often depict him as having an overriding concern with the "restoration of God's honor."[21] Craig summarizes these critics: "Anselm is said to portray God as a sort of feudal monarch, whose wounded ego demands some satisfaction before the insult is forgiven. Since God would be all the greater if He magnanimously forgave the insult without demanding satisfaction, Anselm's theory fails to show that Christ's atoning death was necessary."[22]

However, a close reading of *Cur Deus Homo* indicates that Anselm's overriding concern is with "God's essential justice and its moral demands."[23] Sin does in fact dishonor God; however, a wounded ego is not the reason God requires satisfaction. Nor does he demand satisfaction because he is bound by moral duties.[24] He requires satisfaction because his nature demands it. God must deal with sin according to his freedom to be both fittingly compassionate and just. Anselm explains, "For the term 'freedom' relates only to the freedom to perform what is advantageous or fitting, and one should not give the name of 'benevolence' to something which brings about a result unfitting for God."[25] God cannot simply command forgiveness and/or deliverance in a way that is incongruent with his very nature. Divine justice then demands that God deal with humanity's sin either by way of punishment or compensation and in a way that is "proportional to the size of the sin."[26] Anselm chose compensation, or satisfaction, rather than punishment.[27] The incarnate Christ, as the perfect God-man, offers in his death the compensation for God-dishonoring humans whose offense incurred a debt far beyond their capacity to pay. God's justice then rewards Christ, who neither needs nor owes anything. Therefore, Christ gives his reward to those who believe in him.[28] The result is salvation through Christ's compensation or work of satisfaction.

Summary

Scripture supports the notion that God's justice must be satisfied, even if it is not ultimately in the precise manner that Anselm suggests. Anselm's theory has loomed large within atonement discussions since the medieval era.

---

21. Craig, *Atonement and the Death of Christ*, 114.
22. Craig, *Atonement and the Death of Christ*, 114.
23. Craig, *Atonement and the Death of Christ*, 114.
24. Craig, *Atonement and the Death of Christ*, 116.
25. Anselm, "Why God Became Man," 285.
26. Anselm, "Why God Became Man," 300–305. See also Craig, *Atonement and the Death of Christ*, 116–17.
27. Craig explains, "Anselm thus presents the atonement theorist with a choice: since the demands of divine justice must be met, there must be either punishment of or compensation for sin. Anselm chose the second alternative, since he naturally assumed that punishment would result in mankind's eternal damnation" (Craig, *Atonement and the Death of Christ*, 117).
28. Craig, *Atonement and the Death of Christ*, 118.

Craig summarizes his impact, noting, "Anselm thus presents the atonement theorist with a choice: since the demands of divine justice must be met, there must be either punishment of or compensation of sin."[29] Anselm chose the latter while subsequent figures, such as some Reformers, chose the former (Questions 6, 16, and 17). McGrath suggests that from Anselm to the sixteenth century three models emerged that attempted to link forgiveness to the death of Christ, which were challenged in subsequent generations: (1) *representation:* believers stand with and share in the benefits won by Christ, their representative before God; (2) *participation:* believers participate by faith in the risen Christ and the benefits secured by him; and (3) *substitution:* believers receive the righteousness of Christ who stood in the place of sinners.[30]

REFLECTION QUESTIONS

1. How would you explain the theory of satisfaction to someone?

2. What two options does Anselm present to atonement theorists?

3. How have Anselm's critics perhaps misrepresented him?

4. Does the OT support a satisfaction idea? Explain.

5. Does the NT support a satisfaction idea? Explain.

---

29. Craig, *Atonement and the Death of Christ*, 117.
30. McGrath, *Christian Theology*, 402–3.

What Is the Governmental Theory of Atonement?

And he judges the world with righteousness; he judges the peoples with uprightness.

~Psalm 9:8

In ancient Rome, authorities often crucified criminals at the very place in which they committed their crimes. Quintilian, a first-century rhetorician, explains the purpose of this practice: "That the sight may deter others from such crimes and be a comfort to the relatives and neighbours of those whom they have killed, the penalty is to be exacted in the place where the robbers did their murder."[1] The sight of a crucified criminal functioned as a deterrent to other potential criminals and rebels. Broadly speaking, such is the function of Jesus's death, according to the governmental theory of atonement. It is a penal example meant to deter sin whereby God maintains his moral governance of the universe.

As with many theories of atonement, this theory has variations, its seminal proponents, and its misrepresentations. Consideration of all these factors helps us answer more fully the question, "What is the governmental theory of atonement?"

Main Emphases in the Moral Government Theory

Oliver Crisp describes the main emphases of the theory as an attempt to preserve Reformation thought on the atonement while also responding to

---

1. As cited in Martin Hengel, *Crucifixion in the Ancient World and the Folly of the Message of the Cross* (Philadelphia: Fortress, 1977), 50.

Socianism (Question 11).[2] First, the moral government theory distinguishes between "rectoral justice," which refers to God governing the world according to his holy law, and "retributive justice," which refers to how God metes out justice according to the penalty that sin deserves. In his rectoral justice, God is the moral governor of the universe who cannot cease from exercising his justice and must do so according to his holy character. Contrastively, God's retributive justice can be "relaxed."[3] God puts forward the crucified Christ as a penal example for how he could judge sinners; however, he sets that judgment apart in Christ because his death "has a deterrent effect upon fallen human beings."[4] As Crisp asserts in the divine first person, "My moral government of the universe will be upheld because Christ will have shown you what would happen to human sin. His atoning work means that I am able to relax the need to visit retribution upon you. Instead, I may forgive you your sins."[5]

Second, in this theory, a human being's sin and guilt are not transferred to Christ. Rather, Christ takes on the "penal consequences," not the sin and guilt themselves, that God could rightly dole out to sinful human beings.[6]

Third, in response to the Socinian claim that divine retribution is unjust and that God could simply forgive sin rather than punish it, the governmental proponent leans into the distinction between rectoral and retributive justice. The former is "fundamental to God's nature" while the latter is not.[7] Consequently, as noted above, God can relax his retribution while maintaining his moral government of the world as its rector.

Fourth, given the Socinian criticism that it was illogical/unjust that an innocent Christ could stand in for sinners, the moral government theorist replaces penal substitution with a penal example.[8] Rather than Christ literally suffering the full extent God's punishment against the sinner, he is an example of what could happen to the sinner, though he himself does not suffer the sinner's eternal death.

Finally, in response to the Socinian criticism that Christ's punishment on the cross is not equal in value to eternal punishment in hell, the moral government theorist appeals to the notion of a "suitable equivalent (*solutio tantidem*)."[9] Christ does not have to suffer exactly what sinners suffer in eternal damnation. He must perform an act that is equivalent in moral value before God, which he performs in his crucifixion.

---

2. Oliver D. Crisp, *Approaching the Atonement: The Reconciling Work of Christ* (Downers Grove, IL: IVP Academic, 2020), 116–20.
3. Crisp, *Approaching the Atonement*, 118.
4. Crisp, *Approaching the Atonement*, 118.
5. Crisp, *Approaching the Atonement*, 118.
6. Crisp, *Approaching the Atonement*, 119.
7. Crisp, *Approaching the Atonement*, 119.
8. Crisp, *Approaching the Atonement*, 119.
9. Crisp, *Approaching the Atonement*, 120.

Hugo Grotius's Moral Government Theory

Hugo Grotius, a seventeenth-century respondent to Socinus, is often linked to the governmental theory, though not always correctly. Grotius's 1617 work *A Defense of the Catholic Faith concerning the Satisfaction of Christ, against Faustus Socinus* reflects a "non-necessitarian penal substitutionary theory."[10] God chose (contingency) to punish Jesus in place of sinners for their forgiveness and salvation because it was the best way to secure reconciliation; however, he did not have to do so (necessity).[11] The explicit governmental aspect of Grotius's theory stems from his response to Socinus in which he distinguishes between God as sovereign (*dominus*) and God as rector.[12] Privately, as *dominus*, God could forgive sin without punishment; however, publicly, as *rector*, God had to punish sin as part of his government of the world.[13] Additionally, in addressing Socinus's criticism that one person could not absorb eternal death for so many other people, Grotius argues that Jesus did not have to experience eternal death. Rather, "the death of Christ was of the same worth as the guilt of humankind."[14]

For Grotius, divine justice is "consequentialist," meaning God can adjust laws for the community's good, and it is "functional," meaning God could regard Jesus's death "as a satisfaction to justice," even if he did not suffer eternal death for many others.[15] Grotius, an Arminian, drew criticism from Reformed opponents at this point, who argued that God's unalterable righteous nature determined the scope of Christ's punishment rather than a supposed "consequentialist" and "functional" implementation of justice. Some critics did not agree with Grotius's position that God decided to regard Christ's death as a satisfaction for sins, even though his death did not include the same punishment that sinners deserved because his death had the same worth as such punishment.[16] Other critics, however, may have misrepresented Grotius altogether. Crisp suggests that Grotius saw himself as a defender of atonement, as the Reformers understood it, while also defending it against Socinus.[17]

---

10. William Lane Craig, *Atonement and the Death of Christ: An Exegetical, Historical, and Philosophical Exploration* (Waco, TX: Baylor University Press, 2020), 137.
11. For a discussion of divine contingency and necessity in relation to atonement, see Craig's discussion of Anselm and Aquinas in Craig, *Atonement and the Death of Christ*, 120–21.
12. See Gert van den Brink, "Hugo Grotius," in *T&T Clark Companion to Atonement*, ed. Adam J. Johnson (London: Bloomsbury T&T Clark, 2017), 523–25.
13. van den Brink, "Hugo Grotius," 523.
14. Gert van den Brink goes on to explain, "Grotius infers from the fact that both options lead to the same result: whether sinners die in their own persons, or whether Christ dies for all, in both cases God maintains the rulership of his creation" (van den Brink, "Hugo Grotius," 524).
15. van den Brink, "Hugo Grotius," 524.
16. van den Brink, "Hugo Grotius," 524.
17. Crisp, *Approaching the Atonement*, 115.

Regardless of how his critics viewed him, Grotius's discussion of atonement helped shape subsequent Arminian and Wesleyan thoughts on the matter.[18]

New Divinity's Moral Government Theory

In addition to Hugo Grotius, theologians often link the moral government theory to the so-called New Divinity, which is a pejorative reference to Jonathan Edwards's (1703–58) theological successors.[19] Edwards provided "the seeds of the New England governmental view" in multiple ways.[20] Edwards held to a kind of penal substitution while also describing God as "the supreme Rector of the universality of all things."[21] Human beings have sinned against a God who, as moral governor of the universe, is a "being of infinite worth"; therefore, he must punish sin in one of two ways: (1) through "infinite punishment" of the sinner, or (2) through a substitute to whom God can transfer "the infinite penal consequences" incurred by the sinner.[22] Christ, as the fully human and fully divine "vicar of the elect," is qualified to do the latter.[23] Edwards's view influenced his New Divinity successors in several ways.[24] However, his successors departed from him at the point of his belief in penal substitution.[25]

In 1750, Joseph Bellamy, who studied in Edwards's home after his graduation from Yale, penned *True Religion Delineated and Distinguished from Counterfeits*, which included the New Divinity's view of atonement.[26] Crisp has labeled Bellamy's view as "the doctrine of penal non-substitution."[27] He

---

18. Crisp, *Approaching the Atonement*, 115. According to van den Brink, Grotius's critics include Albert Ritschl and F. C. Baur who, in the nineteenth century, concluded that Grotius's view of the atonement differed little from Socinus. American theologians such as Charles Hodge, A. A. Hodge, and B. B. Warfield, along with the Dutch theologian Herman Bavinck, likewise adopted this criticism. As van den Brink explains, "They stated that both Socinus and Grotius saw the death of Christ only as a moral cause on human beings, who, being moved by his severe sufferings, come to faith and repentance. In their view, the only difference was that in Socinus the exhortation was encouraging (people being impressed by God's great love), while in Grotius it was threatening (Christ's death as a deterrent manifestation of God's wrath)" (van den Brink, "Hugo Grotius," 525).

19. See Obbie Tyler Todd, "An Edwardsean Evolution: The Rise and Decline of Moral Governmental Theory in the Southern Baptist Convention," *Journal of the Evangelical Theological Society* 62 (2019): 792.

20. Oliver D. Crisp, "The Moral Government of God: Jonathan Edwards and Joseph Bellamy on the Atonement," in *After Jonathan Edwards: The Courses of the New England Theology*, eds. Oliver D. Crisp and Douglas A. Sweeney (Oxford: Oxford University Press, 2012), 78.

21. Crisp, "The Moral Government of God," 82.

22. Crisp, "The Moral Government of God," 83–84.

23. Crisp, "The Moral Government of God," 83–84.

24. Crisp, "The Moral Government of God," 84.

25. Crisp, "The Moral Government of God," 85.

26. Crisp, "The Moral Government of God," 85. See also Richard L. Bushman, ed., *The Great Awakening: Documents on the Revival of Religion, 1740–1745* (Chapel Hill: University of North Carolina Press, 1989), 134.

27. Crisp, "The Moral Government of God," 85.

explains, "On this view, Christ's work is a penal example that vindicates God's moral governance by showing that the consequences of sin must be dealt with, in order that he may pardon (some) human beings."[28] Edwards and Bellamy agreed at multiple points: (1) sin deserves infinite condemnation; (2) human beings have a natural ability for faith in Christ that saves them from this condemnation, but sin renders them morally incapable of believing; and (3) God bestows faith on the elect "for whom the work of Christ is effectual through faith."[29]

Bellamy departs from Edwards at the point of penal substitution, preferring instead a penal example. Christ's death is penal in the sense that it exemplifies what sin deserves, namely, "infinite punishment."[30] However, Christ is only a substitute for the sinner inasmuch as his death is a suitable equivalent to infinite punishment and a sufficient example of the sinners' fate if they were infinitely punished. Christ's death is not, from Bellamy's perspective, an experience of the infinite consequences for sin that are absorbed on the sinners' behalf. As to the question of why Edwards endorsed Bellamy's work, when their penal substitution and penal example views of atonement clearly diverge from one another, Crisp suggests they differ at the point of "their understanding of the mechanisms by means of which Christ's work is said to atone for sin."[31] Edwards identifies the "mechanism" by which Christ atones for sin as his experience of the punishment that sinners deserved (penal substitution).[32] Contrastively, Bellamy identifies the "mechanism" as the example of the punishment that sinners deserved (penal non-substitution), which is a kind of governmental theory of atonement.

Summary

Even after correcting caricatures and misrepresentations of moral governmental theorists, scriptural and logical problems remain. This theory requires us to treat classic atonement passages through the lens of an example. According to a moral governmental theory, if Paul says that God set Jesus forth as a propitiation (*hilasterion*) for sins, he means that God set Jesus forth as an example for what could happen to sinners rather than what really happened to Jesus. Moreover, logical gaps remain within the view so that it may not qualify as a theory at all. In this view, Jesus only "removes an obstacle" to reconciliation rather than accomplishes sinners' reconciliation with God.[33]

---

28. Crisp, "The Moral Government of God," 85.
29. Crisp, "The Moral Government of God," 86.
30. Crisp, "The Moral Government of God," 87.
31. Crisp, "The Moral Government of God," 88. Regarding Edwards's support of Bellamy, he wrote the preface to Bellamy's *True Religion Delineated*.
32. Crisp, "The Moral Government of God," 88–89.
33. See Crisp, *Approaching the Atonement*, 121.

REFLECTION QUESTIONS

1. What is the difference between "penal substitution" and "penal example"?

2. Does this theory shed light on an aspect of Jesus's death that might otherwise go unrecognized?

3. What is the difference between "deterring" sinners and "reconciling" sinners to God?

4. Should we distinguish between God's "rectoral justice" and his "retributive justice"?

5. Can you find scriptural support for this theory?

What Is the Amyraldian Theory of Atonement?

The position that God intended Christ's death to atone for the sins of all humanity on the condition that they believe has long been an alternative position to both Calvinist limited atonement and Arminian unlimited atonement views.[1]

~Jeff Fisher

Moïse Amyraut (1596–1664) was a seventeenth-century professor who taught at the French Protestant Academy of Saumur, where he found himself embroiled in multiple theological debates within the Reformed tradition, including the extent of Christ's atonement.[2] His views came to take on his namesake, resulting in the Amyraldian theory of atonement.[3] As with many atonement theorists, it is not always clear if subsequent critics have rightly understood, represented, or expanded upon Amyraut. The rhetoric can get heated here as Amyraut's theory is entangled with larger questions regarding the universalist versus particularist understanding of atonement. In general, universalism is "the view that the extent of the atonement is such that it is not only universally offered to all human beings but also universally

---

1. Jeff Fisher, "Amyraut in Context: A Brief Biographical and Theological Sketch," in *Unlimited Atonement: Amyraldism and Reformed Theology*, eds. Michael F. Bird and Scott Harrower (Grand Rapids: Kregel Academic, 2023), 152.
2. Roger Nicole observes that Amyraut also involved himself in controversies over the scope of divine grace and predestination. See Roger Nicole, "Amyraldism," in *New Dictionary of Theology: Historical and Systematic*, eds. Martin Davie, Tim Grass, Stephen R. Holmes, et al. (Downers Grove, IL: IVP Academic, 2016), 21–22.
3. For one of the most recent treatments of Amyraldism, see Bird and Harrower, *Unlimited Atonement*.

effective for all human beings."[4] A particularist understanding of atonement holds that salvation is only available to those who trust in the atoning work of Christ. Within the particularism view, Amyraut claimed that his view came closer to John Calvin than Calvin's successor Theodore Beza and subsequent Reformed theologians, which has caused not a little stir.[5] Within the past century, some have called for a charitable reconsideration of Amyraut's theory rather than merely dismissing the Frenchman as a heretic.[6] The conversation here also has implications for how we understand atonement within the Reformed tradition (Question 21). Given these considerations, what, then, is the Amyraldian theory of atonement?

John Cameron and the Atonement

Amyraut's theory did not arise in a theological vacuum. John Cameron (1579–1625), a Scottish transplant whose universalist view of the atonement drew both ire and emulation among French Protestants, directly impacted Amyraut's own view.[7] It will be helpful to summarize a few salient points related to Cameron's view of the atonement.

First, in his reading of texts such as 1 Timothy 2:4, where Paul describes God as one "who desires *all* people to be saved and to come to the knowledge of the truth," Cameron stresses that God obviously wills salvation with a condition. He explains:

> For if you think that God equally wills the salvation of all without any condition, you are most foolish—not to say anything worse. For do you think that God either does not want to effect what he wills *absolutely* (which is incoherent) or else cannot do it (which is blasphemous)? Therefore, if God wills absolutely the salvation of all, if he wills absolutely that all come to a knowledge of the truth, he will provide this effect.[8]

---

4. Tom Greggs, "Christian Universalist View," in *Five Views on the Extent of the Atonement*, ed. Adam Johnson, Counterpoints: Bible and Theology (Grand Rapids: Zondervan Academic, 2019), 197.

5. See Matthew S. Harding, "Atonement Theory Revisited: Calvin, Beza, and Amyraut on the Extent of the Atonement," *Perichoresis* 11 (2013): 49–50.

6. As Harding explains, "Throughout the bulk of the Reformed Tradition's history within both Europe and the United States, most scholars have dismissed pastor and theologian Moïse Amyraut as a seventeenth century French heretic whose actions and theology led to the demise of Huguenots in France" (Harding, "Atonement Theory Revisited," 49).

7. See Albert Gootjes, "John Cameron (ca. 1579–1625) and the French Universalist Tradition," in *The Theology of the French Reformed Churches: From Henri IV to the Revocation of the Edict of Nantes*, ed. Martin I. Klauber (Grand Rapids: Reformation Heritage, 2014), 123–24.

8. Gootjes, "John Cameron and the French Universalist Tradition," 129.

The condition Cameron has in view is belief in what God has accomplished in Christ.

Second, Cameron's condition of belief must be understood in relation to the distinction he makes between the two degrees of God's "antecedent love."[9] In the first degree, pointing to texts such as John 3:16, Cameron argues that God gave and willed Christ for the salvation of the world to those who repent and believe (see also 1 Tim. 2:4; 1 John 2:2). He then explains how the condition of repentance and belief is met in relation to the second degree of God's love wherein God gives and wills the salvation of the elect.[10]

Third, Cameron acknowledges the distinction that theologians of his day made between the "sufficient" and "efficient" nature of Christ's death; however, as Gootjes explains, he wanted to go beyond this distinction. In keeping with the Canons of Dort, Christ's death can be regarded as "sufficient" to save all people while being "efficient" to save only the elect.[11] Cameron, however, suggests that "sufficiency" means more than is typically assumed.[12]

Finally, Cameron's universalist theory also rests upon his understanding of eternal and/or soteriological decrees (*decreta/décrets*). Brian Armstrong suggests that Cameron distinguished between God's "decree of sending Christ for all men" and his "decree to give faith to the elect."[13] For Cameron, God's general, or universal, decrees involve the divine work in Christ, but particular decrees apply Christ's work to believers.[14] God hypothetically (potentially) redeems all people in his universal decree "to redeem the world in Christ."[15]

Here is the heart of Cameron's "hypothetical universalism" in which he famously marshaled sunlight as a metaphor to explain it, noting that the sun "shines on all men, but those who sleep or voluntarily close their eyes do not receive its light."[16] This is not the fault of the sunlight but of those who do not open their eyes to receive it. Similarly, Cameron concludes that

---

9. Gootjes, "John Cameron and the French Universalist Tradition," 129.
10. Gootjes, "John Cameron and the French Universalist Tradition," 129.
11. See Michael Horton, "Response to Fred Sanders," in Johnson, *Five Views on the Extent of the Atonement*, 189–90.
12. Gootjes, "John Cameron and the French Universalist Tradition," 130.
13. Brian G. Armstrong, *Calvinism and the Amyraut Heresy: Protestant Scholasticism and Humanism in Seventeenth-Century France* (Eugene, OR: Wipf and Stock, 1998), 58. Cameron explains, "The first decree has to do with the restoration of the image of God in the creature, but so as to be consistent with God's justice; the second with the sending of the Son who saves each and every one who believes in Him . . . ; the third with rendering men capable of believing; the fourth is to save those who believe. The first two decrees are general, the last two are particular" (Armstrong, *Calvinism and the Amyraut Heresy*, 58).
14. Armstrong, *Calvinism and the Amyraut Heresy*, 58.
15. Armstrong, *Calvinism and the Amyraut Heresy*, 59.
16. Armstrong, *Calvinism and the Amyraut Heresy*, 59.

"Christ died for all, but his death makes blessed only those who lay hold of him by faith."[17]

Amyraut's Theory

Cameron's influence on Amyraut's view of the atonement is clear. One example of this influence is the way Amyraut separates Christ's atoning work as "absolute" on the one hand, and "conditional" on the other. It is absolute in the sense that Christ has obtained salvation for all people; however, it is conditional in the sense that his saving work is only effective for those who believe.[18] If one does not believe, which is the stipulation for receiving the benefit of Christ's work, it follows that Christ does not will it.[19]

Amyraut also articulates his view by distinguishing between "objective" and "subjective" grace. Echoing Cameron's sunlight analogy, Amyraut explains, "Objective grace is as the sun, subjective grace as the faculty of seeing with our eyes."[20] "Seeing with our eyes" refers to faith in Christ and union with him so that one can share in his saving benefits. How, though, is the eye opened or faith exercised? As with Cameron, Amyraut believed that human beings possess "the faculties necessary to respond to grace," namely, understanding and a will. However, sin has corrupted those faculties, making it ultimately impossible for people to respond to God's grace in Christ. Amyraut, at this point, appeals to the "operation of God's absolute will" that "fulfills the conditional will."[21] He senses here the mysterious outworking of divine election that results in faith, noting, "It is revealed to us that all those who believe, believe by virtue of the election through which God has separated them from the others."[22] While election is the cause of faith, that faith by which one shares in the benefits of Christ's atoning work comes through the Spirit's work in concert with the word of God.[23]

---

17. Armstrong, *Calvinism and the Amyraut Heresy*, 59.
18. As Armstrong writes, "By Christ's satisfaction salvation has been obtained for us, but with this stipulation attached—provided that we believe. That is, the work of Christ is explained in terms of God's conditional will and the conditional covenant in which man is required to fulfill his part of the contract before it will become effective" (Armstrong, *Calvinism and the Amyraut Heresy*, 210).
19. Armstrong, *Calvinism and the Amyraut Heresy*, 212.
20. Armstrong, *Calvinism and the Amyraut Heresy*, 213.
21. Armstrong, *Calvinism and the Amyraut Heresy*, 216–17.
22. Armstrong, *Calvinism and the Amyraut Heresy*, 218.
23. As Armstrong summarizes Amyraut's thought at this point, "The Holy Spirit alone works subjectively in man, illumining the mind and disposing the will so that faith may be born. But the work of the Spirit is in turn both tied up with and dependent on the revelation of the work of Christ through the Word" (Armstrong, *Calvinism and the Amyraut Heresy*, 220).

Amyraut's Theory Today

More current engagement with Amyraut has often revolved around claims that Amyraldianism is an "authentic Calvinism" as opposed to "Bezan Calvinism, Owenite Calvinism," and the like.[24] Some see the suggestion that Cameron and Amyraut better captured Calvin's thought than others who are altogether misguided.[25] Donald Macleod explains that John Calvin never faced the direct atonement question that the Amyraldians faced, namely, "whether Christ by his death obtained redemption for all men."[26] Contrastively, Macleod observes that such a question is the Amyraldians' very *raison d'être* (i.e., their reason for existing).

However, some see their response to this aspect of the atonement as problematic. Simply put, what advancement is made by distinguishing the absolute and conditional effects of Jesus's death? How does a hypothetical death, redemption, and forgiveness illuminate one's understanding of God's reconciling work in Christ?[27] As some critics note, even if one distinguishes between the "decretive" will of God and the "revealed" will of God, the only ones effectively reconciled to God are those whom he chose to believe the gospel.[28] This leaves one precisely where Arminians and Calvinists find themselves, that is, debating God's secret will.[29]

Summary

It is not clear to me that Amyraut's thoughts on atonement, or at least what gets highlighted from his thought, constitute an entire atonement theory. If an atonement theory, account, or model explains how Christ reconciles sinners to God, Amyraut primarily wrestles with one aspect of it.[30] He, or at least those who discuss him, mainly focuses on the extent and/or the means of how one receives the benefits of Christ's atoning work. Nevertheless, even if it does not constitute an entire model, it does offer an alternative to discussions on the extent of the atonement.

---

24. Donald Macleod, "Amyraldus Redivivus: A Review Article," *Evangelical Quarterly* 81 (2009): 210.

25. Macleod, "Amyraldus Redivivus," 210–211. See, e.g., Paul Helm, *Calvin and the Calvinists* (Edinburgh: Banner of Truth Trust, 1982); Richard Muller, *Christ and the Decree: Christology and Predestination in Reformed Theology from Calvin to Perkins* (Grand Rapids: Baker, 1986).

26. Macleod, "Amyraldus Redivivus," 211.

27. Macleod, "Amyraldus Redivivus," 211.

28. Macleod, "Amyraldus Redivivus," 211.

29. Macleod, "Amyraldus Redivivus," 212.

30. Once again, Oliver Crisp questions the use of "theory" to describe what he calls "accounts" or "models" of the atonement. See Oliver D. Crisp, *Approaching the Atonement: The Reconciling Work of Christ* (Downers Grove, IL: IVP Academic, 2020), 25.

REFLECTION QUESTIONS

1. What do you find helpful or unhelpful about a *hypothetical* aspect of sharing in the benefits of atonement?

2. How do you understand passages such as 1 Timothy 2:4?

3. Is it problematic to separate the *objective* will of God from his *subjective* will?

4. How does the sunlight metaphor align with what Scripture says about the relationship between the gospel and faith?

5. What other questions does Amyraldianism need to address to qualify as an entire theory or model of atonement?

What Is the Penal Substitutionary Theory of Atonement?

But he was pierced for our transgressions; he was crushed for our iniquities; upon him was the chastisement that brought us peace, and with his wounds we are healed.

~Isaiah 53:5

The noun "Punishment" (*poena/poinē*), or the adjective "penal," is a word that makes many of us wince. It may evoke the thought of someone in an authoritative position who mercilessly wounds, tortures, or even kills another person as retribution for a perceived or actual crime. Perhaps it engenders connotations of a punishing political figure, parent, or employer. Therefore, when theologians employ it as a descriptor for understanding the atoning effect of Jesus's death, some are morally repulsed by it. For God to punish his innocent Son seems unbecoming of a righteous and loving Father. Others find it incoherent in the Socinian sense (Question 11) or on other logical grounds.[1]

Nevertheless, at least since the Protestant Reformation, the penal substitutionary theory of atonement has for many in the Christian tradition served as the definitive explanation of God's atoning work in Christ.[2] Like unfavorable dispositions toward the theory, favorable dispositions toward it can be

---

1. E.g., Mark C. Murphy argues, "The penal substitution account of the atonement fails for conceptual reasons: punishment is expressive action, condemning the party punished, and so is not transferable from a guilty to an innocent party" (Mark C. Murphy, "Not Penal Substitution but Vicarious Punishment," *Faith and Philosophy* 26 [2009]: 253–73).

2. As William Lane Craig observes, "The theological revolution wrought by the Protestant Reformers brought to full bloom the theory of the atonement that has come to be known as penal substitution" (*Atonement and the Death of Christ: An Exegetical, Historical, and Philosophical Exploration* [Waco, TX: Baylor University Press, 2020], 125).

equally intense. The late J. I. Packer recalled an evangelical theologian who remarked as he neared death, "I am so thankful for the active obedience [righteousness] of Christ. No hope without it." Packer reworked the thanksgiving as, "I am so thankful for the penal substitutionary death of Christ. No hope without it."[3] Given both the disdain and fondness for this theory, it is necessary to clearly articulate what it is.

A Basic Definition of Penal Substitution

William Lane Craig largely credits the Protestant Reformers with shaping the definition of penal substitutionary atonement. Given this influence, he provides the following definition:

> Christ voluntarily bore the suffering that we were due as the punishment for our sins. There is therefore no longer any punishment due to those who are the beneficiaries of Christ's death. God's wrath is propitiated by Christ's substitutionary death, for the demands of divine justice have been met.[4]

The contours of penal substitution then are threefold: (1) Christ bore the deserved punishment for sinners in their place, (2) Christ's punishment guarantees that beneficiaries of his death will not face their own punishment from God, and (3) Christ's substitutionary punishment fulfills the standard of divine justice and satisfies/propitiates divine wrath.

Biblical Support for Penal Substitution

Here some might suggest that biblical support for this theory is in the eye of the beholder. Opposing theorists either marshal some of the same texts for their own positions or interpret those texts in a way that challenges penal interpretations (e.g., the interpretation of Rom. 3:21–26). Therefore, rather than focus only on exegetical minutiae, as important as that is, it may be more helpful to ask some broader biblical-theological questions about God's engagement with sinners in both Testaments.

First, does Scripture indicate that God punishes or penalizes sinners? The simple answer is yes. From the first couple's removal from the garden to John's apocalyptic vision of divine enemies being cast into a lake of fire, God enacts punishment upon those who rebel against him (Gen. 3:22–24; Rev. 20:11–15). Not coincidentally, the protological judgment of the Noahic flood provides a cognitive framework for understanding eschatological judgment, which is evidenced in multiple typological treatments of the flood narrative in the NT

---

3. J. I. Packer and Mark Dever, *In My Place Condemned He Stood: Celebrating the Glory of the Atonement* (Wheaton, IL: Crossway, 2007), 21.
4. Craig, *Atonement and the Death of Christ*, 125.

(e.g., Matt. 24:37–39; 1 Peter 3:20; 2 Peter 2:5; 3:1–7). Between these two poles of divine punishment, Scripture recounts several instances of God's punishing those who sin against him (see Gen. 6:1–7:24; Rev. 20:11–15).

Second, how does God punish or penalize sinners? Broadly speaking, God punishes sin through disease, famine, economic hardship, military defeat, exile, death, and his own absence.[5] In this regard, one motif found in both Testaments is that of God "handing over" rebels to his judgment, that is, exacting punishment.[6] Paul describes God's wrath against all idolaters on a cosmic scale: "Therefore God gave them up in the lusts of their hearts to impurity, to the dishonoring of their bodies among themselves" (Rom. 1:24; cf. 1:26, 28). Such punishment is both temporal and potentially eternal.

Third, does Scripture indicate that God transfers the punishment of sin to others? Here the sacrificial system as described in Leviticus is informative. Gestures such as the placing of hands on a sacrificial animal symbolize the transfer of sin and its punishment to something else: "He shall lay his hand on the head of the burnt offering, and it shall be accepted for him to make atonement for him" (Lev. 1:4).[7] As John Hartley observes, "The offerer certainly recognizes that the animal's death is necessary, because the penalty for sin is death."[8]

Fourth, how does the transfer of punishment impact God's disposition toward sinners? If the theology of Leviticus is any indication, the transfer of punishment from ancient Israelites to sacrificial animals simultaneously results in the expiation and propitiation of sinners before God. The "sacrificial forgiveness" outlined in Leviticus 1–15 is "climactically realized" in Leviticus 16, which then opens the way to "ethical holiness" in Leviticus 17–26.[9] The removal of sin (expiation) through the sacrifice at the same time satisfies God's righteous indignation (propitiation) against the sinner. It is axiomatic to Leviticus, and the rest of the biblical canon, that without sacrificial forgiveness, God's wrath remains (cf. Heb. 9:22).

NT writers take these four scriptural strands and more to describe Christ's atoning work. Historically, crucifixion is unquestionably a punishment.[10] To

---

5. The covenantal curses in Deuteronomy sum up such punishment (see Deut. 28:15–68).

6. See the use of נתן/παραδίδωμι in the MT, LXX, and GNT, as the psalmist observes in recalling certain moments in Israel's history: "And God's anger burned against his people, and he loathed his inheritance. So, he handed them over into the hand of the nations, and those who hated them ruled over them" (Ps. 106:40–41).

7. See, e.g., Lev. 1:4; 3:2, 8, 13; 4:4, 24, 29, 33; 8:14, 18, 22; 16:21; 24:14. John Hartley notes this gesture in Leviticus has a variety of explanations; however, many of them maintain a notion of "transference." See John E. Hartley, *Leviticus*, WBC 4. (Nashville: Thomas Nelson, 1992), 19–21.

8. Hartley, *Leviticus*, 21.

9. See Stephen G. Dempster, *Dominion and Dynasty: A Theology of the Hebrew Bible*, New Studies in Biblical Theology 15 (Grand Rapids: IVP Academic, 2003), 108.

10. In his review of perceptions of crucifixion in antiquity, David W. Chapman explains, "Crucifixion is almost universally viewed as a horrendous penalty, often being mentioned

borrow from Calvin, "The very form of the death embodies a striking truth" (*Inst.* 2.17.6). NT writers theologize Jesus's crucifixion as a punishment— though not only a punishment—using the atonement structure of OT theology. Christ's crucifixion is a sacrifice whereby God transfers the punishment for sinners to Jesus. His death is sacrificial in the sense that it both expiates sin and propitiates God's righteous indignation against sinners (Isa. 53:1–12; Rom. 3:21–26; 5:6–10; 1 John 2:1–2; 4:10).

Protestant Reformers and Penal Substitution

Watershed moments always have precursors; however, historical summaries by nature require oversimplification, which is what I offer here. Therefore, while penal substitution does not begin with the Protestant Reformation, it is often a starting point within historical theology, given its importance in this era and its subsequent effect. I will simply stipulate that the Reformers did not create this doctrine *ex nihilo*, as critics too often insinuate.[11] As Polycarp told the Philippians as early as the second century, "Let us, therefore, hold steadfastly and unceasingly to our hope and the guarantee of our righteousness, who is Christ Jesus, who bore our sins in his own body upon the tree, who committed no sin, and no deceit was found in his mouth; instead, for our sakes he endured all things, in order that we might live in him" (*Pol. Phil.* 8:1).[12]

With that said, Martin Luther (1483–1546) emerged as a proponent of penal substitution. In his lectures on Isaiah 53, Luther observes: "Note the wonderful exchange: one sins, another pays the penalty; one deserves peace, the other has it. The one who deserves peace has discipline, while the one who deserves discipline has peace."[13] Luther links this "wonderful exchange," in which Christ is punished in place of the sinner, to forensic justification. Simply put, through faith in Christ and his atoning work, God declares sinners as righteous before him rather than guilty. Faith is directed toward the Christ who was punished with God's wrathful presence and absence at the cross. The result is that believers who deserve such a fate do not have to experience it.[14]

among the most extreme forms of death" (David W. Chapman, *Ancient Jewish and Christian Perceptions of Crucifixion* [Grand Rapids: Baker Academic, 2010], 96).

11. E.g., N. T. Wright, *The Day the Revolution Began: Reconsidering the Meaning of Jesus's Crucifixion* (New York: HarperOne, 2016), 28–37. Cf. Daniel J. Hill and Joseph Jedwab, "Atonement and the Concept of Punishment," in *Locating Atonement: Explorations in Constructive Dogmatics*, eds. Oliver D. Crisp and Fred Sanders (Grand Rapids: Zondervan Academic, 2015), 150–53.

12. See Michael W. Holmes, ed., *The Apostolic Fathers: Greek Texts and English Translations*, 3rd ed. (Grand Rapids: Baker Academic, 2007), 291.

13. *TAL* 6:363.

14. On this point, see Alister E. McGrath, *Luther's Theology of the Cross: Martin Luther's Theological Breakthrough* (Oxford: Blackwell, 1990), 172–73.

Similarly, John Calvin (1509–1564) regarded Jesus's death as a divine punishment that is efficacious for sinners, because their sins are imputed to him.[15] Calvin observed:

> But it is especially necessary to attend to the analogy which is drawn by Paul as to his having been a curse for us. It had been superfluous and therefore absurd, that Christ should have been burdened with a curse, had it not been in order that, by paying what others owed, he might acquire righteousness for them. There is no ambiguity in Isaiah's testimony, "He was wounded for our transgressions, he was bruised for our iniquities: the chastisement of our peace was laid upon him; and with his stripes we are healed" (Isa. 53:5). For had not Christ satisfied for our sins, he could not be said to have appeased God by taking upon himself the penalty which we had incurred. To this corresponds what follows in the same place, "for the transgression of my people he was stricken" (Isa. 53:8). We may add the interpretation of Peter, who unequivocally declares that he "bore our sins in his own body on the tree" (1 Peter 2:24), that the whole burden of condemnation, of which we were relieved, was laid upon him.[16]

Here we find a clear penal interpretation based upon Calvin's interpretation of various texts in which he finds "no ambiguity." In summarizing Calvin's position, Craig avers, "We find here the affirmation of expiation of sins and propitiation of God's wrath through Christ's satisfaction of divine justice by means of substitutionary punishment. The efficacy of penal substitution depends upon the imputation of our sin and guilt to Christ."[17]

Summary

The penal substitution theory insists that reconciliation with God entails the transfer of the sinner's punishment to the crucified Christ. For those who believe, Christ's punishment on the cross both expiates and propitiates sinners before a holy and righteous God. An innocent Christ endures and satisfies divine wrath on behalf of others so they do not face the same judgment. What some regard as illogical, repulsive, and unbecoming of God, others find gracious and definitive of him.

---

15. See Craig, *Atonement and the Death of Christ*, 126–27.
16. John Calvin, *Institutes of the Christian Religion*, trans. Henry Beveridge, 2 vols. (Grand Rapids: Eerdmans, 1989), 2:456.
17. Craig, *Atonement and the Death of Christ*, 127.

REFLECTION QUESTIONS

1. Why might some people find penal substitution unbecoming of God?

2. What kind of scriptural support does this theory have?

3. How does the OT sacrificial system inform our understanding of this theory?

4. Is it unjust for God to punish his innocent Son?

5. What is the difference between Christ's *expiation* of sin and *propitiation*?

Does Scripture Have a Primary Theory of Atonement?

He himself bore our sins in his body on the tree, that we might die to sin and live to righteousness.

~1 Peter 2:24

Some theologians prefer to highlight various features of Christ's atoning work rather than adopt a singular view that defines those features. As Adam Johnson observes, "We reject the pursuit of the one theory of the atonement that is at the heart of the biblical witness and allows us to account for and systematize the others, and the ensuing temptation to fight skirmishes with other competing theories."[1] Johnson worries that such a pursuit will eclipse the "mutually complementary theories of Christ's saving work which are founded in Scripture and developed throughout the history of the Church."[2] While I agree that various views/theories of atonement have a complementary quality, it does not follow that Scripture is entirely devoid of a primary theory that organizes and informs those complementary features of God's atoning work in Christ. Moreover, if Scripture itself prioritizes and organizes features of atonement, that prioritization and organization must inform our theories and views of the matter.

Readers will probably not be surprised to learn that I believe the primary theory of atonement in Scripture is penal substitution (Question 16), which

---

1. Adam J. Johnson, *Atonement: A Guide for the Perplexed*, Guides for the Perplexed (London: Bloomsbury T&T Clark, 2015), 5–6. Along these same lines, see also Jeremy R. Treat, *The Crucified King: Atonement and Kingdom in Biblical and Systematic Theology* (Grand Rapids: Zondervan Academic, 2014).
2. Johnson, *Atonement*, 6.

William Lane Craig defines as "the doctrine that God inflicted upon Christ the suffering that we deserved as the punishment for our sins, as a result of which we no longer deserve punishment."[3] Many have made a similar suggestion about the centrality of this view based on scriptural, theological, and even philosophical factors. For example, Craig argues:

> Essential to any biblically adequate theory of the atonement, it seems to me, is penal substitution. No atonement theory that neglects penal substitution can hope to account adequately for the biblical data we have surveyed, particularly Isaiah 53 and its NT employment. Moreover, penal substitution, if true, could not be a merely tangential, minor facet of an adequate atonement theory, for it is foundational, as we shall see, to so many other aspects of the atonement, such as satisfaction of divine justice, redemption from sin, and the moral influence of Christ's example. So a biblically adequate atonement theory must include penal substitution at its center.[4]

Indeed, penal substitution is neither "tangential," "minor," nor one feature/ view equal to others. Instead, it has the most explanatory power in relation to the scriptural characterizations of God, humanity, Christ, and the salvation-historical metanarrative. Moreover, it has an unmatched ability to incorporate other atonement theories/models and features.

The Character of God and Humanity Necessitates Penal Substitution

God's holiness and righteousness, as described in Scripture, juxtaposed with human rebellion against it necessitates a penal substitution view of atonement (Question 6). In Scripture, human defilement of God's holy and righteous standards has consequences that are a measure of divine holiness and his righteousness. Examples of these consequences include the diluvian (flood) judgment, the fatal stoning of Achan and his family, Phinehas's divinely approved execution of the Israelite man and Midianite woman who defiled the Israelite camp, mass destruction of the occupants in Canaan whose ungodly behavior defiled it, and the destruction of Jerusalem punctuated by its residents' deaths or exile (Question 24). In one sense, these examples are iterations of God's removal of Adam and Eve from his holy presence in Eden, which ended in death for the first couple and all their progeny. However, in another sense, these examples and others like them are rightly labeled as divine punishment. Their very nature indicates the kind of judgment experienced,

---

3.   William Lane Craig, *Atonement and the Death of Christ: An Exegetical, Historical, and Philosophical Exploration* (Waco, TX: Baylor University Press, 2020), 147.
4.   Craig, *Atonement and the Death of Christ*, 147.

which is undeniably punitive. Why, in the aforementioned examples, do people not simply experience a peaceful judgment of death in sleep rather than the judgment of death by drowning, stoning, famine, war, and the like? It is because God does not merely bring life to an end in his judgment against those who defile his holiness and righteousness. He punishes them.[5]

It follows that death in Scripture is neither merely a natural part of life in the Stoic sense nor merely a consequence of the fall. Death is God's punishment for humanity's rebellion against him in his holiness and righteousness. Along these lines, death of sacrificial animals within the Levitical system is thoroughly symbolic of the punishment that those offering the sacrifice deserve. The priest transfers the guilt and punishment of the human agents to the animal who stands in their place (see Lev. 1:4).

How, though, is the incongruence between God's character and the human condition related to a primary theory of atonement, specifically penal substitution? The answer is that nothing salvific can transpire between God and sinners without the righteous allotment of punishment that is warranted by the human affront against divine holiness and righteousness. If God is to act in accordance with his character, he must dispense punishment in a way that is simultaneously just and merciful, that is, in his righteousness. To put it another way, salvation requires and includes forgiveness that cannot be granted without punishment for transgressions. As the writer of Hebrews insists, under the influence of Leviticus, "Indeed, under the law almost everything is purified with blood, and without the shedding of blood there is no forgiveness of sins" (Heb. 9:22; cf. Lev. 17:11). Death, to reiterate, is divine punishment for sin; therefore, the death of a sacrificial animal and/or person is tantamount to divine punishment of them.

Of course, Scripture portrays death as more than divine punishment for sin. Death is an impurity and the last enemy that God overcomes in Christ (see 1 Cor. 15:26; Heb. 2:14).[6] However, it is first and always the divinely appointed consequence of sin from Eden until the eschaton. As Paul asserts,

---

5. Of course, not all death is a direct form of punishment from God, and we should exercise great caution in drawing such conclusions. Nevertheless, all deaths are an indirect result of the punishment first instituted in the garden of Eden: "By the sweat of your face you shall eat bread, till you return to the ground, for out of it you were taken; for you are dust, and to dust you shall return" (Gen. 3:19).

6. On regarding death as an impurity within the first-century era and the Synoptic Gospels, Matthew Thiessen avers, "The Gospel writers portray Jesus first destroying impurities that he encounters, then giving his disciples the power and authority to do what he does, and then personally entering into the source of all impurity: death" (Matthew Thiessen, *Jesus and the Forces of Death: The Gospels' Portrayal of Ritual Impurity within First-Century Judaism* [Grand Rapids: Baker Academic, 2020], 184). What gives me pause with Thiessen's fascinating study is that it lacks adequate emphasis upon human guilt and the need for repentance. Those infected by the "impurity" that is death are not neutral parties. While the Synoptic writers generally do not attribute a person's impurity or ailment to their own sin, Jesus's miracles encode larger soteriological affects, such as a healing symbolizing forgiveness.

under the influence of the Mosaic law, "The wages of sin is death" (Rom. 6:23a; cf. Deut. 27:26; Gal. 3:10). To overcome death, one must experience it as a penalty for sin, which is precisely what Christ did.

Christological Identity and Penal Substitution

In the NT, seminal examples of divine punishment against sinners in the OT and the transfer of divine punishment from humans to sacrificial animals via the priesthood typify God's work in Christ (see Rom. 3:21–26; Heb. 7:1–28; 9:1–27; 1 Peter 1:18–19; 2:21–25). A key passage in this regard is Isaiah 53, which combines priestly and messianic motifs in a way that demonstrates how the incongruence between God's character, particularly his holiness and righteousness, and human rebellion require punishment for sin. As Isaiah declares in describing the suffering servant:

> But he was *pierced* for our transgressions;
>   he was *crushed* for our iniquities;
> upon him was the *chastisement* that brought us peace,
>   and with his wounds we are healed.
> All we like sheep have gone astray;
>   we have turned—every one—to his own way;
> and the LORD has laid on him
>   the iniquity of us all.
>
> He was oppressed, and he was afflicted,
>   yet he opened not his mouth;
> like a lamb that is led to the *slaughter*,
>   and like a sheep that before its shearers is silent,
>   so he opened not his mouth. (Isa. 53:5–7, italics added)
>
> Yet it was the will of the LORD to *crush* him. (Isa 53:10a, italics added)

Several of the lexemes here indicate a punitive death of the servant, including "pierce," "crush," "chastisement," and "slaughter."[7] The last lexeme is tied to the way Isaiah likens the servant to a slaughtered sheep, which evokes the motif of a sacrificial animal and thereby the punishment that such animals endured on behalf of human transgressors.[8] Additionally,

---

7.   For the senses of "pierce" (חלל), "crush" (דכה/נכה), "chastisement" (מוסר), and "slaughter" (טבח), see *HALOT* 1:221; 1:319–20; 1:368; 1:418–19; 1:697–98.

8.   To reiterate, if the death of a sacrificial animal is not ultimately punishment, what is it? Reward? Ritual? This is one of the logical problems I believe critics of penal substitution face.

Isaiah asserts that God "delighted," or willed, to punish his servant on behalf of his people.[9]

NT writers consciously take up Isaiah 53 to describe Jesus's atoning work. Jesus frames his mission as God's sending him to the "lost sheep" of Israel (Isa. 53:4; Matt. 8:17). Jesus, as the "Son of Man," likens himself to the Isaianic servant who must "suffer many things and be treated with contempt" (Mark 9:12b; cf. Isa. 53:3). In describing Philip's evangelization of the Ethiopian, Luke explains the Ethiopian was struggling to understand the identity of the one whom Isaiah described as a sheep led to slaughter (Isa. 53:7; Acts 8:32). In short, Isaiah 53 functions as one of the key templates for the NT's understanding of Jesus's identity and the nature of his death which, in keeping with the prophecy, is thoroughly punitive.[10]

Besides Isaiah 53, other OT texts as well as the details surrounding Jesus's death are best understood in relation to penal substitution. One example is the mode of Jesus's death. Historically, imperial Rome implemented crucifixion to torture and shame their victims and deter those who witnessed such ignominious deaths. As the late Martin Hengel expressed it, "Crucifixion as a penalty was remarkably widespread in antiquity."[11] Similarly, from a specifically Jewish perspective, David Chapman maintains that "post mortem bodily suspension," such as Jesus's crucifixion, was often regarded as punishment as far back as prior to the Davidic monarchy.[12]

Jesus's identity according to the NT writers involves more than his fatal punishment in the place of sinners. Other christological actions define him, including his incarnation, teaching, miracles, resurrection, enthronement, and promised return. Nevertheless, none of those actions hold salvific value apart from his death, wherein he suffers the penalty of sinners in their place. That action defines and animates all others. We will return to this below.

Salvation History and Penal Substitution

I begin here with a note of caution about so-called salvation/redemptive history. Contrary to popular belief, Scripture does not offer a seamless meta-narrative from Genesis to Revelation that explains all divine actions and the

---

9. As John N. Oswalt insists, "God wanted to crush this man? God wanted to visit terrible pain on him? Surely not. The faithful God of the Bible would certainly not visit bad things on innocent people, would he? Yes, he would if some greater good would be served (cf. Job)" (John N. Oswalt, *The Book of Isaiah: Chapters 40–66*, The New International Commentary on the Old Testament [Grand Rapids: Eerdmans, 1998], 400).

10. For other NT engagements with Isa. 53, see e.g., Matt. 12:29; 20:28; 26:28; 27:12, 38; Mark 10:45; 14:49, 61; 15:27; Luke 11:22; 22:37; 23:34; John 1:29; 12:38; Acts 3:13; Rom. 4:24–25; 5:1, 15, 19; 10:16; 1 Cor. 15:3; Phil. 2:7; Heb. 9:28; 1 Peter 2:24, 25; 1 John 3:5; Rev. 5:6; 14:5.

11. Martin Hengel, *Crucifixion in the Ancient World and the Folly of the Message of the Cross* (Philadelphia: Fortress, 1977), 86.

12. David W. Chapman, *Ancient Jewish and Christian Perceptions of Crucifixion* (Grand Rapids: Baker Academic, 2010), 174.

experiences of God's people in a clairvoyant manner.[13] Instead, to borrow a line from the psalmist, "Your way was through the sea, your path through the great waters; yet your footprints were unseen" (Ps. 77:19). To put it another way, when God finally answers Job's lament, he does not frame his response with respect to where Job finds himself within the salvation-historical story (Job 38:1–42:6). Instead, God presses upon his superior power and wisdom as Creator in contrast to Job's weakness and lack of understanding as a creature. In other words, mystery always marks God's ways, even within a salvation-historical framework where tracing and understanding his work is more like tracking footprints on the sea rather than on sand.

With that said, various biblical texts present a kind of salvation-historical framework, from Moses's song, to storytelling psalms, to Stephen's speech (see Deut. 32:1–43; Ps. 78:1–72; 105:1–45; 106:1–48; 135:1–21; 136:1–21; Acts 7:1–53). What I want to highlight here is that the salvation story cannot progress without sacrificial deaths that often reflect penal substitution. Two examples will have to suffice here.

First, Passover precedes Israel's exodus from Egypt. The Passover sacrifice stood in place of those who offered it and served as the divine means of protection from divine judgment (see, e.g., Exod. 12:13). Those without the sacrificial substitute experienced divine punishment firsthand. Moreover, without this penal substitutionary sacrifice, Israel never makes it out of Egypt. Second, the conquest of Canaan only continues after Achan and his family are stoned to death. Achan caused trouble for Israel by taking what God had devoted to the ban so that Israel suffered defeat in their battle with Ai (see Josh. 7:1–5). Once the banned items are recovered, Achan confesses his sin and the guilty parties are fatally punished. As the narrator observes, "Then the LORD turned from his burning anger" (Josh. 7:26). God's wrath burned against Israel until the guilty party was punished. As with Jesus's crucifixion, the mode of death here, stoning, clearly conveys punishment that is meted out upon one figure and his associates rather than the whole nation.[14]

Both examples typify Jesus's atoning death that does not merely push the salvation-historical narrative forward. Nor is it merely the *climax* of the narrative. *Climax* cannot account for the unique personhood of Jesus and its implications for the larger *story*. Stories that involve human agents rightfully move toward a climax. However, the hypostatic union that defines Christ's identity means that he was present in the story all along, just as Paul and Jude well note (see 1 Cor.

---

13. One must be careful about detecting a metanarrative that stands behind the written word itself, which then functions as the dominant hermeneutic for interpreting that very word. On this point, see Mark A. Seifrid, "Storylines of Scripture and Footsteps in the Sea," *Southern Baptist Journal of Theology* 12 (2008): 88–106.

14. As Mark J. Boda explains in his analysis of Josh. 7, "So serious is this sin that the offending party is eradicated from the community" (Mark J. Boda, *A Severe Mercy: Sin and Its Remedy in the Old Testament*, Siphrut 1 [Winona Lake, IN: Eisenbrauns, 2009], 131.

10:1–13; Jude 1:5). Therefore, Jesus's atoning death defines the entirety of salvation history. Specifically, his death, like the Passover lamb and Achan, which typify him, is the defining form of divine punishment in the place of others.

Summary

As discussed in Questions 9–15, Christian theology contains a multiplicity of atonement theories. However, none of them ultimately work without penal substitution. Within the *Christus Victor* view, God cannot grant victory over sin, death, and Satan unless he addresses human rebellion against him in a way that is consistent with his holiness and righteousness (Question 9). That consistent *way* is the punishment of a substitute, which cannot be accounted for in the Socinian theory (Question 11). Similarly, God cannot *ransom* sinners unless he addresses their rebellion against him, which he does through Jesus's penal substitutionary death. If God is to rule the universe well, which is the concern of the governmental theory (Question 14), it follows that he must address the rebellion against his holiness and righteousness through the punishment of his Son.

In short, other theories of atonement highlight key aspects of Jesus's atoning work; however, on their own, they cannot address the prerequisite need to those aspects, which is nothing less than the justification of God whereby he sufficiently deals with sinners in a way consistent with his holiness, righteousness, and faithfulness within salvation history. That sufficient way is the punishment of Jesus to the point of death on a cross, which John the Baptist foreshadowed in his baptism of sinners. Luke uniquely characterizes this baptism as God's self-justification: "When all the people heard this, and the tax collectors too, they declared God *just*, having been baptized with the baptism of John" (Luke 7:29, italics added). A custom that represented death before God signaled that God was right to punish sinners. Therefore, the actual death of Jesus stands for the justification of God's punishment of sinners in the sinless one.

REFLECTION QUESTIONS

1. Why does God's character require punishment for sin?

2. What is the connection between Jesus's identity and penal substitution?

3. How does penal substitution move salvation history forward?

4. What does the penal substitution view accomplish that other theories cannot?

5. What does the nature of Jesus's death tell us about how it should be viewed?

PART 3

Views on Atonement
in the Christian Tradition
and World Religions

What Is the Roman Catholic View of Atonement?

It is called the sacrament of reconciliation, because it imparts to the sinner the love of God who reconciles: "Be reconciled to God."
~CCC Para. 1424

There exists no official theory of atonement either in Protestant or Catholic theology. From a Catholic perspective, as Frederick Bauerschmidt and James Buckley remind us, "Because the Church has never defined a particular vocabulary or approach to the work of Christ, there is a greater 'pluralism' in soteriology than in Christology."[1] Moreover, with the specific question "What is the Roman Catholic view of atonement?" one must also specify what era is in view. Many of the same texts, creeds, and theologians, such as Anselm of Canterbury, have shaped the views of Catholics and Protestants alike. Given these considerations, the answer provided here will focus especially upon influences that shaped Catholic views as they came to be expressed at the Council of Trent (1545–63) and beyond.

A Roman Catholic Definition of Atonement

While the term "atonement" is not as prevalent in Catholic theology as it is in Protestant theology, the former contains extensive reflection on Christ's reconciling work.[2] Diverse approaches and images mark Catholic reflection. As Bauerschmidt and Buckley observe:

---

1. Frederick Bauerschmidt and James J. Buckley, *Catholic Theology: An Introduction* (Chichester, UK: Wiley-Blackwell, 2017), 145.
2. See, e.g., the absence of "atonement" language in the index of *CCC* 757–60.

The Catholic understanding of Christ's work of salvation is embodied in an incredible variety of approaches and images, even within the work of individual theologians. The relationship between these varying approaches is generally thought to be complementary and not competitive. We need a variety of theological languages in order to speak truthfully of the great mystery of human redemption in Christ.[3]

What binds these approaches together is the "creedal affirmation" that the "work of Christ is 'for us and for our salvation.'"[4] God saves through Christ in the sense that he "does something to bring humans to their fulfillment as well as to eradicate sin and suffering."[5] Catholic explanations of what Christ does to accomplish this work and how he accomplishes it can vary; however, the variations typically work within established parameters.

During the Counter-Reformation, the Council of Trent helped establish some of those parameters. For example, in its "Decree concerning Original Sin," the council affirmed "the merit of the one mediator, our Lord Jesus Christ, who has reconciled us to God in his own blood, made unto us justice, sanctification, and redemption."[6] In keeping with Trent, the modern *Catechism of the Catholic Church*, prepared after the Second Vatican Ecumenical Council (1962–1965), affirms, "Jesus atoned for our faults and made satisfaction for our sins to the Father."[7] These simple definitions align nicely with Protestant definitions of atonement. However, differences arise in how some of this atonement language is defined and in how one appropriates the benefits of Christ's reconciling work.[8]

Patristic Influences on the Catholic View

Prior to Trent, Vatican II, and other summations, what teachings have shaped the Catholic view of atonement? Among the various historical influences, patristic theology stands out.[9] It is not possible here to summarize all the ways that patristic theology may have shaped the Catholic view of atonement.

---

3. Bauerschmidt and Buckley, *Catholic Theology*, 145.
4. Bauerschmidt and Buckley, *Catholic Theology*, 145.
5. Bauerschmidt and Buckley, *Catholic Theology*, 146.
6. *Canons and Decrees of the Council of Trent*, 5th Session, Decree concerning Original Sin, 3, as cited in William G. Witt and Joel Scandrett, *Mapping Atonement: The Doctrine of Reconciliation in Christian History and Theology* (Grand Rapids: Baker Academic, 2022), 3.
7. *Catechism*, para. 615.
8. The difference between a shared term and its divergent meaning within Catholicism and Protestantism is reflected in the 1999 *Joint Declaration on the Doctrine of Justification*. See David E. Aune, *Reading Paul Together: Protestant and Catholic Perspectives on Justification* (Grand Rapids: Baker Academic, 2006).
9. Of course, both patristic theology and Thomas Aquinas also impacted Protestant views of atonement.

However, two key themes from the patristic era have enjoyed a lasting effect: (1) the link between incarnation and atonement, and (2) ransom as an atonement model.

Both Irenaeus (AD 130–202) and Athanasius (AD 297–373) highlight the link between Jesus's incarnation and his work of reconciliation. William Witt and Joel Scandrett suggest that Irenaeus offers both an ontological and restorative explanation for the incarnate Christ's redemptive work.[10] Ontologically, the Word became flesh because sinful humanity could not save itself.[11] As fully man and fully God, Jesus acts as an effective mediator who joins sinners to God. The incarnate Word both actualizes atonement and reveals the image of God so that people learn about God firsthand and what it means to commune with him.[12] Restoratively, Irenaeus's well-known emphasis on *recapitulation*, that is, Jesus's work of successfully retracting the steps of the human experience marred by Adam, means the incarnate Christ "has 'regathered' or brought into unity that which has become separated, restoring humanity to its intended unity."[13]

Within this recapitulation paradigm, Irenaeus employs a variety of atonement images: (1) an obedient Jesus undoes the effect of a disobedient Adam; (2) Jesus is the "new man" who cleanses and washes humans enslaved through Adam's disobedience so they can share life with God; (3) communion by the Spirit through sharing in a crucified and risen Jesus; (4) a humanity enslaved to sin through violence is saved, or "persuaded," through the cross; (5) the incarnation makes sinful enemies "friends" with God; (6) Jesus's death "for us" includes his entire human existence for our benefit; and (7) Jesus's work is victory over sin, death, and Satan.[14] Similar images emerge in later Catholic views of atonement.

Athanasius's influence includes his depiction of Jesus's death as an "inside job."[15] Simply put, in the incarnation, God saves through the inner transformation of the human being. Sin's corruption came from within the human

---

10. Witt and Scandrett, *Mapping Atonement*, 21.
11. Witt and Scandrett, *Mapping Atonement*, 21.
12. On the relationship between the ontological and pedagogical aspects of Christ's reconciling work, Witt and Scandrett note, "There are similarities between Irenaeus's understanding of Jesus's task as teacher and the later 'exemplarist' models of the atonement. However, in Irenaeus's understanding of atonement, the incarnate Jesus Christ did more than provide an example for others to follow. Jesus Christ's reconciling work is not merely pedagogical; it accomplishes something ontologically. Jesus's incarnate life, death, and resurrection are constitutive, not merely illustrative, of atonement" (Witt and Scandrett, *Mapping Atonement*, 23).
13. Witt and Scandrett, *Mapping Atonement*, 24. Irenaeus develops his thoughts on "recapitulation" from the use of *anakephalaiosis* in Rom. 13:9 and Eph. 1:10, translated in Latin as *recapitulatio*.
14. Witt and Scandrett, *Mapping Atonement*, 23–26.
15. Witt and Scandrett, *Mapping Atonement*, 31.

being; therefore, salvation must be accomplished in like manner as it is in the incarnate Word.[16] Given this framework, Witt and Scandrett identify several themes in Athanasius's reflection on the atonement that can be summarized as follows: (1) the incarnate Word recreates the image of God marred through sin; (2) this re-creation is via the "union of the Word with humanity"; (3) the Word reverses "sin, death, and corruption"; (4) it is not just Jesus's death but his incarnation and resurrection that produces atonement; (5) an "exchange" occurs between fallen humanity and the Word so that the former possess the characteristics of the latter and vice versa; (6) Jesus's incarnation, death, and resurrection are collectively a kind of representation, substitution, and ransom; and (7) atonement occurs through *Christus Victor* (Question 9).[17] Similar themes appear in later Catholic views of atonement.

Aquinas's Influence on the Catholic View

Thomas Aquinas's (1225–1274) influence on Roman Catholic theology is immense.[18] That influence includes his thoughts on the atonement, wherein he engages Anselm's theory of satisfaction (Question 13).[19] In his summary of Aquinas's thoughts on Christ's passion, William Lane Craig observes, "Christ's passion, he says, has a threefold effect: insofar as it frees us from the servitude of guilt, it acts by way of *redemption*; insofar as it reconciles us to God, it acts by way of *sacrifice*; and in so far as it liberates us from the debt of punishment, it acts by way of *satisfaction*."[20]

As with Anselm, Aquinas's reflection on satisfaction stands out. For example, Aquinas observes, "He properly atones for an offense who offers something which the offended one loves equally, or even more than he detested the offense. But by suffering out of love and obedience, Christ gave more to God than was required to compensate for the offense of the whole human race."[21] Aquinas does not regard Jesus's death as a substitutionary punishment (Question 16).[22] Rather, in his death Jesus rescues sinners from the punishment they deserve.[23] For Aquinas, unlike Anselm, God could have achieved

---

16. Witt and Scandrett, *Mapping Atonement*, 31.
17. Witt and Scandrett, *Mapping Atonement*, 31–34.
18. See Brian Davies, *Thomas Aquinas's Summa Theologiae: A Guide and Commentary* (Oxford: Oxford University Press, 2014), 346–47.
19. See, e.g., the use of *satisfactio* in Aquinas, *Summa Theologiae*, 3.48.2.
20. William Lane Craig, *Atonement and the Death of Christ: An Exegetical, Historical, and Philosophical Exploration* (Waco, TX: Baylor University Press, 2020), 119. See also Aquinas, *Summa Theologiae* 3.48.6.
21. Aquinas, *Summa Theologiae*, 3.48.2, as cited in Craig, *Atonement and the Death of Christ*, 119.
22. Thomas White observes that in Catholic theology substitutionary atonement does *not* "note that Christ suffers the wrath of God the Father, or that he is punished as one deemed guilty on our behalf" (Thomas White, *The Light of Christ: An Introduction to Catholicism* [Washington, DC: Catholic University of America Press, 2017], 170).
23. White, *The Light of Christ*, 119.

this satisfaction by means other than Christ's death; however, his death is the "best way of achieving human salvation."[24]

Finally, as Adam Johnson asserts, the central feature of Aquinas's approach to atonement is the "concept of 'fittingness' (*convenire*)," which accentuates why an action is "fitting, or appropriate, for God."[25] God chose Jesus's satisfactory death as the means for atonement because it brings about "the greatest number of desired effects."[26] Aquinas does not adopt a single theory of atonement. Instead, as Johnson explains, "He brings together a wide range of effects flowing from Christ's work, acknowledging each in its unique significance."[27] Later Catholic articulations of atonement reflect Aquinas's "fittingness" approach.

Unique Emphases in the Catholic View

Catholic views of atonement tend to describe Jesus's work through the lenses of ransom, victory, and satisfaction, in keeping with the influence of patristic theology, Aquinas, and others. Obvious overlap exists here with Protestant usage of these atonement models, though not without differences.

First, Christ's descent into hell is a key part of his victory over death and Satan on the sinner's behalf (Question 28). The *Catechism* explains, "Jesus did not descend into hell to deliver the damned, nor to destroy the hell of damnation, but to free the just who had gone before him."[28] Jesus's descent is "solidarity with us in death" and thereby "the source of our authentic hope in God for participation in eternal life."[29] The soul of Jesus experiences hell on Holy Saturday, though not "eternal damnation."[30] As White explains, in this descent, Jesus "leads into the light of heaven (the beatific vision) all the souls of the faithful departed who had died in a state of grace."[31]

Second, Catholic thought is unique with respect to how one participates in the benefits of Christ's atoning work. Participation here naturally involves sacraments administered by the church that are "necessary for salvation" and are described as "efficacious because in them Christ himself is at work."[32] For example, baptism, performed through bishops and priests in the church, is the foremost sacrament of forgiveness because it unites one with Christ, who died for sins and rose for justification.[33] For the baptized who have since confessed

---

24. White, *The Light of Christ*, 120. See also Davies, *Thomas Aquinas's Summa Theologiae*, 314.
25. Adam J. Johnson, "A Fuller Account: The Role of 'Fittingness' in Thomas Aquinas' Development of the Doctrine of the Atonement," *International Journal of Systematic Theology* 12 (2010): 304.
26. Johnson, "A Fuller Account," 305.
27. Johnson, "A Fuller Account," 317.
28. *Catechism*, para. 633.
29. White, *The Light of Christ*, 171.
30. White, *The Light of Christ*, 171.
31. White, *The Light of Christ*, 171–72.
32. *Catechism*, para. 1127, 1129.
33. *Catechism*, para. 977–999.

their faith and live "in friendship" with God but remain "imperfectly purified," they experience purgatory at the time of death wherein they undergo their "final purification."[34] Additionally, the Eucharist functions as the "source and summit of the Christian life" whereby one participates in Christ's death because he is "really present under the species of bread and wine," so one has increased union with Christ and forgiveness from venial sins (i.e., a slighter transgression that does not incur the penalty of eternal condemnation) and preservation from grave sins (i.e., a transgression that potentially leads to eternal condemnation unless the transgressor repents).[35] One must also consider the sacrament of penance that "makes sacramentally present Jesus' call to conversion."[36] For those who sin after baptism, penance calls for three actions: (1) repentance, (2) confession, and (3) reparation.[37] Among other things, the sacrament results in "reconciliation with God" and with the church.[38]

Summary

Catholic and Protestant views of atonement overlap at several points. Neither holds to an official view of atonement. They share similar influences, such as the patristic writers, Aquinas, and Anselm. However, one of the main points of divergence pertains to how one shares in the benefits of Christ's atoning work. Catholic thought underscores sacramental participation and allows for a postmortem share in Christ's atoning work through its doctrine of purgatory. In contrast, Protestant thought underscores faith, repentance, and baptism, though in a variety of ways across denominations, and generally does not allow for a postmortem share in Christ's atoning work in the vein of purgatory.

REFLECTION QUESTIONS

1. How does Roman Catholicism define atonement?

2. What is the difference between the influences of Irenaeus and Athanasius?

3. What role has Aquinas played in the Catholic view of atonement?

4. Describe some of the unique aspects of the Catholic view.

5. Where do Catholic and Protestant views of atonement overlap?

---

34. *Catechism*, para. 1030–32.
35. *Catechism*, para. 1324, 1410, 1413–16.
36. *Catechism*, para. 1423.
37. *Catechism*, para. 1491.
38. *Catechism*, para. 1496.

What Is the Eastern Orthodox View of Atonement?

I weep and I wail when I think upon death, and behold our beauty, fashioned after the image of God, lying in the tomb, disfigured, dishonored, bereft of form. O marvel!

~St. John of Damascus

This poetic flourish is part of a funeral service hymn penned by St. John of Damascus (AD 675–749). In its fuller context, St. John goes on to ask, "What is this mystery which befalls us? Why have we been given over into corruption, and why have we been wedded to death?"[1] His thoughts magnify two significant motifs in the Eastern Orthodox view of atonement, namely, incarnation and mystery. Eastern Orthodox thought finds an indissoluble link between the incarnation and the death of Christ. At the same time, in keeping with the broader theological ethos of Eastern Orthodoxy, much emphasis is placed on the mysterious and indescribable nature of God's work in Christ (Question 40). That is not to say that Eastern Orthodoxy contributes nothing to the discussion of atonement. However, it does so in awe and with an eye toward the goal of *theosis*, which is "The term used by the Orthodox to describe salvation as the transformative process of sharing in the divine nature."[2]

---

1. As cited in John Behr, "Irenaeus on 'Atonement,'" in *On the Tree of the Cross: George Florovsky and the Patristic Doctrine of Atonement*, eds. Matthew Baker, Seraphim Danckaert, and Nicholas Marinides (Jordanville, NY: Holy Trinity Seminary Press, 2016), 50.
2. Eve Tibbs, *A Basic Guide to Eastern Orthodox Theology: Introducing Beliefs and Practices* (Grand Rapids: Baker Academic, 2021), 189.

The State of Eastern Orthodoxy

The so-called Great Schism in AD 1054 marks the official split between Eastern and Western Christianity; however, long before this date cultural and political differences were driving a wedge between the Latin-speaking Western church and the Greek-speaking Eastern church.[3] Differences in language, the dissolution of political unity, and some theological differences, including the so-called *filioque* clause controversy, resulted in differences between these two wide branches of Christianity that can still be felt today.[4] The label "Eastern Orthodox," though not entirely accurate given ongoing emigration and globalization, can refer to families of churches determined by national groups, including Greek Orthodox, Russian Orthodox, Romanian Orthodox, Bulgarian Orthodox, Serbian Orthodox, Georgian Orthodox, and others.[5] Some might also include the Coptic Orthodox, the Syrian Orthodox, the Armenian Orthodox, the Ethiopian Orthodox, and the Eritrean Orthodox churches.[6] Overall, as Andrew Louth observes, borrowing from Alexander Schmemann, the road to Eastern Orthodoxy began with Greek-speaking apostles, progressed with the rise of the Byzantine Empire (AD 395–1453), and expanded through various diaspora groups expelled through the collapse of empires and persecution.[7]

Within this wide spectrum of Eastern Orthodoxy, views on the atonement vary. The East, like the West, currently does not have a single view of the atonement equivalent to their incarnational or Trinitarian doctrine.[8] Understanding these variations can prove difficult given differences in language, concepts, and a general lack of familiarity with Eastern Orthodoxy among those in the West. As Andrew Louth admits, "To ask what Orthodox theology makes of original sin, or the atonement, is to first ask for an effort

---

3. From a broad perspective, Justo L. González maintains, "In the West, the demise of the Empire created a vacuum that the church filled, and thus ecclesiastical leaders—particularly the pope—also came to wield political power. In the East, the Empire continued for another thousand years. It was often beleaguered by foreign invasion or by inner turmoil, but it survived. And its autocratic emperors kept a tight rein on ecclesiastical leaders" (Justo L. González, *The Story of Christianity: Volume 1, The Early Church to the Dawn of the Reformation* [New York: HarperSanFrancisco, 1984], 251).
4. See Tony Lane, *A Concise History of Christian Thought* (Grand Rapids: Baker Academic, 2006), 67.
5. Andrew Louth, *Introducing Eastern Orthodox Theology* (Downers Grove, IL: IVP Academic, 2013), xiv.
6. Louth notes, "These are Churches that refuse to accept some of the Ecumenical Councils endorsed by the Eastern Orthodox. Most accept the first three (Nicea I: AD 325; Constantinople I: AD 381; and Ephesus: AD 431), but not the fourth (Chalcedon: AD 451) or any later ones" (Louth, *Introducing Eastern Orthodox*, xiv–xv).
7. Louth, *Introducing Eastern Orthodox*, xv–xviii. See also Alexander Schmemann, *The Historical Road of Eastern Orthodoxy* (London: Holt, Rinehart & Winston, 1963).
8. On this point, see Petro Kovaliv, "Rediscovering a Biblical and Early Patristic View of Atonement through Orthodox-Evangelical Dialogue," *Religions* 12 (2021): 2–3.

of translation of an unfamiliar concept into something recognizable on the terrain of Orthodox theology."[9] Nevertheless, based upon shared readings of scriptural texts, influence from the patristic era, and other developments, it is possible to provide a sketch of the matter. One way to frame the discussion here is to consider how Eastern Orthodoxy understands the *problem* between humanity/cosmos and God as well its *solution*.[10]

The *Problem* According to Eastern Orthodoxy

Eve Tibbs suggests the "deepest and widest chasm" between Eastern Orthodox and Western Christian theologies is their views on "the fall" with its subsequent results.[11] While Western Christianity stresses the inheritance of Adamic guilt and a thoroughly corrupted nature, Eastern Christianity stresses that the fall led to the forfeiture of communion with God. The fall inhibited the divine image in humans; however, their natures have not been corrupted to the point they are incapable of choosing to follow God's will.[12] Humanity has not inherited Adamic guilt in the Western sense. Rather, humanity has inherited the loss of communion with God so that it is subjected to inimical forces such as "death, decay, and evil."[13] As Tibbs summarizes the problem according to Eastern Orthodoxy, "We thus contracted something like a disease––the disease of death and decay––and we are desperately subject to a world in which the Evil One presently has a stronghold."[14]

Along similar lines, Georges Florovsky avers, "The Fall was already a kind of death, an exclusion from the only source of life and immortality, a loss of the life-giving Spirit."[15] This loss destabilized human nature and the entire cosmos. Florovsky explains:

> Human death becomes a cosmic catastrophe. Nature loses its immortal center in the dying human person and dies itself in the human person. The human person is a kind of "microcosm." All kinds of life exist in him. Only through and in the human person will the whole world come into a relationship

---

9. Andrew Louth, "Eastern Orthodox View," in *Five Views on the Extent of the Atonement,* ed. Adam J. Johnson, Counterpoints: Bible and Theology (Grand Rapids: Zondervan Academic, 2019), 19.

10. I am helped here by Tibbs, *A Basic Guide to Eastern Orthodox Theology,* 99–124.

11. Tibbs, *A Basic Guide to Eastern Orthodox Theology,* 103.

12. Tibbs writes, "Orthodox Christianity teaches that following God's will is a choice available to everyone, even after the Fall, since free will is still active" (Tibbs, *A Basic Guide to Eastern Orthodox Theology,* 105).

13. Tibbs, *A Basic Guide to Eastern Orthodox Theology,* 106.

14. Tibbs, *A Basic Guide to Eastern Orthodox Theology,* 106.

15. Georges Florovsky, "*In Ligno Crucis*: The Church Father's Doctrine of Redemption Interpreted from the Perspective of Eastern Orthodoxy Theology," in Baker, Danckaert, and Marinides, *On the Tree of the Cross,* 145.

with God. The fall of humanity alienated the whole creation from God. It destroyed the cosmic harmony. Through the Fall, humanity became subject to the course of nature.[16]

Of course, Florovsky observes that human death outweighs death in animals. While the extent of an animal's death is that it ceases to enjoy "individual existence," human death "strikes at the personality" so that "the whole person dies."[17] To put it bluntly, "The image of God fades. Death reveals that the human person, this creature made by God, is only a body. The fear of death reveals a deep metaphysical anguish and not only a sinful attachment to earthy things."[18]

The *Solution* According to Eastern Orthodoxy

If the *problem* between humanity and God is the loss of communion, and humanity's concomitant subjection to evil and death, it follows that restoration would stand at the heart of the Eastern Orthodox *solution*. As Florovsky avers, "Redemption is, above all, the salvation from death and destruction, a restoration of the original unity and stability of human nature."[19] How, though, does Christ accomplish this restoration? Eastern Orthodoxy underscores at least four features of God's work in Christ.

First, given the loss of communion between God and people, along with the injury to the image of God within humanity, Eastern Orthodox thought stresses the incarnation of Christ that reunites the divine and the human.[20] As Athanasius expressed it, "The Word of God came in His own Person, because it was He alone, the Image of the Father, Who could recreate man made after the Image."[21] In one of his most well-known analogies, Athanasius explains the soteriological import of the incarnation by noting:

> You know what happens when a portrait that has been painted on a panel becomes obliterated through external stains. The artist does not throw away the panel, but the subject of the portrait has to come and sit for it again, and then the likeness

---

16. Florovsky, "*In Ligno Crucis*," 145.
17. Florovsky, "*In Ligno Crucis*," 145–46.
18. Florovsky, "*In Ligno Crucis*," 146.
19. Florovsky, "*In Ligno Crucis*," 146.
20. As Tibbs observes, "Salvation in Orthodoxy is therefore conceived in terms of reuniting the human and the divine to restore the communion lost by our primal ancestors. The Incarnation solves the problem, so stated, since in Jesus Christ the communion between human and divine nature has been restored" (Tibbs, *A Basic Guide to Eastern Orthodox Theology*, 120).
21. St. Athanasius, *On the Incarnation*, trans. a religious of the Community of St. Mary the Virgin (Crestwood, NY: St. Vladimir's Seminary Press, 1996), 41.

is re-drawn on the same material. Even so was it with the All-holy Son of God. He, the Image of the Father, came and dwelt in our midst, in order that He might renew mankind made after Himself, and seek out His lost sheep, even as He says in the Gospel: "I came to seek and to save that which was lost."[22]

In short, the Word became flesh to *redraw* the image of God within human creatures. This kind of renewal animates Eastern Orthodox soteriology, which begins with the Incarnation.[23]

Second, in Orthodox soteriology, Jesus's death plays a definitive role in the restoration of human beings; however, it is generally not regarded as a form of divine satisfaction. Instead, Jesus's death solves the dilemma of subjection to mortality. Florovsky explains, "The decisive reason for the death of Christ is the mortality of mankind. Christ suffered death, but He conquered death and corruptibility and destroyed the power of death. In the death of Christ, death itself receives new meaning."[24] This death results in the defeat of death for fallen humanity and restores the corrupted divine image. Jesus's death is not efficacious in this way because of his innocence but rather the incarnation of his deity.[25]

Third, Orthodox thought regards Jesus's death and resurrection as equally "essential to salvation" and "part of the same saving action" (see Rom. 4:25).[26] As Florovsky maintains, "The death of Christ is by itself a victory over death not only because it is followed and crowned with the resurrection, for this only reveals and manifests the victory of the Cross. The power of the resurrection is the same as the 'power of the Cross.'"[27] There is no place then for the Western notion of God's forsakenness at the cross.[28] Instead, though Eastern Orthodoxy recognizes the solemnness of Good Friday, it ultimately regards

---

22. St. Athanasius, *On the Incarnation*, 41–42.
23. As Tibbs explains, "The troparion (or hymn) of the Orthodox Great Feast of the Annunciation, celebrated on March 25 (exactly nine months before the Nativity of Christ), proclaims that our salvation begins in the Incarnation: 'Today is the beginning of our salvation and the revelation of the pre-eternal mystery; the Son of God becomes the son of the Virgin'" (Tibbs, *A Basic Guide to Eastern Orthodox Theology*, 120).
24. Florovsky, "*In Ligno Crucis*," 146.
25. As Florovsky explains, "The death on the Cross was not efficacious because it was the death of an innocent man, but because it was the death of the incarnated Lord. It was not a human being who died on the cross but God. But God died in His own humanity" (Florovsky, "*In Ligno Crucis*," 148).
26. Tibbs, *A Basic Guide to Eastern Orthodox Theology*, 121.
27. Florovsky, "*In Ligno Crucis*," 149.
28. As Tibbs observes while reflecting upon Florovsky's view, "Fr. Florovsky repudiates Calvin's view that Christ was forsaken by God, or that Christ needed to satisfy God's anger, since this view does injustice to Christ's acceptance of death out of love for his creation. Moreover, the 'hypostatic union' of Christ's two natures cannot be divided, broken, or destroyed––not even in death. Remember, the incarnate Word is not a divine part next to a

Jesus's death on the cross as the glorious revelation of divine life. In his death and resurrection, Christ renders death powerless and gives the "whole human nature" the "ability to be resurrected."[29]

Finally, Eastern Orthodoxy regards salvation in the incarnate, crucified, and risen Christ as an "unending movement in response to the love of God," which reaches its goal in *theosis*.[30] Forgiveness, restoration, and healing of the divine image in human beings are not ends in themselves. Rather, redemption in Christ is, as Sergius Bulgakov regards it, a means of "the elevation of man to divine-humanity."[31] Louth identifies this dimension of Orthodox theology as that which outpaces Anselm's satisfaction theory of atonement with its forensic emphasis (Question 13). Louth contends the narrative "arc" reflected in Anselm only runs from "the fall to redemption." However, the Orthodox view reflects a "greater arc" from "God's creation to his final union with creation in deification."[32]

Summary

As noted from the outset, it is difficult to translate Eastern Orthodox views on God's work in Christ into the language of *atonement*. Nevertheless, Eastern theologians have plenty to say about the *problem* with humanity before God and the *solution* in Christ, which means they have an atonement theology. Christ defeats death/evil, restores the corrupted image of God, restores an unstable humanity, and thereby propels people to the goal of *theosis*, which, to reiterate, is the "transformative process of sharing in the divine nature."[33] To be sure, the Eastern view accentuates the continuity between various aspects of Christ's atoning work, particularly the relationship between incarnation, death, and resurrection. Moreover, it challenges us to think about the ultimate divine purposes behind God's atoning work in Christ.[34]

However, these Orthodox reflections do not necessarily constitute a full-blown theory of atonement. What we find are ideas about what God gives in Christ to fallen humanity. But one does not find robust and integrated discussions about human guilt, God's righteous indignation with sinners, or even

---

human part but an inseparable union of both natures" (Tibbs, *A Basic Guide to Eastern Orthodox Theology*, 122).

29. Florovsky, "*In Ligno Crucis*," 150.
30. Tibbs, *A Basic Guide to Eastern Orthodox Theology*, 112.
31. See Sergius Bulgakov, *The Lamb of God*, trans. Boris Jakim (Grand Rapids: Eerdmans, 2008), 446.
32. Louth, "Eastern Orthodox View," 42.
33. Tibbs, *A Basic Guide to Eastern Orthodox Theology*, 189.
34. As Fred Sanders explains in his response to Andrew Louth's explanation of how Eastern Orthodoxy views the extent of the atonement, "God's ultimate purposes with regard to the creature need to be invoked and held steadily in mind throughout the entire doctrine, or atonement theology itself will be distorted, cramped, and impoverished" (Sanders, "Response to Andrew Louth," in Johnson, *Five Views on the Extent of the Atonement*, 58).

Final Judgment in relationship to Christ's atoning work. By not fully engaging these issues, the Eastern view offers no real explanation as to how God reconciles himself to sinners, which stands at the heart of the doctrine of atonement. However, Eastern Orthodox liturgy does commend the sacrament of confession as an act of reconciliation with God and the church.[35]

REFLECTION QUESTIONS

1. What is the ultimate and eternal purpose of God's reconciling work in Christ?

2. According to Eastern Orthodox thought, what is the problem that plagues humanity?

3. According to Eastern Orthodox thought, what is the proposed solution to what plagues humanity?

4. How are Christ's incarnation and atoning work related to one another?

5. Why might there be limitations to describing sin only as a "disease"?

---

35. Tibbs, *A Basic Guide to Eastern Orthodox Theology*, 161.

What Is the Lutheran View of Atonement?

For when we had been created by God the Father, and had received from Him all manner of good, the devil came and led us into disobedience, sin, death, and all evil, so that we fell under His wrath and displeasure and were doomed to eternal damnation, as we had merited and deserved.

~Martin Luther (LC II:2)

This reflection from Luther's *Large Catechism* captures how he saw the human predicament, namely, as sinners who succumb to the devil and are thereby under divine wrath. Therefore, God's atoning work in Christ is both the defeat of Satan and the removal of divine indignation. However, as with the Lutheran tradition in general, Martin Luther's view on the atonement is not necessarily the view held by all subsequent Lutheran theologians. Since the Reformation, Lutheran articulations of the doctrine of atonement have both aligned with their founder and drastically diverged from him.

Martin Luther's View(s) of the Atonement

"It may be roundly stated that no side of Luther's theology has been more summarily treated or more grossly misinterpreted than his teaching on the Atonement. The fundamental mistake has been the assumption that his teaching on this subject belongs to the Anselmian type."[1] This is Gustaf

---

1. Gustaf Aulén, *Christus Victor: An Historical Study of the Three Main Types of the Idea of Atonement,* trans. by A. G. Hebert (Austin, TX: Wise Path, 2016), 108. Similarly, see Paul Althaus's analysis of Albert Ritschl in Paul Althaus, *The Theology of Martin Luther,* trans. Robert C. Schultz (Philadelphia: Fortress, 1966), 218.

Aulén's assertion in his 1930 seminal work on atonement, *Christus Victor* (Question 9). By contrast, Ian Siggins retorts, "Luther has no theory of atonement," at least if one means by theory a "coherent explanatory discourse about how the atonement works."[2] However, Aulén and Siggins represent extreme and even misguided positions on the matter. Robert Kolb acknowledges that Luther did not attempt a systematic explanation of how the atonement works.[3] However, Luther offers some organized reflection on the matter that includes the language of substitution or satisfaction (Question 13), victory (Question 9), and ransom (Question 12).[4] Therefore, it will be helpful to briefly summarize Luther's thoughts and compare them to subsequent Lutheran views of atonement.[5]

First, Luther employs images to explain the "benefits of Christ's dying and rising" that reflect his thoughts on atonement.[6] Kolb identifies the two main images as a "joyous exchange" and a "magnificent duel."[7] The former refers to the way that Christ "has made his righteousness my righteousness and my sin his sin."[8] The latter refers to the way that, in his death and resurrection, Christ "conquers all enemies of the believer."[9] Luther combines both images through a wedding metaphor in *The Freedom of a Christian*:

> For Christ is God and a human being in one and the same person, who does not and cannot sin, die, or be damned; and his righteousness, life, and salvation are unconquerable, eternal, and all-powerful. When, I say, such a person shares in common, and, indeed, takes as his own the sins, death, and hell of the *bride* on account of the *wedding ring* of faith, and when he regards them as if they were his own and as if he himself had sinned—suffering, dying, and descending into hell—then, as he *conquers* them all and as sin, death,

---

2. Ian D. Kingston Siggins, *Martin Luther's Doctrine of Christ* (New Haven, CT: Yale University Press, 1970), 109, as cited in Robert A. Kolb, *Martin Luther: Confessor of the Faith* (Oxford: Oxford University Press, 2009), 118.
3. Kolb, *Martin Luther*, 119.
4. Kolb, *Martin Luther*, 120–21.
5. One could also consider the shift that Luther had in this thinking about atonement from a mixture of Anselm and Abelard, as presented to him through his university instructor Peter Biel, to evangelical insights in the late 1510s and forward. On this point, see Robert A. Kolb, "Martin Luther," in *T&T Clark Companion to Atonement*, ed. Adam J. Johnson (London: Bloomsbury T&T Clark, 2017), 613.
6. Kolb, *Martin Luther*, 120.
7. Kolb, *Martin Luther*, 120–21.
8. *LW* 25:188.
9. Kolb, *Martin Luther*, 121.

and hell cannot devour him, they are devoured by him in an *astounding duel* (emphasis added).[10]

Luther's image does not point to believers sharing in Christ's obedience, who are now empowered to do likewise.[11] Rather, as Kolb explains, "Luther spoke of this joyous exchange with Christ to show how God's wrath against the sinner is taken away through Christ's dying for sin and guilt."[12] With respect to the "astounding duel" imagery, Luther asserts that "Christ's victory is a victory over the Law, sin, our flesh, the world, the devil, death, hell, and all evils; and this victory of his he has given to us."[13]

Second, while Luther's equivalent thoughts on what we are calling "atonement" can be found scattered across various works, his *Large Catechism* provides a collective description of Jesus's death as victory, ransom, and substitution. In his comments on the second article of the Apostles' Creed, we find this interrelated triad of atonement views.[14] With respect to victory, Luther writes, "Those tyrants and jailers now have been routed, and their place has been taken by Jesus Christ, the Lord of life and righteousness and every good and blessing. He has snatched us, poor lost creatures, from the jaws of hell, won us, made us free, and restored us to the Father's favor and grace."[15] Regarding Jesus's death as a ransom, Luther writes, "Let this be the summary of this article, that the little word 'Lord' simply means the same as Redeemer, that is, he who has brought us back from the devil to God, from death to life, from sin to righteousness, and now keeps us safe there."[16] With respect to satisfaction, in the same section Luther writes, "That is to say, he became man, conceived and born without sin, of the Holy Spirit and the Virgin, that he might become Lord over sin; moreover, he suffered, died, and was buried that he might make satisfaction for me and pay what I owed, not with silver and gold but with his own precious blood."[17] Luther closes his comments on the second article of the Apostles' Creed by encouraging further reflection on Christ's death through the medium of "sermons throughout the year."[18]

---

10. *TAL* 1:500.
11. Kolb, *Martin Luther*, 120.
12. Kolb, *Martin Luther*, 120.
13. *LW* 26:21–2, as noted in Kolb, *Martin Luther*, 121,
14. The second article of the Apostles' Creed as Luther understands it reads, "And in Jesus Christ, his only Son, our Lord: who was conceived by the Holy Spirit, born of the virgin Mary, suffered under Pontius Pilate, was crucified, dead, and buried: he descended into his hell, the third day he rose from the dead, he ascended into heaven, and is seated on the right hand of God, the Father almighty, whence he shall come to judge the living and the dead" (Martin Luther, *The Large Catechism* [Philadelphia: Fortress, 1959], 57).
15. Luther, *The Large Catechism*, 57.
16. Luther, *The Large Catechism*, 57.
17. Luther, *The Large Catechism*, 57.
18. Luther, *The Large Catechism*, 57–58.

However, he ultimately concludes that the second article is "so rich and broad that we can never learn it fully."[19]

Finally, while Luther may not provide the kind of synthesis that some require to constitute a theory of atonement, two interrelated concerns hold much of his atonement thought together, namely, the wrath of God and life in Christ. Jesus's victory and ransom of the sinner is not merely deliverance from enemies but from God who handed sinners over to the devil according to his righteous indignation.[20] Therefore, contrary to Aulén's bold assertion, Luther did in fact see Jesus's death as a kind of satisfaction as well as a victory.[21] However, Luther also stresses that the crucified, risen, and ascended Christ is then, now, and always the source and guarantee of one's reconciliation with God. As Oswald Bayer summarizes Luther at this point, "One goes astray theologically if one either speaks only speculatively about the 'person' of Christ or discusses his work of salvation only in terms of the historical effect it has. Neither Christology nor soteriology can be understood apart from one another, neither the 'person' nor the action of salvation."[22] One does not share in the atoning work and benefits of Christ apart from union by faith with the living Christ.[23]

Melanchthon and Chemnitz on Atonement

Sixteenth-century peers of Luther offered some key insights on atonement that helped shape subsequent Lutheran views on the issue. Two prominent peers in this regard are Philipp Melanchthon (1497–1560) and Martin Chemnitz (1522–1586).[24]

In his 1555 *Loci communes* (i.e., *Common Topics*), Melanchthon emphasizes that Jesus needed to both "atone for sin" in his humanity and "defeat death and the devil" in his divinity.[25] Given these emphases, Jack Kilcrease declares that, in *Loci communes*, Melanchthon laid out six explanations for the necessity of the incarnation and the cross: (1) humanity fell into sin so that the penalty had to be paid by a sinless person; (2) if the payment was going to be of equal value and/or surpass the penalty, it had to be paid by a divine person; (3) only

---

19. Luther, *The Large Catechism*, 58.
20. Paul Althaus notes that, for Luther, "The powers with which Christ struggled had their power and authority only through God's wrath. They are his instruments against the sinner" (Althaus, *The Theology of Martin Luther*, 220).
21. Althaus, *The Theology*, 222.
22. Oswald Bayer, *Martin Luther's Theology: A Contemporary Interpretation* (Grand Rapids: Eerdmans, 2008), 234.
23. As Mark A. Seifrid quips, echoing the sentiment of Luther, "Our righteousness is not properly ours, but an alien righteousness given us in Christ" (Seifrid, *Christ Our Righteousness: Paul's Theology of Justification*, New Studies in Biblical Theology 9 [Downers Grove, IL: IVP Academic, 2000], 184).
24. See Jack D. Kilcrease, *The Doctrine of Atonement: From Luther to Forde* (Eugene, OR: Wipf and Stock, 2018), 51–65.
25. Kilcrease, *The Doctrine of Atonement*, 53.

the omnipotent and merciful Son of God could sufficiently bear divine wrath for sin; (4) only a divine mediator such as Jesus could carry out his high priestly work; (5) only a divine person could conquer death and give life; and (6) only a divine Redeemer within the redeemed could sustain them and create obedience and life in them.[26] Kilcrease also observes that, in contrast to Luther, Melanchthon's opaque Christology resulted in "dividing up Christ's human and divine actions in redemption."[27] Overall, like Luther, Melanchthon regarded Christ's death as both a penal substitution (Questions 13 and 16) and the defeat of death/Satan (Questions 9 and 12). As Melanchthon summarizes it, "Christ was given to us to remove both these sins (actual and original) and these punishments, and to destroy the kingdom of the devil, sin and death."[28]

Martin Chemnitz attempted to clarify various "theological proposals" of both Luther and Melanchthon.[29] With respect to atonement, Chemnitz suggested that both Christ's human and divine natures are necessarily involved in redemption. This suggestion is reflected in the *Formula of Concord* (1577) with entries such as, "Christ is called our Righteousness in the affair of justification, namely, that our righteousness rests not upon one or the other nature, but upon the entire person of Christ, who as God and man is our Righteousness in His only, entire, and complete obedience."[30] It is not that Christ atoned for sins in his humanity and defeated Satan/death in his divinity. Rather, atonement for sin that removed wrath required the God-man just as the defeat of Satan/death did.

After the influential works of Melanchthon, Chemnitz, and others, the Lutheran tradition entered an "Age of Orthodoxy" (1580–1725).[31] Some advancements in the Lutheran view of atonement developed here, such as in Johann Gerhard's teaching on the "threefold office of Christ" (Question 21).[32] However, according to Kilcrease, this age was marked by a "remarkable consistency" with respect to atonement. He explains that all theologians of this era "held to the doctrine of penal substitution as a corollary of the proper articulation of the doctrine of justification."[33]

Moderate Revisions in the Lutheran Doctrine of Atonement

Since the "Age of Orthodoxy," several developments have occurred in the Lutheran doctrine of atonement. Kilcrease categorizes these developments as "moderate" and "radical" revisions respectively.[34] Ultimately, however,

---

26. Kilcrease, *The Doctrine of Atonement*, 54.
27. Kilcrease, *The Doctrine of Atonement*, 54.
28. Kilcrease, *The Doctrine of Atonement*, 55.
29. Kilcrease, *The Doctrine of Atonement*, 56.
30. FC 3.55.
31. Kilcrease, *The Doctrine of Atonement*, 60.
32. Kilcrease, *The Doctrine of Atonement*, 61. Cf. *Inst.* 2.15.
33. Kilcrease, *The Doctrine of Atonement*, 65.
34. Kilcrease, *The Doctrine of Atonement*, 66–100.

he asserts that modern Lutheran theologians do not agree on the issue of substitutionary atonement.

"Moderate" revisions, under the influence of figures such as Werner Elert (1885–1954), Gustaf Aulén (1879–1977), and Gustaf Wingren (1910–2000), include more emphases on Jesus's earthly ministry, divine love, and the defeat of demonic forces. According to Elert, Jesus's life demonstrates how profoundly and efficaciously different he is from those who follow him. Elert sees it as a "total difference, the difference between the whole Christ and the whole man—as a sinner."[35] Nevertheless, he becomes the "equal" of human beings, a friend of sinners, and even "carries the guilt of the whole of humanity" in his death.[36] Christ's cross shows that he had the "same attitude" toward sinners in his death as he did in his life.[37]

With respect to Aulén's *Christus Victor*, his attempt to dispense with the rational theory of penal substitution is ultimately problematic (Question 9). Aulén touts his view as a recovery of what the early church espoused concerning God's atoning work in Christ, namely, the victory of divine love over divine wrath.[38] However, by reducing penal substitution to a rational mirage upon the landscape of later Christian history, Aulén denies "the underlying assumptions of all the biblical authors," which is that "the law must be fulfilled in order that redemption might be achieved."[39] God does not overcome his own demands but satisfies them.

According to Kilcrease, Wingren's revisions are largely in line with the "Age of Orthodoxy." Although his "accent falls very heavily on Christ's conquest of demonic forces in his understanding of atonement," Wingren maintains the need for the fulfillment of divine law and thereby Christ's substitution for sinners.[40]

Radical Revisions in the Lutheran Doctrine of Atonement

Among the radical revisionists, Kilcrease critiques Wolfhart Pannenberg (1928–2014) and Robert Jenson (1928–2017).[41] "Radical" refers to their tendency to "subordinate" traditional Lutheran concerns with salvation to "secular and philosophical ones."[42]

Although Pannenberg was most interested in how people could obtain a rational knowledge of God, that interest did not preclude some reflection on atonement. In *Jesus—God and Man*, Pannenberg dedicates a full section

---

35. Werner Elert, *Law and Gospel,* trans. Edward H. Schroeder (Philadelphia: Fortress, 1967), 23.
36. Elert, *Law and Gospel,* 28.
37. Elert, *Law and Gospel,* 26.
38. Kilcrease, *The Doctrine of Atonement,* 72.
39. Kilcrease, *The Doctrine of Atonement,* 73.
40. Kilcrease, *The Doctrine of Atonement,* 78.
41. He also critiques Eberhard Jüngel (1934–2021).
42. Kilcrease, *The Doctrine of Atonement,* 79.

to the meaning of Jesus's death.[43] He reviews various theories of atonement and concludes that Luther rightly understood Paul as holding to "a vicarious penal suffering."[44] However, he also underscores participation in Jesus's death and resurrection, which leads to eschatological hope.[45] Moreover, the conclusive significance of Jesus's person and work is that it "inaugurates a new creation."[46] Nevertheless, overall, Pannenberg's "radical" revision lies in the fact that the atonement, like all theological knowledge for him, must conform to his view of "universal human rationality."[47] As Kilcrease observes, even though Pannenberg's views of atonement often conform with Scripture, he reduces Jesus to the agent of obtaining "genuinely rational knowledge of God" and "only secondarily" the agent of "salvation from sin."[48]

Robert Jenson discusses atonement as part of a larger theological program in which he focuses on "the identification of God by the Resurrection of Jesus" in the church.[49] As Kilcrease remarks in his analysis of Jenson, "By engaging in the theological task, the people of God are able to identify and explain the reality of the one God through their participation in his ongoing narrative."[50] Within this experience, Jenson largely regards sin as "alienation from God."[51] Consequently, the solution is not a divine payment for sin or the removal of righteous wrath. It is simply "the adjustment of a wrong attitude on the part of humanity toward an already gracious God."[52]

Summary

The preceding discussion is by no means exhaustive.[53] It is fair to say that Luther himself would likely have vehemently, and humorously, objected to some of the theologians within the tradition that bears his name. For Luther, Christ's defeat of sin and removal of divine wrath went hand in hand. To

---

43. Wolfhart Pannenberg, *Jesus—God and Man*, trans. Lewis L. Wilkins and Duane A. Priebe, 2nd ed. (Philadelphia: Westminster, 1968), 245–80.
44. Pannenberg explains, "Luther was probably the first since Paul and his school to have seen with full clarity that Jesus's death in its genuine sense is to be understood as vicarious penal suffering. Subsequent Protestant theology, unfortunately, did not maintain this insight. Both Melanchthon and Calvin returned to Anselm's theory of satisfaction with the somewhat baroque revision that not the man Jesus, but the divine-human person was the bearer of the accomplishment of satisfaction" (Pannenberg, *Jesus—God and Man*, 279).
45. Kilcrease, *The Doctrine of Atonement*, 83.
46. Kilcrease, *The Doctrine of Atonement*, 83.
47. Kilcrease, *The Doctrine of Atonement*, 84.
48. Kilcrease, *The Doctrine of Atonement*, 84.
49. Robert W. Jenson, *Systematic Theology, Volume 1: The Triune God* (Oxford: Oxford University Press, 1997), 42.
50. Kilcrease, *The Doctrine of Atonement*, 85.
51. Kilcrease, *The Doctrine of Atonement*, 91.
52. Kilcrease, *The Doctrine of Atonement*, 92.
53. E.g., Kilcrease dedicates two chapters to Gerhard Forde's view of the atonement. See Kilcrease, *The Doctrine of Atonement*, 101–65.

favor either element at the expense of the other would be inconsistent with his thought. Even worse, to jettison both entirely would be anathema to him.

REFLECTION QUESTIONS

1. What is the relationship between the work of Satan and divine wrath?

2. How does God's work in Christ deal with Satan and divine wrath?

3. What problems might Luther have had with Aulén's depiction of him?

4. How does a theologian's view of the human condition influence his or her view of atonement?

5. How do the "radical revisionists" align with the scriptural witness regarding atonement?

What Is the Reformed View of Atonement?

When we say, that grace was obtained for us by the merit of Christ, our meaning is, that we were cleansed by his blood, that his death was an expiation for sin, "His blood cleanses us from all sin."

~John Calvin

The descriptor "Reformed" can be overused, misunderstood, or viewed with suspicion. Here it refers to a theological tradition that originated with the French theologian John Calvin (1509–1564) and has a discernible successive line from him.[1] Not surprisingly, the Reformed view of atonement both overlaps with views outside its own tradition and has its own internal variations. In answering the question "What is the Reformed view of atonement?" it is necessary to consider the prominence of Calvin and some key developments that followed after him.

John Calvin and Penal Substitution

Many associate John Calvin with the theory of penal substitutionary atonement.[2] However, as William Witt and Joel Scandrett note, Calvin's atonement theology "is not monolithic but a rich tapestry of themes."[3] While penal substitution stands at the center of his atonement theology,

---

1. See Alister E. McGrath, *Christian Theology: An Introduction*, 2nd ed. (Oxford: Blackwell, 1997), 575.
2. Much of Calvin's atonement theology can be found in *Inst.* 2.12.1–2.17.6.
3. William G. Witt and Joel Scandrett, *Mapping Atonement: The Doctrine of Reconciliation in Christian History and Theology* (Grand Rapids: Baker Academic, 2022), 127.

certain themes precede, shape, and emanate from that center and help to explain it.

One position that precedes and shapes Calvin's penal substitution view is how he regards the depth of sin's effect on human beings. He explains this effect in multiple interrelated ways. For example, sin has not destroyed entirely the image of God in human beings; however, sin has left that image as a "frightful deformity."[4] Along with original sin, which Calvin sees as hereditary and corrosive to human nature, whereby people heap upon themselves divine wrath and perpetuate evil, he also stresses the totality of sin's effect on human beings.[5] He asserts that "the whole man, from crown of the head to the sole of the foot, is so deluged, as it were, that no part remains exempt from sin, and therefore, everything which proceeds from him is imputed as sin" (*Inst.* 2.2.9).[6]

A second formative position is that an individual's horribly sinful state results in a "dramatic separation" from God that requires Christ's mediating work.[7] Christ is the "mediator" that humanity needs both before and especially after Adam's transgression.[8] As Calvin explains, "Our iniquities, like a cloud intervening between Him and us, having utterly alienated us from the kingdom of heaven, none but a person reaching to him could be the medium of restoring peace" (*Inst.* 2.12.1). Such a predicament required the mediator be "very God and very man" (*Inst.* 2.12.1).

Also integral to Calvin's emphasis on Jesus as "mediator," and thereby instructive for his atonement view, is his emphasis on the "threefold office" (*triplex munus*) of Christ: (1) prophet, (2) king, and (3) priest.[9] Each office has a divine purpose. With respect to Jesus as prophet, Calvin insists, "The purpose of this prophetical dignity in Christ is to teach us, that in the doctrine which he delivered is substantially included a wisdom which is perfect in all its parts" (*Inst.* 2.15.2). Jesus's kingly office is a spiritual reign in which he fulfills the prior promise of a Davidic king, "enriches" those in his kingdom with "all things necessary to eternal salvation, strengthens his people against "spiritual foes," including "the devil, sin, and death, strengthens his people to endure "insults of the world" by being "clothed with his righteousness," dispenses gifts to the church by the Spirit, and stands in judgment against his enemies (*Inst.* 2.15.3–5). With respect to his priesthood, to effectively perform the duties of the office, Jesus first offers himself as an expiating sacrifice as a "priest employed to appease the wrath of God," whereby he "may reinstate us in his favour" (*Inst.* 2.15.6). As Calvin

---

4. Witt and Scandrett, *Mapping Atonement*, 129. See Calvin, *Inst.* 1.15.4.
5. Witt and Scandrett, *Mapping Atonement*, 129.
6. Calvin points here to Rom. 8:7.
7. Witt and Scandrett, *Mapping Atonement*, 129–31.
8. Witt and Scandrett, *Mapping Atonement*, 130.
9. Witt and Scandrett, *Mapping Atonement*, 131–32.

concludes, "Thus we see, that if the benefit and efficacy of Christ's priesthood is to reach us, the commencement must be with his death" (*Inst.* 2.15.6). In commencing his priesthood via his sacrificial death, Jesus then acts as a "perpetual intercessor" who not only reconciles sinners to his Father (*Inst.* 2.15.6) but also admits sinners into an "alliance" with God and entrance to the "heavenly sanctuary," where prayers and praise can be appropriately offered to him (*Inst.* 2.15.6).

This brings us directly to Calvin's penal substitution view. According to Witt and Scandrett, for Calvin, atonement not only requires that Christ be a mediator but also that the mediator "would remedy human disobedience through his obedience."[10] Such a requirement means that Calvin expands atonement beyond the death of Christ to the entire life of Christ to accomplish what he regards as constitutive of atonement, namely, "salvation from sin, exchange, and obedience."[11] In explaining this atoning work, Calvin takes up various biblical metaphors; however, "these are explained in *terms* of penal substitution."[12] These six metaphors, each explained in penal terms, include:

1. *Satisfaction:* Unlike Anselm, who regarded satisfaction as an alternative to punishment, Calvin sees satisfaction and punishment as synonymous aspects of Christ's death.[13]

2. *Substitution:* In his death, the innocent Jesus stands in for the guilty so his innocence is transferred to the guilty and vice versa (*Inst.* 2.16.1–19).

3. *Punishment:* Reconciliation with God necessitates punishment.[14]

4. *Divine Wrath:* Jesus's death necessarily "appeased" God's wrath, though God was angry with sinners, not his Son.[15]

---

10. Witt and Scandrett, *Mapping Atonement*, 133. On this point, see also Paul Dafydd Jones, "The Fury of Love: Calvin on the Atonement," in *T&T Clark Companion to Atonement*, ed. Adam J. Johnson (London: Bloomsbury T&T Clark, 2017), 227–28.
11. Witt and Scandrett, *Mapping Atonement*, 133.
12. Witt and Scandrett, *Mapping Atonement*, 134–35.
13. I am helped with this outline by Witt and Scandrett, *Mapping Atonement*, 134–37. With respect to satisfaction, pointing to Isa. 53:5 as an indication that God punished Christ at the cross, Calvin suggests, "There is no ambiguity in Isaiah's testimony" (*Inst.* 2.17.4).
14. As Calvin asserts, "But what is the correction of our peace, unless it be the punishment due to our sins, and to be paid by us before we could be reconciled to God, had he not become our substitute? Thus you clearly see that Christ bore the punishment of sin that he might thereby exempt his people from it" (*Inst.* 3.4.30). Calvin references here Isa. 53:5 and 1 Peter 2:24.
15. Witt and Scandrett, *Mapping Atonement*, 136. See also Calvin, *Inst.* 2.16.6; 2.17.5.

5. *Sacrifice and Redemption:* In his sacrificial death, Jesus is a substitute for the sinner whose substitutionary punishment satisfies God's wrath and pays what is owed in the redemptive sense.[16]

6. *Merit:* Negatively, Jesus's obedience, most of all his death, purchases/merits grace for sinners with God so that sin is not imputed to them (*Inst.* 2.17.3–4). Positively, Christ's obedience, most of all his death, results in the imputation of his righteousness (*Inst.* 2.17.3–5).

Finally, in Calvin's view, union with the risen Christ makes it possible to share in this atoning work.[17] No one can share in the benefits of Christ's atoning work apart from this union. As Calvin notes in his reflection on Galatians 2:20, "The love of Christ led him to unite himself to us, and he completed the union by his death. By giving himself for us, he suffered in our own person; as, on the other hand, faith makes us partakes of everything which it finds in Christ."[18]

Historical Developments with Calvin's View

Reformed theologians engaged Calvin's view of the atonement for different purposes and from various perspectives. I will briefly highlight three developments between the seventeenth and twentieth centuries, though one could follow several different trajectories.[19]

To begin, partly in response to Socinus (Question 11), Francis Turretin (1623–1687), a Genevan Reformed theologian, provides a structured explanation of the atonement. Craig summarizes Turretin's structure in three parts: (1) union with Christ "as our head" through faith and by Christ's status as mediator, (2) union with Christ is the cause of the imputation of Christ's righteousness to us, and (3) this imputation is the cause of forgiveness rooted in the satisfaction of God's justice by way of "Christ's vicarious suffering and death," which grants life to adopted sons.[20] Turretin stresses Christ's mediator role as both priest and victim whose substitutionary death brings penal satisfaction.[21] For God to impute sin to Christ and to impute righteousness to us is for God "to hold him

---

16. However, Witt and Scandrett note, "Calvin never specifies what we owed to God's justice or what the penalty was that Christ paid" (Witt and Scandrett, *Mapping Atonement*, 136). For the redemptive sense of Jesus's death, see Calvin, *Inst.* 2.17.5.

17. Witt and Scandrett, *Mapping Atonement*, 137–38.

18. John Calvin, *Commentaries on the Epistles of Paul to Galatians and Ephesians* (1542; repr., Grand Rapids: Baker, 2003), 75.

19. E.g., one could trace the development of Reformed views geographically in the Netherlands, Germany, Switzerland, France, Great Britain, Eastern Europe, and North America. See the discussion in Herman J. Selderhus, ed., *A Companion to Reformed Orthodoxy* (Leiden: Brill, 2013), 119–349.

20. William Lane Craig, *Atonement and the Death of Christ: An Exegetical, Historical, and Philosophical Exploration* (Waco, TX: Baylor University Press, 2020), 137.

21. Craig, *Atonement and the Death of Christ*, 134.

who has not done a thing as if he had done it" and "to hold him who has done a thing as if he had not done it."[22] The imputation of Christ's righteousness, which is predicated on his lifelong obedience and culminated in his death, is not a "sham righteousness" or legal fiction.[23] Rather, God's declaration actually delivers sinners from their debt and consequent judgment.

Next, later engagements with Calvin's theory also resulted in a protracted conversation about so-called federal Calvinism in which "covenant" serves as a central concept for understanding God's relationship with people.[24] Covenants between God and people have certain conditions and operate according to the principle of reward and punishment. The "federal" modifier refers to a "head," or representative, of humanity within the covenants.[25] Within this covenantal approach, whether the one articulated by Johannes Cocceius (1603–1699) or in the so-called Princeton theology, Adam fails as humanity's head within a covenant of works so that everyone is included in his disobedience and consequent judgment.[26] However, a prior covenant between the Father and the Son existed, wherein the Father rewards the Son for successfully carrying out his tasks, including obedience to the law and his sacrifice for sins.[27] A covenant of grace also exists in which God gives grace to his elect given the Son's fulfillment of the covenant with his Father. However, human beings only enjoy these atoning benefits by faith.

Finally, many associate Reformed views of the atonement with particular, or limited, atonement which emerged from the Synod of Dort (1618–1619) (Questions 22 and 36). However, as the preceding discussion demonstrates, a Reformed view of atonement is more robust than how it discusses the extent of the atonement.

Summary

Though it may come as a surprise to some, Calvin's view of the atonement did not place the preponderance of its attention on divine predestination and election. Instead, he highlights Christ's threefold office of prophet, priest, and king. Within this threefold office, Calvin clearly describes God's atoning work along penal substitutionary lines. He also stresses sinners' union with Christ by faith whereby they share in the benefits of his atoning

---

22. Craig, *Atonement and the Death of Christ*, 134. See also Frances Turretin, *Institutes of Elenctic Theology*, ed. James T. Dennison Jr., trans. George Musgrave Giger, 3 vols. (Phillipsburg, NJ: P&R Publishing, 1992–1997), 16.3. The Latin term behind "impute" is *imputo* and broadly bears the sense of "to lay a charge, enter in an account," or "to reckon as a merit or a fault in someone." *CLD*, s.v. "imputo."
23. Craig, *Atonement and the Death of Christ*, 135.
24. See Witt and Scandrett, *Mapping Atonement*, 140–43.
25. Witt and Scandrett, *Mapping Atonement*, 141.
26. Witt and Scandrett, *Mapping Atonement*, 43, 142.
27. Witt and Scandrett, *Mapping Atonement*, 142.

work. Some subsequent developments within the Reformed tradition reflect Calvin's original emphases; however, historical exigencies and other factors have also resulted in other points of emphases within Reformed discussions on the atonement.

REFLECTION QUESTIONS

1. What are some key biblical texts that describe Jesus's threefold office?

2. What is the relationship between Jesus's death and his threefold office?

3. Where do Calvin's six metaphors for atonement find biblical support?

4. How does "union" with Christ impact Calvin's view of atonement?

5. How does Turretin's view of penal substitutionary atonement address criticisms raised by Socinus (Question 11)?

What Is the Arminian View of Atonement?

Christ the Savior of the world died for all and every human being, so that he obtained, through his death on the cross, reconciliation and pardon for all, in such a way, however, that only the faithful actually enjoy the same.

~Remonstrance (ca. AD 1610)

Jakob Arminius (1560–1609) is often remembered for his reaction to the "Reformed doctrine of particular redemption," or limited atonement, as well as the emergence of the movement known as Arminianism and its repudiation at the Synod of Dort (1618–1619).[1] However, in considering the Arminian view of atonement, we must avoid oversimplifications and misrepresentations. No single Arminian view exists.[2] Some Arminians hold to a governmental theory (Question 14), while others subscribe to a penal substitution theory (Question 16). If we are to understand the Arminian view of atonement, we need to consider the actual position of Jakob Arminius and

---

1. Alister E. McGrath, *Christian Theology: An Introduction*, 2nd ed. (Oxford: Blackwell, 1997), 454–55. Tony Lane contextualizes the origin of Arminius's reactions against John Calvin and Arminius's own mentor, Theodore Beza: "In 1589 Arminius was called upon to defend the Calvinistic doctrine of predestination against the attacks of Dirk Coornhert. But on weighing up the rival arguments, Arminius found himself siding with Coornhert and prudently kept silent. In the early 1590s, while lecturing on Romans, Arminius questioned the Calvinist interpretation of chapters 7 and 9. This led to controversy and to questions about his orthodoxy, which were to continue until his death" (Lane, *A Concise History of Christian Thought* [Grand Rapids: Baker Academic, 2006)], 183).
2. See Roger E. Olson, *Arminian Theology: Myths and Realities* (Downers Grove, IL: IVP Academic, 2006), 221.

how Remonstrants, and other subsequent followers, held to or diverged from his position.[3]

Jakob Arminius on Atonement

Contrary to popular belief, Jakob (Jacobus/Jacob) Arminius did not hold to a governmental theory of atonement.[4] Instead, he held to a view that combined both Anselm's satisfaction theory and a penal substitution view that resembled the Reformed view of his day.[5] In summarizing Arminius's theory along these lines, Matthew Pinson analyzes five key aspects of the Dutch theologian.

First, Arminius stresses Christ's role as a priestly mediator much in the same way that Calvin does (Question 21).[6] Christ is both the priest and sacrifice whose priestly work expiates and propitiates human sin while also acquiring righteousness and eternal life for believers.[7] Pinson observes that for Arminius, as with Anselm, such a priest must be both divine and human, given the inability of sinful humanity to carry out the work.[8]

Second, within Christ's priestly work, God simultaneously satisfies his love for people and love for his own justice.[9] William den Boer maintains that Arminius's reflection on God's "twofold love" (*Duplex amor Dei*), first his love for justice and then for humankind, is "foundational" to all of his thought.[10] This especially informs Arminius's view that God expresses both his love for people and his hatred for sin through the death of his Son, whom he punishes in place of sinners.[11] Arminius suggests, "But it has pleased God not to exercise his mercy in restoring man, without the declaration of his justice, by which he loves righteousness and hates sin."[12]

---

3. Remonstrants is a reference to forty-six Arminian pastors who in 1610 produced a five-point "Remonstrance," or "protest," against Calvinist doctrine, especially underlining Arminius's position that "God's grace makes our salvation *possible*, not *inevitable*" (Lane, *A Concise History of Christian Thought*, 184).

4. J. Matthew Pinson, "The Nature of Atonement in the Theology of Jacob Arminius," *Journal of the Evangelical Theological Society* 53 (2010): 773. See also, J. Matthew Pinson, *40 Questions About Arminianism* (Grand Rapids: Kregel Academic, 2022).

5. See Olson, *Arminian Theology*, 225.

6. James Arminius, *The Works of Arminius: The London Edition*, trans. James Nichols and William Nichols, 3 vols. (Grand Rapids: Baker, 1986), 2:220.

7. Pinson, "The Nature of Atonement," 776.

8. Pinson, "The Nature of Atonement," 777.

9. Arminius, *Works*, 2.221.

10. William den Boer, "Jacobus Arminius: Theologian of God's Twofold Love," in *Arminius, Arminianism, and Europe*, eds. Marius van Leeuwen, Keith D. Stanglin, and Marijke Tolsma, Brill's Series in Church History 39 (Leiden: Brill, 2009), 40.

11. Pinson summarizes Arminius's thought as "God's love for the creature expresses itself in his desire to save sinners. His love for justice expresses itself in 'a hatred against sin'" (Pinson, "The Nature of Atonement," 778).

12. Arminius, *The Works of Arminius*, 2:378.

Third, Arminius describes divine wrath as "an expression of divine justice against humanity's violation of divine law and gospel," violations that deserve divine punishment.[13] Christ's death propitiates this wrath for those who believe.[14] For those who reject the gospel, Arminius noted that God's wrath remains upon them.[15]

Fourth, "satisfaction" is a key aspect of Arminius's view on atonement. Pinson explains, "Arminius speaks of God as having the 'right' to demand satisfaction from sinners 'for the injuries which He has sustained' because of their sin."[16] God operates with a rigid sense of justice and a love for that justice. He abhors sin and does not permit sinners to dwell before him; therefore, God demands satisfaction.[17] God righteously and mercifully provides this satisfaction through Christ, whose obedience unto death expiates/propitiates sin and meets the demand of the law, since Christ carries it out on the sinner's behalf. Christ's mediation satisfies both the obedience and the punishment demanded in the law.[18]

Fifth, in describing the satisfaction for divine justice, Arminius sometimes refers to Jesus's death as a "payment." The payment is a penalty that sinners owe to God that Jesus, as the "sinless priest," pays to him.[19]

In summarizing Arminius's view, and juxtaposing it with the Reformed view of Arminius's day, Pinson explains:

> In Christ's oblation, Arminius argues, Christ as priest and sacrifice suffers the divine punishment that is due for human sin. This suffering constitutes the satisfaction or payment to the divine justice for redemption of humans from sin, guilt, and wrath. Thus, Arminius presents an understanding of atonement in the context of his view of the priestly office of Jesus Christ that is consistent with the penal substitution motifs regnant in sixteenth- and early seventeenth-century Reformed theology.[20]

Historical Developments of Arminius's View

Followers of Arminius's theology came to be known as Arminians.[21] In 1610, a year after Arminius's death, the Dutch Arminian party published a

---

13. Pinson, "The Nature of Atonement," 780–81.
14. Olson, *Arminian Theology*, 229.
15. Boer, "Jacobus Arminius," 39.
16. Pinson, "The Nature of Atonement," 782. See also John 3:36.
17. Pinson, "The Nature of Atonement," 782.
18. Pinson, "The Nature of Atonement," 782. See Arminius, *Works*, 3:477.
19. Pinson, "The Nature of Atonement," 784.
20. Pinson, "The Nature of Atonement," 785.
21. Interestingly, Lane observes that Jakob Arminius's given name was Jakob Hermandszoon; however, he "took the Latin name Arminius" (Lane, *A Concise History of Christian Thought*, 183).

"Remonstrance" (protest) that detailed their opposition to Calvinist doctrine.[22] Consequently, Arminius's followers also received the moniker "Remonstrants." Among these followers both then and now, developments of Arminius's view of the atonement have tended to move in one of two directions.

First, some Arminians adopted a governmental theory of atonement. This development originated with Hugo Grotius (1583–1645), a supporter of the Remonstrants, who argued that God could have forgiven sin without requiring a sacrifice for sin; however, Jesus's death demonstrated the seriousness of sin from God's perspective and thereby maintained his moral governance of the universe (Question 14).[23] Olson maintains that Grotius's theory "has often been read back into Arminius, who does not seem to have known anything about it."[24]

According to Olson, misreading Arminius's view as a governmental theory flourished in the nineteenth century due especially to the influence of Charles Finney and John Miley.[25] However, Finney (1792–1875) was either not an Arminian at all or a *sui generis* (i.e., "of its own kind" or "unique") one.[26] Even more, Finney's view of the atonement may not have been singularly governmental but, at least in some instances, an eclectic blend of "*Christus Victor*, the satisfaction theme of Anselm, the substitutionary elements of penal substitution, the rectoral framework of moral government, and the ethical focus of moral influence."[27] In any case, the point here is that the Arminian association lives on.[28] Finney's governmental-laden statements about the atonement tend to stand out and dominate his view of the doctrine. He plainly states, "The atonement of Christ was intended as a satisfaction of public justice."[29]

---

22. Of the five articles that comprise the Remonstrance, the second article is most directly related to atonement as it "affirms that Jesus died for all human beings, although only believers actually receive the benefits of the passion" (Justo L. González, *The Story of Christianity: Volume 2, The Reformation to the Present Day* [New York: HarperCollins, 1985], 181).

23. Olson, *Arminian Theology*, 229.

24. Olson, *Arminian Theology*, 229.

25. Olson, *Arminian Theology*, 237.

26. Olson, *Arminian Theology*, 237. For the conclusion that Finney represents a "*sui generis* Arminianism," see Allen C. Guelzo, foreword in Charles E. Hambrick-Stowe, *Charles G. Finney and the Spirit of American Evangelicalism* (Grand Rapids: Eerdmans, 1996), ix.

27. Obbie Tyler Todd, "Rethinking Finney: The Two Sides of Charles Grandison Finney's Doctrine of Atonement," *Journal of the Evangelical Theological Society* 63 (2020): 343.

28. In explaining how Finney has come to be associated with Arminian views of atonement, Olson suggests, "His theology was closer to semi-Pelagianism; it was without classical Arminian roots and may have been influenced by the late Remonstrant Philip Limborch (as mediated to Finney by Nathaniel Taylor)" (Olson, *Arminian Theology*, 237).

29. Charles G. Finney, *Finney's Lectures on Systematic Theology* (Grand Rapids: Eerdmans, 1953), 271. Finney distinguishes between "retributive justice," which he defines as "treating every subject of government according to character," and "public justice," which he defines

Finney then follows with an interpretation of Romans 3:24–26 that reflects his governmental leanings, noting, "This passage assigns the reason, or declares the design, of the atonement, to have been to justify God in the pardon of sin, or in dispensing with execution of the law."[30]

John Miley (1813–1895), a well-known nineteenth-century Methodist theologian, fully endorsed the governmental theory. Miley dedicated almost two hundred pages to a discussion of atonement that included a review of competing theories.[31] In his preliminary summary, Miley defines atonement: "The vicarious sufferings of Christ are an atonement for sin as a conditional substitute for penalty, fulfilling, on the forgiveness of sin, the obligation of justice and the office of penalty in moral government."[32] Miley clarifies every key term in his definition: (1) *vicarious sufferings* refer to what Jesus suffered for sinners "under the divine judicial condemnation" for their forgiveness, (2) *substitute* is not Christ's punishment but his sufferings that are "sufficient grounds for forgiveness," and (3) Jesus's vicarious sufferings are *conditional* in the sense that they are "a conditional substitute for penalty" so that the "obligation of justice and the office of penalty in moral government" are met.[33] Miley concludes, "Thus the substitution of Christ in suffering fulfills the obligation of justice and the office of penalty in their relation to the ends of moral government."[34]

Second, other Arminians adopted a substitutionary model of atonement.[35] Most famously, John Wesley (1703–1791) held to a penal substitutionary model with "no hint of the governmental theory in his sermons, letters, or essays."[36] Wesley described Jesus's death in terms of ransom, satisfaction, debt, and punishment, with an emphasis on his priestly role.[37] He accentuated divine wrath that only Jesus's punishment could appease.[38] Like Arminius himself, this places Wesley close to the Reformed tradition; however, limited atonement and the relationship between divine sovereignty and human responsibility are obvious divergences that separated Wesley and placed him squarely in the Arminian camp.

---

as "in its exercise, consists in the promotion and protection of the public interests" (Finney, *Finney's Lectures*, 259). Based on this distinction, Finney argues that Christ's death satisfies public justice but not retributive justice.

30. Finney, *Finney's Lectures*, 271.
31. See John Miley, *Systematic Theology*, 2 vols. (New York: Hunt & Eaton, 1892–94), 2:65–253.
32. Miley, *Systematic Theology*, 2:68.
33. Miley, *Systematic Theology*, 2:68.
34. Miley, *Systematic Theology*, 2:69.
35. Olson identifies the following as Arminians who held to a substitutionary view of some kind: John Wesley (1703–1791), Richard Watson (1781–1833), William Burt Pope (1822–1903), and Thomas Summers (1812–1882). See Olson, *Arminian Theology*, 231–37.
36. Olson, *Arminian Theology*, 232.
37. Olson, *Arminian Theology*, 232.
38. See Thomas H. McCall, "Wesleyan Theologies," in *T&T Clark Companion to Atonement*, ed. Adam J. Johnson (London: Bloomsbury T&T Clark, 2017), 797.

Summary

As with the Lutheran (Question 20) and Reformed (Question 21) views of atonement, the Arminian view as it stands does not necessarily reflect the view of its founder, Jakob Arminius, at every point. Arminius himself held to a combination of substitutionary and penal views that were consistent with the Reformed position of his day. Nevertheless, many flatten out Arminius as someone who resisted the Reformed tenets of irresistible grace and limited atonement. Additionally, despite Arminius's commitment to the substitutionary-penal view of atonement, some of his followers adopted a governmental theory. Overall, while it is certainly fair to identify Arminians as the foil of the Reformed tradition, this association neither adequately defines Jakob Arminius's view of atonement nor the Remonstrants nor those who find themselves in the Arminian camp.

REFLECTION QUESTIONS

1. How did Jakob Arminius's view of atonement align with his Reformed contemporaries?

2. Where did Arminius depart from his Reformed contemporaries?

3. What do Martin Luther (Question 20), John Calvin (Question 21), and Jakob Arminius have in common?

4. What biblical passages might Arminians point to as a critique of limited atonement?

5. How did Arminius's subsequent followers remain consistent with his thought and also depart from it?

How Do Non-Christian Religions View Atonement?

Indeed, under the law almost everything is purified with blood, and without the shedding of blood there is no forgiveness of sins.

~Hebrews 9:22

The five major religions in the world today are Christianity, Judaism, Islam, Hinduism, and Buddhism. Each of them have different conceptions of the divine and the state of humanity. While all agree that humanity is flawed, there is no agreement on the cause of those flaws. Consequently, "solutions" to the human predicament tend to be quite different from what is offered in the Christian Bible and tradition. Non-Christian religions have a drastically different view of "atonement" or whatever might qualify as a parallel to it. While the writer of Hebrews insists that the shedding of blood is essential for forgiveness, non-Christian religions do not necessarily concur.

Atonement in Judaism

Atonement within Judaism and Christianity overlaps at multiple points, including their common use of Judaism's Scriptures, the OT (Question 24). Despite this shared literary source, differences exist between the two religions due to their divergent views on the person of Jesus and the evolution of Judaism since AD 70 (the destruction of the Jerusalem temple) as well as since AD 132 (the failed Bar Kokhba revolt). With respect to the outcome of the latter two events, Rabbi Jonathan Sacks avers, "All the institutions of national Jewish life were now gone. There was no Temple, no sacrificial order, no priests, no kings, no prophets, no land, no independence, and no expectation that they might soon return."[1] Regarding the high Day of Atonement, Yom Kippur, Sacks explains, "So long as the Temple stood, the service of the High Priest on Yom Kippur was designed to secure atonement for all Israel."[2] Theological slippage occurred even prior to the destruction of the temple, with the high priesthood going to the "highest bidder."[3] Nevertheless, with the dawn of a "post-temple" age, a new view of atonement emerged in various forms over the next several centuries up until today.

Rabbi Akiva (Akiba) (AD 50–135) saw post-temple Judaism as an opportunity to foster a way of atonement that would bring the sinner "closer to the Divine Presence."[4] Without the temple and the priesthood, forgiveness could be obtained directly from God rather than vicariously through other human agents. Sacks observes that Akiva and other leaders combined priestly, prophetic, and kingly strands of atonement and repentance.[5] From the prophets, they drew the emphasis on repentance, which was not bound to a specific day. From the priests, they drew confession, given that the high priest made three confessions on Yom Kippur. From the kings, they also took the confession of sin. With respect to an atoning ritual akin to what transpired in the temple, especially on Yom Kippur, Sacks writes, "We recount the whole of the High Priest's service—something we do at no other time—telling the story much as we relate the Exodus at the Seder table on Pesah."[6] Additionally, prayer and fasting play vital roles in seeking forgiveness as they signal "a change of heart and deed."[7] Overall, Sacks maintains, "Prayer took the place of sacrifice. The synagogue replaced the Temple. Repentance substituted for the rites of the High Priest."[8]

Other developments that have helped to define atonement in Judaism include reflection on the nature of repentance (*teshuva*), confession, and reflection on atonement-laden passages. For example, Maimonides (AD 1138–1204)

---

1. Sacks adds, "With the possible exception of the Holocaust it was the most traumatic period in Jewish history" (Rabbi Jonathan Sacks, *Ceremony & Celebration: Introduction to the Holidays* [Jerusalem: Maggid, 2017], 56).
2. Sacks, *Ceremony & Celebration*, 57.
3. Sacks, *Ceremony & Celebration*, 57. See, e.g., 2 Macc. 11:3.
4. Sacks, *Ceremony & Celebration*, 57. In the Mishnah, Akiba asserts, "Happy are you, O Israel. Before whom you are made clean, and who makes you clean? It is your Father who is in heaven" (Yoma 8:9).
5. Sacks, *Ceremony & Celebration*, 58.
6. Sacks, *Ceremony & Celebration*, 59. Along with this priestly recollection, Sacks observes an additional service: "We prostrate ourselves four times during Musaf, something we only do on one other occasion, Rosh HaShana, again in memory of the Temple. The custom of men wearing the kittel, a white tunic, on Yom Kippur recalls the white robe the High Priest wore on that day when he entered the Holy of Holies. All of this is priestly" (Sacks, *Ceremony & Celebration*, 59).
7. Sacks, *Ceremony & Celebration*, 60.
8. Sacks, *Ceremony & Celebration*, 66.

derives the act of repentance from the law of the priests (*Torat Kohanim*) in Scripture; sincere repentance and confession is what is left of the temple.[9] Along these lines, what now stands at the heart of atonement in Judaism are prayers of confession/repentance intertwined with reflection upon Scripture in the context of community. Sacks describes the aim of this atoning work in relation to Yom Kippur: "It is a day not just of confession and forgiveness but of a profound liberation. Atonement means that we can begin again. We are not held captive by the past, by our failures."[10]

Atonement in Islam

Broad generalization is necessary here for multiple reasons, including the fact that Islam, as with any religion, has internal variations often represented by inner-religious sects, such as the differences between Sunni and Shia Muslims, along with the denominations embedded in each of them.[11] Moreover, the 114 units (*surahs*) that make up the Qur'an are not mere dogmatic expressions of the Islamic faith.[12] Therefore, one must draw a fair amount of theological inferences regarding atonement or its Islamic equivalent. Additionally, as with Christian Scripture and theology, disagreements among Islamic exegetes do arise. Nevertheless, at the risk of oversimplification, I will summarize what Islamic theology generally regards as the human predicament and its divine solution.

In Islam, ignorance and disobedience that leads to idolatry lay at the heart of the human predicament. Eschatological judgment ultimately awaits those who fail and/or refuse to obey and worship Allah as the one true God and creator. Several passages in the Qur'an bear this out, including:

> There is no god worthy of worship except him. He alone gives life and causes death. He is your Lord, and the Lord of your forefathers. In fact, they are in doubt, amusing themselves. Wait then O Prophet for the day when the sky will be veiled in haze, clearly visible, overwhelming the people. They will cry, "This is a painful torment." (Ad-Dukhan 44:8–11)

---

9. Sacks, *Ceremony & Celebration*, 62–63.

10. Sacks, *Ceremony & Celebration*, 95.

11. As Carole M. Cusack and M. Afzal Upal note, "In common with other faith traditions, Islam has been a dynamic force from the start, with adaptations stemming from individual leaders, diverse ethnic populations, and the cultural contexts in which the religion took root" (Carole M. Cusack and M. Afzal Upal, "Introduction: Islamic Sects and Movements," in *Handbook of Islamic Sects and Movements*, eds. Muhammand Afzal Upal and Carole M. Cusack (Leiden: Brill, 2021), 1. See also Matthew Aaron Bennett, *40 Questions About Islam* (Grand Rapids: Kregel Academic, 2020).

12. See Richard Bell, *Bell's Introduction to the Qur'an*, ed. William Montgomery Watt (Edinburgh: Edinburgh University Press, 1970).

So as for those whose scale is heavy with good deeds, they will be in a life of bliss. And as for those whose scale is light, their home will be the abyss. And what will make you realize what this is? It is a scorching fire. (Al-Qari'ah 101:6–11)

Jonathan Brown points to the vertical and horizontal dimensions of sin within Islam and notes, "Man sins against God, offending upward an all-powerful, invincible Creator. And man sins against man, injuring an all-too-vulnerable fellow human being, a human being whom God has granted the right to repair."[13] According to Islamic theology, such sin originated in Eden, where Iblis (leader of the demons) refused the divine command to bow before Adam and tempted him instead.[14] When Iblis "asks for a respite," it is granted to facilitate the testing of "people's commitment to the divine command and verify their ability to resist and withstand temptation."[15] In short, then, the human predicament in Islamic thought is that human beings commit sins that can result in eternal punishment and that Adam's children are locked in an "eternal battle" against "Iblis and his followers."[16]

What, then, is the solution given this predicament? Several points are in order. First, Allah sends prophets to warn human beings, culminating in the prophet Muhammad who reveals "the true religion of Abraham."[17] Adherence to Muhammad results in absolution: "As for those who believe, do good, and have faith in what has been revealed to Muhammad—which is the truth from their Lord—He will absolve them of their sins and improve their condition" (Muhammad 47:2). Imitation of Muhammad is embodied in the so-called five pillars of Islam: (1) declaration of faith in Allah and his prophet, (2) prayer, (3) almsgiving, (4) fasting, and (5) pilgrimage.

Second, there exists within Islam no atoning sacrifice that reconciles Allah to people. As Richard Bell notes, "Indeed the chief point of difference between the Qur'an and the Old Testament is the absence from the former of any profound conception of sacrifice and a sacrificing priesthood."[18]

---

13. Jonathan A. C. Brown, "Sin, Forgiveness, and Reconciliation: A Muslim Perspective," in *Sin, Forgiveness, and Reconciliation: Christian and Muslim Perspectives*, eds. Lucinda Mosher and David Marshall (Washington, DC: Georgetown University Press, 2016), 14.
14. See Ayman Shabana, "The Concept of Sin in the Qur'an in Light of the Story of Adam," in Mosher and Marshall, *Sin, Forgiveness, and Reconciliation*, 43. See Al-Araf 7:11–27.
15. Shabana, "The Concept of Sin," 43.
16. Shabana, "The Concept of Sin," 61.
17. Bell, *Bell's Introduction*, 157. On the fittingness of Abraham's faith in Allah's sight, see An-Nisa 4:125; Al Mumtahanah 60:4.
18. Bell, *Bell's Introduction*, 158. Bell adds regarding the Qur'an's portrayal of Jesus's crucifixion, "The denial that Jesus died on the cross is primarily a denial that the crucifixion was a Jewish victory; but, in line with the absence of the conception of sacrifice, it means that the Qur'an never speaks of the atonement or the saving work of Jesus" (Bell, *Bell's Introduction*, 158).

Third, even with obedience to Allah and his prophet, certainty about entrance into eternal paradise, rather than eternal hell, remains elusive. As Brown remarks, "Because of the enormity of God's mercy, and because the scope of His cosmic justice so far exceeds our ken, the result is that we cannot know who will enter heaven and who will not."[19]

While some cursory parallels exist between Islam and Christianity with respect to the human condition and Final Judgment, the former contains nothing like God's atoning work in Christ. The Qur'an features no definitive act of God by which he reconciles himself to sinners in the vein of what we find in the Christian Bible.[20]

Atonement in Hinduism

Of the five major world religions, Hinduism (*Sanatana Dharma*: "the eternal path/law") qualifies as the most unlike Christianity.[21] It is notoriously difficult to define in terms of a seamless origin story, sacred texts, a historical founder, doctrines, practices, or even God/gods.[22] According to Harold Coward, the "major obstacle" in Hinduism is not sin but ignorance.[23] Hinduism features a plethora of gods who broadly fit into two categories: (1) *nirguna* Brahman, which is a "formless, impersonal supreme reality without qualities or attributes"; and (2) the *saguna* Brahman, which is "the personified, personal form of the supreme reality."[24] Largen refers to these two categories as "two different ways of perceiving the one true ultimate reality."[25] *Nirguna* Brahman perceives reality along philosophical, intellectual, and meditative lines; *saguna* perceives it in relation to "adoration, sacrifice, and devotion."[26] With respect to the latter, Largen describes its basic narrative parameters as follows:

> Unlike Christianity, which is grounded in a linear understanding of time, Hinduism has a cyclical understanding of

19. Brown, "Sin, Forgiveness, and Reconciliation," 15.
20. Matthew Aaron Bennett, "Atonement Impasse: The Perennial Problem of Communicating Christ's Atonement to Muslims," *Missiology* 50 (2022): 374–85.
21. Even the label "Hinduism" as a reference to a religion is a misnomer. See Kristin Johnston Largen, *Finding God among Our Neighbors: An Interfaith Systematic Theology* (Minneapolis: Fortress, 2013), 14. The etymology of "Hindu" involves the ancient title for the River Indus that runs through northern India.
22. Largen observes, "Scholars agree that Hinduism is the oldest living major religious tradition, but beyond that simple fact there is much debate, since it is clear that what we today call Hinduism is made up of different beliefs and practices that were handed down orally for millennia before they were finally written down" (Largen, *Finding God among Our Neighbors*, 12).
23. Harold Coward, *Sin and Salvation in the World Religions: A Short Introduction* (Oxford: Oneworld, 2003), 89.
24. Largen, *Finding God among Our Neighbors*, 23.
25. Largen, *Finding God among Our Neighbors*, 23.
26. Largen, *Finding God among Our Neighbors*, 23.

time, in which the universe continually cycles into and out of existence, over many eons. In most descriptions of this process, instead of there being a single divinity behind it all, there are three: Brahma is the creator, the one who brings the universe into being; Shiva is the destroyer, the one who, at the right time, causes the universe to fall into nothingness; and during the in-between time stands Vishnu the preserver, the god who sustains the universe and protects it from evil while it is in existence.[27]

In both *saguna* Brahman, with its narrative underpinning, and *nirguna* Brahman, with its philosophical/meditative underpinnings, ignorance defines the human dilemma. Within the hindrance of ignorance, the ultimate objective is to experience *moksha*, which is "release from the cycle of rebirths."[28]

The pathway to such a release constitutes the closest parallel to salvation, and thereby atonement, within the Christian tradition. However, the Hindu move toward release is more a matter of right practice (orthopraxy) than right belief (orthodoxy).[29] Within the diverse beliefs of Hindu deities, Largen highlights the belief that Vishnu periodically comes to the earth in "the endless cycles of history" disguised in various forms (avatars) to "save and preserve creation from a particular demonic force that is threatening the very existence of the cosmos."[30] Within this loose structure, and alongside its various festivals, "salvation" in Hinduism has to do with favorably cycling "in and out of existence" (reincarnation).[31] Karma (right actions that impact the soul's future) and Dharma (proper actions according to one's social caste) dictate the nature of one's reincarnation.

This salvation, or liberation, stems from performing the right actions according to "your station in life," by which "you will continually move up the anthropological hierarchy in subsequent births, eventually being born as a Brahmin and attaining liberation, even if this takes many lifetimes."[32] One's pursuit of liberation can take a variety of equally valuable paths, including: (1) *karma-marga* (the "path of duty or action"), (2) *jnana-marga* (the "path of knowledge"), and (3) *bhakti-marga* ("the path of devotional participation").[33] The latter involves devotion "to one's chosen manifestation of the divine, or to one's guru" in which "god's grace ameliorates the strict causality one's own

27. Largen, *Finding God among Our Neighbors*, 23–24.
28. Robert P. Sellers, "Toward a Multifaith View of Atonement," *Review & Expositor* 118 (2021): 81.
29. See Largen, *Finding God among Our Neighbors*, 13.
30. Largen, *Finding God among Our Neighbors*, 25.
31. Largen, *Finding God among Our Neighbors*, 32.
32. Largen, *Finding God among Our Neighbors*, 32.
33. Largen, *Finding God among Our Neighbors*, 33.

karma and can bring the devotee liberation."[34] Along the way, many Hindus participate in rituals, including sacrificial ones, to secure blessings from various gods.

Atonement in Buddhism

Buddhism originated at some point in the fifth century BC in northeast India under the direction of its founder Siddhartha Gautama, who later received the title "Buddha" ("enlightened one"). Buddha is not a god in the Christian sense but rather a uniquely "awakened human being."[35] He is neither creator nor savior but a "teacher of awakening."[36] According to Buddhists, this awakening unfolded through the "four sights" and the "great renunciation." The former refers to four chariot rides Gautama took around age thirty: (1) a ride in which he witnessed the inevitable toll of old age from which he had been shielded by his father, (2) a ride in which he witnessed a diseased man, whereby he understood power and wealth could not protect from disease, (3) a ride in which he saw his first corpse and realized that, notwithstanding present pleasure, life ended in death, and (4) a ride in which he witnessed a meditating hermit who had taken leave of physical pleasures to find "spiritual liberation from all the suffering and sorrow of the material world."[37] After this experience, Gautama left his family and embarked on "the great renunciation" in which he practiced asceticism and meditation. He ultimately sought a "middle way" between "the two extremes of self-denial and self-indulgence."[38] In this quest, Gautama placed himself under the Bodhi Tree (the tree of awakening) to find enlightenment. However, in this quest, Mara (the god of desire) attempted through various distractions to keep Gautama from reaching a state in which he would not be beholden to desire. But it was to no avail, as Gautama experienced three visions.[39] He then taught for eighty years and chose to end his life and "attain final nirvana" (i.e., a transcendent state of neither suffering nor sense of self).[40]

---

34. Largen, *Finding God among Our Neighbors*, 33.
35. Largen, *Finding God among Our Neighbors*, 73.
36. Largen, *Finding God among Our Neighbors*, 73.
37. Largen, *Finding God among Our Neighbors*, 75.
38. Largen, *Finding God among Our Neighbors*, 76.
39. Largen explains, "In the first watch of the night, he had a vision of all past lives, and he became aware of his personal identity as it had been formed through samsara, the endless cycle of birth and death. In the second watch of the night, he had a vision of the law of karma, or how beings come into being and then go out of being, rising into a more noble birth or falling into a lower birth as a result of their deeds. And in the third watch of the night, in the hours just before dawn, he became awakened" (Largen, *Finding God among Our Neighbors*, 78).
40. Largen maintains, "He entered into final meditation peacefully, lying on his side, surrounded by all manner of animals, disciples, and even gods; and this scene of the Buddha passing into final nirvana is one of the most widely depicted in Buddhist art" (Largen, *Finding God among Our Neighbors*, 79–80).

Buddhism emerged from Gautama's life and experiences. It revolves around "four noble truths": (1) the normal way of life is suffering, evidenced by a frustrating quest for happiness in this life through impermanent means, such as money and pleasure; (2) desire (for sex, money, pleasure, etc.) is the cause of suffering; (3) the true goal of human life is *nirvana* (literally "extinguishing"), that is, "a letting go of the thirst for more," which is not to be confused with heaven or annihilation but is the cessation of misunderstanding and desire; and (4) the truth of an eightfold path whereby one attains nirvana.[41]

While Buddhism can be expressed in a variety of ways and has undergone various developments, the goal remains the attainment of nirvana. In this way, there is nothing inherently soteriological about Buddhism and therefore no real sense of atonement in it. The closest parallel would be a kind of self-reconciliation in which desire is removed and nirvana is achieved through the imitation of Buddha and adherence to his teachings.

Summary

While the major non-Christian religions discussed can agree that humanity is flawed, none of them define that flaw in the way the Christian Bible does. How each religion defines the flaw shapes the perceived solution. Moreover, parallels to atonement as it is found in the Christian tradition are thin. There is no real parallel to the eternal and incarnate Son of God offering himself in a punitive substitutionary death according to the will of his eternal Father, whereby God reconciles himself to his sinful creatures and thereby frees them from the power of sin, death, Satan, and the experience of eternal condemnation.

REFLECTION QUESTIONS

1. How does modern Judaism connect its present expression of atonement to its scriptural past?

2. From a Christian perspective, what would worry you most about God if you were an adherent of Islam?

3. How does Hinduism define the human predicament?

4. How does Buddhism define the human predicament?

5. What do Judaism, Islam, Hinduism, and Buddhism have in common with respect to how people can solve their struggles with God/gods, themselves, and the world?

---

41. Largen, *Finding God among Our Neighbors*, 80–84.

PART 4

The Logic
of Atonement

What Is the Old Testament Concept of Atonement?

Aaron shall make atonement on its horns once a year. With the blood of the sin offering of atonement he shall make atonement for it once in the year throughout your generations. It is most holy to the LORD.

~Exodus 30:10

The phrase "for generations to come" is the description of Israel's need for atonement. All of Abraham's descendants needed atonement. This need is reflected in the seminal moments of the nation's history, in the laws by which Israelites lived, and in the sacrificial system itself. While the need is clear, understanding the nature of OT atonement can prove challenging. However, if we are to understand God's atoning work in Christ, we must understand the OT framework that shapes it. We must answer the question, "What are the OT concepts of atonement?"

The Need for Atonement Shaped Israel's Story

The need for reconciliation between God and all people pervades the OT. Those made in God's image are under judgment and separated from their Creator. These image bearers can neither enjoy life in him nor properly reflect his glory because of sin. The need for atonement precedes Israel's inception, persists with every generation of Abraham's descendants, and follows the nation home from Babylon.

Before Israel's story begins in earnest, atonement shapes humanity's need. Adam and Eve's sin adversely impacts their progeny (Rom. 5:12–14). God carries out his judgments against Adam and Eve by exiling them from his presence. This separation from God finds no permanent resolution until God's work in the crucified and risen Christ. What we find in the meanwhile are temporary measures that foreshadow Israel's sacrificial system and brim with typological implications for understanding Christ's atonement. For example, after the flood, Noah offers a sacrifice to God:

> Then *Noah* built an *altar* to the LORD and took some of every clean animal and some of every clean bird and offered *burnt offerings* on the *altar*. And when the LORD smelled the *pleasing aroma*, the LORD said in his heart, "I will never again curse the ground because of man, for the intention of man's heart is evil from his youth. Neither will I ever again strike down every living creature as I have done." (Gen. 8:20–21, italics added)

Here the contours of Israel's sacrificial system are in plain view. A specific person (*Noah*) had to offer a specific sacrifice (*burnt offerings*) at a particular time and place (*altar*) that pleased God (*pleasing aroma*). The last element stands out. The anthropomorphism (i.e., ascribing human features to God) "the LORD smelled the pleasing aroma," communicates God's pleasure with the sacrifices.[1] Although the narrator does not explain why the sacrifice pleased God, the wider context indicates a link between the judgment in the flood, Noah's sacrifice, and God's promise not to repeat his destruction. The sacrifice pleased God to such a degree that it guaranteed the aversion of future wrath, at least the kind of wrath displayed in the flood. God's acceptance of the sacrifice implies his intent to be gracious to humans who remain under the judgments enacted at Eden and manifested in the flood.[2] That intent takes full bloom in Christ's sacrifice.

As the Genesis narrative narrows its focus to Abraham (Gen. 12:1–3), the need for reconciliation defines seminal moments throughout Israel's history. We repeatedly encounter people who need to be reconciled to God and to one another.[3] This need is implied in the Mosaic law, and it is exacerbated by sin's use of the law (Rom. 7:7–25). The wilderness generation shows a penchant for coming under judgment and creating relational fissures (see Exod. 16:1–6; 32:1–6; Num. 14:1–4; 16:1–50). Even after the wilderness wanderings, Achan's sin momentarily derails the conquest of Canaan (Josh. 7:1–26). The period of the judges oscillates between rebellion and deliverance (Judg. 2:11–23). Though Israel's monarchy flourishes at times, Saul's failure as the

---

1. On this point, see John E. Hartley, *Leviticus*, WBC 4 (Nashville: Thomas Nelson, 1992), 22–23.
2. As William J. Dumbrell observes in his analysis of Gen. 8:21–22, "Nothing is said about the removal of curses resulting from the fall" (William J. Dumbrell, *The Faith of Israel: A Theological Survey of the Old Testament*, 2nd ed. [Grand Rapids: Baker Academic, 2002], 25).
3. See, e.g., the rifts between Jacob and Esau (Gen. 27:41) as well as between Joseph and his brothers (Gen. 37:12–36).

first king portends subsequent royal failures that result in relational fissures (1 Sam. 13:8–15). Relational fissures even mark Israel's "golden age" as David's sin against Bathsheba and murder of her husband Uriah guarantees violence among his descendants (2 Sam. 12:10), and Solomon's unquenchable thirst for foreign women helps to tear the kingdom apart (1 Kings 11:9–13).[4] The fissure of the nation is marked by a host of kings who fail in their responsibilities. Their failures trigger a downward spiral among God's people culminating in both Assyrian invasion and Babylonian exile. Even in the return from exile, relational fissures endure (Ezra 10:18–22; Neh. 13:23–31).

Divine judgments and relational fissures are not limited to seminal moments in Israel's history, a reality made clear in the commands prescribed in the Pentateuch. Many of the instructions assume that individual and corporate life had the potential to separate Israelites from God and from one another. Moses warns the Israelites who are poised to enter the Promised Land that they would either experience God's blessing or curse (Deut. 11:26–28; 28:15; Gal. 3:10). Though death and exile are the ultimate consequences of Israel's disobedience, curses such as pestilence, disease, drought, and defeat at the hands of enemies also mark God's judgment against Israel's sin (Deut. 28:15–68). In short, the reality of judgment and a need for atonement even lurks over the mundane moments of Israel's history.

God Provides Atonement for Israel Through Sacrifice

The judgments and relational fissures outlined above shaped Israel's story. In fact, the need for atonement becomes the subtext of Israel's story from Genesis to Malachi. One of the primary ways God meets that need is by instituting the sacrificial system. This temporary measure provides a process by which Israel could be cleansed from their sin (expiation), avert God's judgment (propitiation), and experience divine blessing. By carrying out prescribed sacrifices, Israel could be, at least momentarily, reconciled to God.

OT sacrifices vary, but their collective function is to "cover/make atonement for" (*kaphar*) sin and impurity. Gordon Wenham describes "make atonement" as a "broad idea involving several subsidiary ones."[5] Through atoning sacrifices, altars and priests are sanctified, lepers and others are cleansed, sinners are forgiven, guilt is carried away, and the effect of sin is reversed from death to life.[6] The animals offered in these sacrifices must be clean and unblemished, according to the standards of the Mosaic law. In these sacrifices, emphasis is often placed on the role of blood in making atonement.

---

4. In both instances, the biblical writers underscore God's anger against his anointed kings (see 2 Sam. 12:10–12; 1 Kings 11:9).

5. Gordon J. Wenham, "The Theology of Old Testament Sacrifice," in *Sacrifice in the Bible*, eds. R. T. Beckwith and M. J. Selman (Carlisle, UK: Paternoster, 1995), 81.

6. See Exod. 29:33, 36, 37; Lev. 10:17; 12:7–8; 14:20; 16:1–34. See also Wenham, "The Theology of Old Testament Sacrifice," 81–82.

The *crux interpretum* (i.e., a crucial passage) here is from Leviticus: "For the life of the flesh is in the blood, and I have given it to you on the altar to make atonement for your souls, for it is the blood that makes atonement by the life" (17:11). Interpreters sometimes struggle to articulate how animal blood secures atonement for those offering the sacrifice. The answer lies in the connection between an animal's blood and its life.[7] An animal's blood gives it life. Consequently, the animal's blood, or life, takes the place of human blood or human life. This connection helps shape the early church's understanding of Jesus's sacrificial death and the theory of penal substitutionary atonement (see Questions 25 and 26).

Besides the frequent sacrifices prescribed by the Mosaic law, the annual sacrifices offered at Passover and on the Day of Atonement stand out. The first Passover sacrifice coincided with the tenth plague that resulted in release from Egyptian bondage (Exod. 12:1–51). Moses instructed all Israelite households to secure an unblemished lamb, slaughter it at twilight, mark their houses with the lamb's blood, eat the roasted flesh of the lamb with unleavened bread and bitter herbs before morning, and burn whatever remains (Exod. 12:1–10). They were to eat the meal dressed for a quick departure as the Lord passed through the land, killing the firstborn male of each household left unmarked by blood (Exod. 12:11–13). Moses instructed Israel to carry out the same ritual year after year, preceded by a seven-day festival of unleavened bread (Exod. 12:14–20). Subsequent Passovers memorialized the exodus in Israel's history. At the heart of this event, one finds a sacrifice that simultaneously protected Israel from God's judgment and delivered them from their enemies.

The annual Day of Atonement also revolved around sacrifices for the sins of Israel: "For on this day shall atonement be made for you to cleanse you. You shall be clean before the Lord from all your sins" (Lev. 16:30). The sacrifices here involved both rare access into the most sacred space of the sanctuary and the exile of a goat into the wilderness. Before a sacrifice could be offered for the people, one had to be offered by the priest for himself, namely, the sin offering of a bull (Lev. 16:6, 11). The priest sprinkled its blood seven times in front of the mercy seat that sat atop the ark of the covenant, where YHWH appeared to the priest in a cloud of incense (Lev. 16:2, 13–14). Only then could he offer the blood from the goat of the sin offering for the people, which he also sprinkled before the mercy seat (Lev. 16:15). The priest had to atone for, or cleanse, the tent of meeting and the altar by sprinkling it with blood and smearing its horns with blood (Lev. 16:16–19). The priest then turned his attention to the living sacrifice, a live goat (Lev. 16:20). The priest placed his hands upon the head of the goat, confessed the sins of Israel upon it, and sent it out into the wilderness to carry away the nation's iniquities (Lev. 16:21–22).

---

7.   On this point, see Wenham, "The Theology of Old Testament Sacrifice," 82.

All these sacrifices functioned to atone for, or cover, the sins of the priest and the nation. The sacrifices cleansed the people from sin and carried their sin away from the presence of God. Without the sacrifices that God provided, Israel could not be reconciled to God, and they thereby risked his wrath.

God Provides Atonement for Israel Through Mediators

God also provides atonement through figures who act as mediators between him and Israel. Some of these mediators, most obviously Levitical priests, offer sacrifices on behalf of the nation. However, others do not. Two examples stand out. First, during the golden calf incident, Moses intercedes for Israel in the face of God's wrath: "But now, if you will forgive sin—but if not, please blot me out of your book that you have written" (Exod. 32:32).[8] God responds by asserting his authority to blot out whom he wants while also relenting from the absolute destruction of the nation that he initially threatened (Exod. 32:33–35). When Moses reflects on this moment in Deuteronomy, he underscores the atoning impact of his intercession (see Deut. 9:18–19). Though it lacked a sacrificial offering, Moses's intercession had an obvious atoning effect. He helped Israel avert God's wrath for its idolatrous rebellion.

A second example can be found in Isaiah's description of a suffering servant: "But he was pierced for our transgressions; he was crushed for our iniquities; upon him was the chastisement that brought us peace, and with his wounds we are healed. All we like sheep have gone astray; we have turned—every one—to his own way; and the Lord has laid on him the iniquity of us all" (Isa. 53:5–6). The sacrificial overtones are clear. Isaiah describes a figure whom God appointed to atone for the sins of his people in the same vein as a sacrificial animal.

What these examples underscore is that OT atonement required mediators whom God approved and appointed. Their work does not mitigate the importance of sacrifices for atonement. To the contrary, just as sacrifices had to be acceptable to God, mediators did as well. The inner life of both Israelites and their mediators mattered to God. We see the divine requirement of appointment and acceptability in figures such as Moses and the Levitical priests.

Old Testament Atonement Typifies the Logic of Christ's Atoning Work

Atonement in the OT provides the typological framework for understanding the logic of Christ's atoning work (see Questions 25–31).[9] The religious elite execute the promised Messiah. In his sovereignty, however, God

---

8. For Moses's other intercessory prayers, see Exod. 32:11–14; 33:12–16; Num. 11:11–15; 12:13; 14:13–19.
9. See Leonard Goppelt, *Typos: The Typological Interpretation of the Old Testament in the New*, trans. Donald H. Madvig (Grand Rapids: Eerdmans, 1982); Mitchell L. Chase, *40 Questions About Typology and Allegory* (Grand Rapids: Kregel Academic, 2020).

uses the climactic example of Israel's need for atonement as the ultimate means of their atonement (Acts 4:8–12, 28). Moreover, the entire sacrificial system anticipates Jesus's sacrificial death (see 1 Cor. 5:7; Heb. 9:13–14; John 1:29). Jesus also fulfills prophecies of a mediator who would atone for sin (Deut. 18:15; Isa. 53:1–12). He excels his mediating predecessors. He longs to do the atoning work the Father wills (Ps. 40:7–9; Mark 14:36; John 4:34; Heb. 10:7). Moreover, Jesus has no need to atone for his own sin. He does not offer animals in an earthly temple, but he offers himself in the very presence of the Father (Heb. 7:1–10:31), where he sits enthroned as the mediator whose atoning work is eternally efficacious.

Summary

God's provision of atonement for Israel signals that his last word to fallen humanity is not a word of judgment. The sacrifices and mediators he provided to ancient Israel speak to his graciousness toward sinners. His affections for Israel could be sensed in every offering. Every sacrifice anticipates the atoning work of Christ, who is the propitiating sacrifice "for the sins of the whole world" (1 John 2:2). In this way, the OT concept of atonement is nothing short of a preamble to the atoning work of Jesus.

REFLECTION QUESTIONS

1. How do the flood narrative and Noah's sacrifice anticipate the work of atonement in the rest of Scripture?

2. What role does atonement play in the seminal moments of Israel's history?

3. How is the need for atonement reflected in the mundane moments of Israel's history?

4. What kind of mediators are required for carrying out God's atoning work in the OT?

5. How does OT atonement provide a framework for understanding God's atoning work in Christ?

How Does Jesus's Death Provide Penal Substitutionary Atonement?

I am the good shepherd. The good shepherd lays down his life for the sheep.

~John 10:11

If one holds to a penal substitutionary theory of atonement, it means he or she believes not only that Christ took the sinner's deserved place at the cross or served as a substitute. It also means they believe Jesus endured divine punishment for sin so believers would not have to experience the same punishment, which they deserved (Question 16).[1] However, even from this vantage point, how, precisely, does Jesus's death provide such a thing? Did God really inflict his Son with all the punishment stored up for sinners? After all, even some proponents of penal substitution stop short of asserting that God the Father literally punished his Son.[2]

What we find then, as with so many questions related to atonement, is a need for theological precision. We need a more precise definition of punishment, a more precise explanation of what Jesus's punishment accomplishes and how it does so, and a more precise understanding of how others share

---

1. William Lane Craig writes, "Penal substitution in a theological context may be defined as the doctrine that God inflicted upon Christ the suffering that we deserved as the punishment for our sins, as a result of which we no longer deserve punishment" (Craig, *Atonement and the Death of Christ: An Exegetical, Historical, and Philosophical Exploration* [Waco, TX: Baylor University Press, 2020], 147).

2. E.g., Craig cites John Stott who plainly asserts, "We must never make Christ the object of God's punishment" (John Stott, *The Cross of Christ* [Leicester: Inter-Varsity Press, 1986], 151). See also Craig, *Atonement and the Death of Christ*, 148.

in that accomplishment. Such precision will help answer how Jesus's death provides penal substitutionary atonement.

Defining Christ's Punishment

Defining terms can sometimes seem pedantic. Nevertheless, how one defines "punishment" should matter to proponents and opponents of penal substitution alike. William Lane Craig's discussion on this matter is instructive. He maintains that defining punishment as "suffering" or even "harsh treatment" is insufficient.[3] At the same time, Craig acknowledges there is currently no consensus "concerning the conditions sufficient for punishment."[4] Nevertheless, from a philosophical perspective, he builds upon Alec Walen's description of the "necessary conditions of punishment."[5] I have summarized here the five conditions that must be met to constitute an act of punishment:

1. An act of punishment must either *impose* a hardship on the *punishee* and/or remove a benefit from him or her.

2. An act of punishment must be intentional. It can neither be accidental nor the result of another pursuit.

3. An act of punishment must be a response to a *punishee's* wrongdoing or at least the belief that wrongdoing has occurred.

4. An act of punishment must signal condemnation/censure of the *punishee's* wrongdoing or perceived wrongdoing.

5. An act of punishment must be handed down by "a recognized authority."[6]

Within the world of legal philosophy, Craig asserts that Walen's characterization of punishment qualifies as "an expressivist theory of punishment," which

---

3. Craig explains, "Harsh treatment is not sufficient for punishment, however. As Socinus recognized, God may inflict suffering on some person without its being punishment" (Craig, *Atonement and the Death of Christ*, 151).
4. Craig, *Atonement and the Death of Christ*, 151.
5. Craig, *Atonement and the Death of Christ*, 151.
6. This is Craig's specific addition to Walen's characterization of punishment. Craig explains, "Most theorists would also want to require that the hardship or loss be imposed by a recognized authority, so as to distinguish punishment from personal vengeance or vigilantism" (Craig, *Atonement and the Death of Christ*, 151).

means whatever "harsh treatment" is meted out, it "must express condemnation or censure in order to count as punishment."[7]

The manner of Jesus's death expresses such punishment historically and scripturally. Historically, death on a cross in imperial Rome only ever expresses one fact about the victims of crucifixion: they are being shamefully punished.[8] While it is true that NT writers hold Roman and Jewish authorities culpable for Jesus's punishment on the cross, they also note that God the Father ultimately handed his Son over to this specific kind of death.[9] That is, God gave him to punishment. As Paul expressly declares, God "*did not spare his own Son but gave him up for us all*" (Rom. 8:32, italics added).[10] In this way, with respect to an act of punishment, Jesus's death meets conditions 1, 2, and 5 outlined above.

Scripturally, both the passion narratives in the Gospels and reflections on Jesus's death elsewhere in the NT indicate that God punished his Son at the cross. For example, Jesus's prayer at Gethsemane/the Mount of Olives indicates he understood his impending death as divine punishment: "Father, if you are willing, remove this cup away from me" (Luke 22:42a; cf. Matt. 26:39; Mark 14:36; John 18:11). "Cup" in this context is a metaphor for divine wrath as expressed in the OT: "Wake yourself, wake yourself, stand up, O Jerusalem, you who have drunk from the hand of the Lord the cup of his wrath, who have drunk to the dregs the bowl, the cup of staggering" (Isa. 51:17).[11] Jesus, then, likens his death to a cup of wrath from God that he must drink. Dialogue at the crucifixion scene also signals that Jesus's death is divine punishment, including the exchange between the two criminals in the Lukan scene. The penitent, or lamenting, criminal says to the sardonically mocking criminal, "And we indeed justly, for we are receiving the due reward for our deeds; but this man has done nothing wrong" (Luke 23:41). While the penitent criminal identifies Jesus as innocent, he also maintains he is sharing in the "same judgment" ultimately being meted out by God.

Along the same lines, as Paul describes Jesus's death to the Galatians, "Christ redeemed us from the *curse* of the law by becoming a curse for us—for it is

---

7. Craig, *Atonement and the Death of Christ*, 151. See also Joel Feinberg, *Doing and Deserving: Essays in Theory of Responsibility* (Princeton, NJ: Princeton University Press, 1970).

8. See David W. Chapman, *Ancient Jewish and Christian Perceptions of Crucifixion* (Grand Rapids: Baker Academic, 2010); Martin Hengel, *Crucifixion in the Ancient World and the Folly of the Message of the Cross* (Philadelphia: Fortress, 1977).

9. See, e.g., Acts 4:23–31, which holds the tension between human responsibility and divine sovereignty as it relates to Jesus's death.

10. In the LXX and GNT, the use of παραδίδωμι with God as the subject often conveys an act of punishment, as it does here. For a detailed discussion of the Synoptic versions of this scene, see Channing L. Crisler, *A Synoptic Christology of Lament: The Lord Who Answered and the Lord Who Cried* (Lanham, MD: Lexington, 2023).

11. See also the divine cup metaphors in Pss. 11:6; 75:8; Isa. 51:22; Jer. 28:7; 30:6; 32:15, 28; Ezek. 23:31, 32, 33.

written, '*Cursed* is everyone who is hanged on a tree'" (Gal. 3:13, italics added; cf. 2 Cor. 5:21). A "curse" (*katara*), in the wider Deuteronomic context that Paul draws from, refers to the overt punishment that YHWH doles out for disobedience to his law. It is the antithesis of the reward that he doles out for obedience (Deut. 11:26, 28, 29; 23:6; 27:13; 28:15, 45; 29:26; 30:1, 19). In Deuteronomy 21:22–23, a person whose crime is worthy of capital punishment is hung upon a tree; however, his corpse must be removed from the tree before nightfall, since his display there indicates he is "cursed by God." Therefore, for Paul, Jesus's death is tantamount to a divine curse that is inherently a punitive experience. In this way, with respect to an act of punishment, Jesus's death also meets condition 4 as outlined above, namely, Jesus's death is clearly a divine censure.

Efficacy of Christ's Punishment

If Jesus experienced punishment at his Father's hand, how is that punishment efficacious with respect to atonement? It is efficacious in three interrelated ways. First, the identity of Christ makes his punishment efficacious for reconciliation, because his divine and human perfections make him uniquely qualified to bear the punishment of sinners in an acceptable way. Both Jesus's sinlessness and willingness to bear divine punishment make his experience of that punishment acceptable to God.[12] If Jesus were sinful, including an unwillingness to be a substitute for sinners, he could not effectively bear the punishment of sinners. At the same time, if Jesus were merely a man, not God incarnate, he could not sufficiently reconcile sinners to God.

Second, God counts, or imputes, humanity's sins to Jesus so he can effectively bear the punishment reserved for sinners, though he himself remains sinless. Paul points to this transfer of sin in 2 Corinthians: "For our sake he made him to be sin who knew no sin, so that in him we might become the righteousness of God" (5:21; cf. Rom. 8:3; Gal. 3:13).

Third, by punishing Jesus in the place of sinners, God satisfies his own justice and righteousness. Scripture repeatedly underscores that God is a righteous judge who always acts in accordance with justice. As the psalmist declares, "God is a righteous judge, and a God who feels indignation every day" (Ps. 7:11). On a cosmic and eternal scale, God must satisfy his justice in complementary ways. He must punish sinners according to the full measure of his righteous fury against their disobedience as promised (see Ps. 1:6). At the same time, he must show sinners mercy according to his righteous character as promised.[13] In the crucified Jesus, God pours out the full measure of

---

12. For the assertion of Jesus's sinlessness, see Luke 23:41; John 8:46; Heb. 4:15; 1 Peter 1:19. For descriptions of Jesus's willingness to die, see Gal. 2:20; 5:2.

13. To be sure, "must" here does not imply that God is beholden to a law or entity that stands above him. God has obligated himself in this manner given his revealed character and prior promise.

his righteous fury against sinners while also providing their forgiveness. As Paul asserts in his description of Jesus to the Romans, he is the one whom "God put forward as a propitiation [*hilasterion*] by his blood, to be received by faith. This was to show God's righteousness, because in his divine forbearance he had passed over former sins. It was to show his righteousness at the present time, so that he might be just and the justifier of the one who has faith in Jesus" (Rom. 3:25–26).

Paul's typological use of "mercy seat" (*hilasterion*), often translated as propitiation or expiation, is a theological abbreviation for how Jesus becomes the "place" where God satisfies both dimensions of his own righteousness. Jesus's death propitiates God's righteous indignation against the sinner and expiates their sin so they might experience God's mercy.

Sharing in Christ's Punishment

How then does one share in the benefits of Christ's punishment? It is only through faith (*pistis*). God counts faith in the crucified and risen Jesus as righteousness (see Rom. 4:23–25; Gal. 2:15–21; 3:1–14). A key aspect of that faith is the believers' trust that Christ has experienced God's righteous condemnation, which they deserve. As Paul summarily declares in Romans 8:1, "There is therefore now no condemnation for those who are in Christ Jesus." Such understanding is critical given that believers live in a world ruled by Satan and under God's wrath, which could lead to the false inference that their suffering should be interpreted as divine judgment on them (2 Cor. 4:4). While God might discipline believers harshly, even then the aim is to keep them from sharing in the world's condemnation (see 1 Cor. 11:27–34). The believer's divine punishment presently and eschatologically has been meted out on their Savior.

Summary

It does not have to be the case that penal substitution functions as "a timeless focus on the negative judgment on sin in the death of Jesus."[14] The prophet Isaiah, who reflected on Jesus's punishment at the hands of his Father even before the apostles did, portrayed his suffering as the quintessential demonstration of divine love for sinners. As he notes in the closing line of Isaiah 53: "Therefore I will divide him a portion with the many, and he shall divide the spoil with the strong, because he poured out his soul to death and was numbered with the transgressors; yet he bore the sin of many, and makes intercession for the transgressors" (v. 12). Paradoxically, nothing demonstrates the beauty and depth of God's love for human beings like the brutal punishment on the incarnate Christ. It is why in his Apocalypse, even in the vision of an

---

14. William G. Witt and Joel Scandrett, *Mapping Atonement: The Doctrine of Reconciliation in Christian History and Theology* (Grand Rapids: Baker Academic, 2022), 149.

eternal new creation, John sees that God Almighty and the scarred *Lamb* eternally illuminate the new heaven and the new earth where they always receive the praise they deserve (Rev. 21:22–27).

REFLECTION QUESTIONS

1. Why must God punish sin rather than merely let it go?

2. How does Jesus's death fit the conditions necessary to be considered divine punishment?

3. Do you find anything difficult to understand about penal substitutionary atonement?

4. How does referring to Jesus as a mercy seat summarize so much about the results of his death?

5. Why is it important for believers to understand the punitive aspect of Jesus's death?

What Are the Moral, Logical, Scriptural, and Theological Challenges to Penal Substitutionary Atonement?

As I grow old I want to tell everyone who will listen: "I am so thankful for the penal substitutionary death of Christ. No hope without it."

~J. I. Packer

The late J. I. Packer summed up his theological sentiments about the importance of holding to the view of penal substitutionary atonement by stating that there is "no hope without it."[1] For him, it was the very essence of Christian hope. However, not everyone shares his sentiment. Many find penal substitutionary atonement morally reprehensible and/or logically incoherent. A growing chorus of critics have emerged from the fields of biblical studies, historical theology, systematic theology, and pastoral ministry. Mark Murphy bluntly states, "The classical penal substitution view of the Atonement is incoherent."[2] With more subtlety, N. T. Wright suggests that attributing penal substitutionary atonement to the NT writers stems from an anachronistic reading of first-century texts in which we unwittingly, or perhaps intentionally, sneak medieval and Renaissance atonement theories into the biblical text.[3] With great passion, others assert, "Atonement theology

---

1. J. I. Packer and Mark Dever, *In My Place Condemned He Stood: Celebrating the Glory of the Atonement* (Wheaton, IL: Crossway, 2007), 21.
2. Mark C. Murphy, "Not Penal Substitution but Vicarious Punishment," *Faith and Philosophy* 26 (2009): 260.
3. In keeping with Wright's familiar presumption to correct the guild and the church, he insists, "We need to learn to think like first-century Jews (and then like first-century

takes an act of state violence and redefines it as intimate violence, a private spiritual transaction between God the Father and God the Son."[4] Along these lines, some even refer to Jesus's death, particularly in the vein of penal substitutionary atonement, as a kind of divine child abuse. Even some who hold to a penal substitutionary atonement view strongly challenge the notion that God literally punished Christ. The late I. Howard Marshall threw down the proverbial gauntlet in this way: "Indeed, at some point that challenge needs to be issued: where are these evangelicals who say that God punished Christ? Name them!"[5]

We find then a variety of challenges to penal substitutionary atonement that need to be addressed. I have categorized the challenges here as moral, logical, scriptural, and theological in nature.

Answering Moral Challenges to Penal Substitutionary Atonement

Those who find penal substitutionary atonement morally questionable make a variety of arguments. I will summarize and briefly respond to five of them here. First, penal substitutionary atonement is "antithetical to the shared life and love of God."[6] Summarizing the views of feminist theologians who reject *Christus Victor*, satisfaction, and especially penal substitutionary atonement, Adam Johnson writes, "They abhor any explanation of the death and resurrection of Christ by means of a dynamic between himself and the Father in which the Father intends the crucifixion of the Son and relates to him as a sinner or as bearing our sin."[7] For example, Rita Nakashima Brock and Rebecca Ann Parker observe, "The liberal theologians rejected the substitutionary atonement because it depicted God as less moral than human beings at our best. Their concern was with the picture of God that the atonement presented. Mine was with the victims of misused power, a perspective absent in liberal work."[8]

Second, some critics of penal substitutionary atonement claim it promotes abuse. Rebecca Parker observes, "If God is imagined as a fatherly

---

Jews who believed that Jesus of Nazareth was God's promised Messiah), not like medieval or Renaissance theorists who used ancient texts to address questions quite foreign to their original intention" (N. T. Wright, "Foreword," in David M. Moffitt, *Rethinking the Atonement: New Perspectives on Jesus's Death, Resurrection, and Ascension* [Grand Rapids: Baker Academic, 2022], xvii–xviii).

4. Rita Nakashima Brock and Rebecca Ann Parker, *Proverbs of Ashes: Violence, Redemptive Suffering and the Search for What Saves Us* (Boston: Beacon, 2001), 60.

5. I. Howard Marshall, "The Theology of the Atonement," in *The Atonement Debate: Papers from the London Symposium on the Theology of Atonement*, eds. Derek Tidball, David Hilborn, and Justin Thacker (Grand Rapids: Zondervan, 2008), 63.

6. Adam J. Johnson, *Atonement: A Guide for the Perplexed*, Guides for the Perplexed (London: Bloomsbury T&T Clark, 2015), 67.

7. Johnson, *Atonement*, 68.

8. Brock and Parker, *Proverbs of Ashes*, 149.

torturer, earthly parents are also justified, perhaps even required, to teach through violence. Children are instructed to understand their submission to pain as a form of love. Behind closed doors, in our own community, spouses and children are battered by abusers who justify their actions as necessary, loving discipline."[9]

Third, critics argue that penal substitutionary atonement eclipses other aspects of Jesus's death and resurrection. Kathryn Tanner criticizes penal substitutionary atonement and other atonement models along these lines, noting, "The public ministry of Jesus is not obviously important on any of the models and this point in particular feminist and womanist theologians make forcefully."[10]

Fourth, from the perspective of historical theology, critics assert that penal substitutionary atonement itself "has never historically included the assertion that God punished Christ."[11] While one might countenance that Christ took on sin and the penalty of sin is death, it does not follow that God punished his Son.[12]

Fifth, Jesus's death exemplifies his sharing in human suffering, not his punishment at God's hands. As Brock and Parker maintain, "On the cross, God experienced the full meaning of human existence. To be human includes humiliation, betrayal, physical torment, abandonment, isolation, and the collapse of hope. On the cross God is finally, fully at one with humanity."[13]

In answering the moral objections to God's punishment of Jesus at the cross, four points are in order. First, misuse of a doctrine, such as the deplorable justification of abuse on a political or individual level, does not invalidate the doctrine itself. Both the scriptural witness and history of interpretation contain expressions of the doctrine which neither encourage nor inevitably lead to misuse. Those expressions cannot be held responsible for the misuse unless it can be demonstrated that such an intent propelled the expressions in the first place. And this simply is not the case.

Second, although it is possible for presentations of penal substitutionary atonement to overshadow other aspects of Christ's work, that possibility does not require one to totally relinquish the theory. Rather, we must strive to articulate how the theory complements and helps explain the totality of Christ's atoning work. The solution is not to soften, or even eliminate, the doctrine from theological discourse. The NT bears witness to a risen Christ who never

9. Brock and Parker, *Proverbs of Ashes*, 30–31. See also John A. Buehrens and Rebecca Ann Parker, *A House for Hope: The Promise of Progressive Religion for the Twenty-First Century* (Boston: Beacon, 2010), 63, 65.

10. Kathryn Tanner, *Christ the Key* (Cambridge: Cambridge University Press, 2010), 250.

11. Daniel J. Hill and Joseph Jedwab, "Atonement and the Concept of Punishment," in *Locating Atonement: Explorations in Constructive Dogmatics*, ed. Oliver D. Crisp and Fred Sanders (Grand Rapids: Zondervan Academic, 2015), 150.

12. Once again, see Marshall, "The Theology of the Atonement," 63.

13. Brock and Parker, *Proverbs of Ashes*, 57.

ceases to be the incarnate and crucified Christ who in his divinity and humanity brings healing between God and man, a healing that is expressed with multiple atonement metaphors. Nevertheless, the multiplicity of metaphors that reflect the dynamic atoning work of Christ should not crowd out the prophetic image of a God who crushed his Messiah nor the divinely orchestrated instrument of death, namely a Roman cross which assured both shame and punishment to its victim.

Third, it simply is not the case that historical theology lacks voices who have described God as punishing his Son based on their reading of the biblical text. Athanasius provides a helpful and prominent example in *The Letter to Marcellinus* wherein he explains how one should interpret Psalms. Not surprisingly, he interprets various psalms christologically and accentuates the fact that Christ endured God's wrath, or punishment, at the cross. Athanasius, in fact, finds Christ bearing witness to this punishment in texts such as Psalms 69 and 88:

> And it says again through his own lips in Psalm 87 [88], "Your wrath has pressed heavily upon me," and in Psalm 68, "Then I restored that which I did not take away." For although he was not himself obliged to give account for any crime, he died—but he suffered on our behalf, and he took on himself the wrath directed against us on account of the transgression, as its says in Isaiah, "He took on our weakness."[14]

Athanasius's comments reflect the fact that OT theology is replete with references to God's wrath which often function as theological abbreviations for the punishment God inflicts upon those who rebel against him. It strikes me as exegetically incredulous to find nothing punitive about references such as "in my wrath I struck you" (Isa 60:10). Athanasius helpfully identifies Christ as the ultimate recipient of such punishment. Moreover, Hill and Jedwab provide an impressive list of voices, including Gregory the Great, who explained, "For our Mediator deserved not to be punished for Himself, because He never was guilty of any defilement of sin. But if He had not Himself undertaken a death not due to Him, He would never have freed us from one that was justly due to us."[15]

Finally, although it is true that Christ's death demonstrates his share in humanity's pain, that truth does not eliminate the necessity of his punishment for the guilty. This is where critics of penal substitutionary atonement miss the mark, that is anthropologically. If Jesus shared fully in the human condition at the cross, as Brock and Parker contend, it follows that Jesus shared in

---

14. Athanasius, The Life of Antony and the Letter to Marcellinus, 105.
15. See the full list in Hill and Jedwab, "Atonement and the Concept of Punishment," 150–52.

humanity's guilt, though as the sinless one, before a righteous God who is just to punish sin in accordance with his revealed character.

Answering Logical Challenges to Penal Substitutionary Atonement

Mark Murphy provides a recent example of penal substitutionary atonement critics who dismiss the view based on alleged logical incoherence.[16] William Lane Craig summarizes the "crucial premises" of Murphy's argument as follows:

1. If Christ were sinless, God could not have condemned Christ.

2. If God could not have condemned Christ, God could not have punished Christ.

3. If God could not have punished Christ, penal substitution is false.[17]

Although Craig responds to Murphy at multiple points, the heart of his retort is that God *imputes* human sin and guilt to Christ, which counters Murphy's assertion that God could not have condemned and punished a sinless Christ. The result of this imputation is that "Christ, though personally without moral fault, is legally guilty and so condemned by God for our sins."[18]

Far from a legal fiction, imputation of sin to Christ entails that God holds Christ responsible for human sin at the cross, even though Christ is not guilty of it. In this way, God punishes his innocent Son in place of guilty human beings by holding his Son as legally responsible for their sin and thereby deserving of their punishment.

Answering Scriptural Challenges to Penal Substitutionary Atonement

Critics of penal substitutionary atonement argue that a sacrificial death is not tantamount to divine punishment in Scripture. As William Witt and Joel Scandrett conclude,

> Contemporary biblical scholars do not tend to consider Old Testament sacrifices as a form of divine appeasement. Key passages in the New Testament speak of Jesus dying "for us" and "in our place" and speak of deliverance from sin, but

---

16. Murphy, "Not Penal Substitution but Vicarious Punishment," 253–73.
17. William Lane Craig, *Atonement and the Death of Christ: An Exegetical, Historical, and Philosophical Exploration* (Waco, TX: Baylor University Press, 2020),
18. William Lane Craig, *Atonement and the Death of Christ*, 161.

they nowhere suggest that Jesus's death was a punishment intended to satisfy God's justice, or even more, God's wrath.[19]

However, such a conclusion overlooks key scriptural texts and axioms. Propitiation and expiation stand at the heart of the OT's theology of sacrifice. Even if the OT does not fully explain how sacrifices cleanse the guilty from sin, and thereby reconcile them to God, without such sacrifices, the guilty clearly remain under divine wrath.[20] This is on display when the wilderness generation grumbles against Moses and Aaron following Korah's rebellion (Num. 16:1–40). YHWH threatens to consume the entire congregation (Num. 16:35). Moses intercedes for the people by instructing Aaron to offer a sacrifice (Num. 16:46). Aaron's atoning sacrifice halts the plague (Num. 16:47–48). Such an impromptu sacrifice that halts judgment reflects the overarching function of sacrifices within the priestly system. Sin caused a breach in Israel's relationship with YHWH, who demonstrated both his wrath against and mercy for the transgressor in the prescribed sacrifice.[21] Otherwise, what did any sacrifice in the OT really accomplish?

The OT's theology of sacrifice provides the conceptual framework for understanding Christ's death. Christ's sacrifice cleanses sinners and thereby removes the righteous indignation against them by directing that wrath to himself. To say otherwise is to ignore or alter clear descriptions of Jesus's person and work in the NT. For example, Paul describes Jesus as God's *hilasterion*, that is, the propitiating sacrifice associated with the priest's work at the mercy seat on the Day of Atonement (Rom. 3:25).[22] Similarly, the writer of Hebrews, while discussing the saving efficacy of the incarnate Christ's priestly work, insists, "Therefore he had to be made like his brothers in every respect, so that he might become a merciful and faithful high priest in the service of God, to make propitiation for the sins of the people" (Heb. 2:17). Additionally, John refers to Jesus as "the *propitiation* [*hilasmos*] for our sins, and not for ours only but also for the sins of the whole world" (1 John 2:2; cf. 4:10).

Although many interpreters have attempted to strip this terminology of its connection to divine wrath, the results of Morris's classic study still stand:

---

19. William G. Witt and Joel Scandrett, *Mapping Atonement: The Doctrine of Reconciliation in Christian History and Theology* (Grand Rapids: Baker Academic, 2022), 150.
20. As Robin Rutledge explains, "How the death of an animal provides cleansing and reconciliation is not explicitly stated in the OT. It may include the idea of making reparation to God for offending against him" (Robin Routledge, *Old Testament Theology: A Thematic Approach* [Downers Grove, IL: IVP Academic, 2008], 189).
21. John E. Hartley, *Leviticus*, WBC, vol. 4 (Nashville: Thomas Nelson, 1992), 65.
22. See Daniel P. Bailey, *Jesus as the Mercy Seat: The Semantics and Theology of Paul's Use of Hilasterion in Romans 3:25* (Cambridge: Cambridge University Press, 1999).

In both testaments, the means of propitiation envisaged in the Bible is one which involves an element of substitution. In both Old and New Testaments the means of propitiation is the offering up of a gift, the gift of a life yielded up to death by God's own appointment. The Scripture is clear that the wrath of God is visited upon sinners or else that the Son of God dies for them.[23]

Answering Theological Challenges to Penal Substitutionary Atonement

Theological challenges to penal substitutionary atonement take various forms. Eleonore Stump has recently argued that penal substitutionary atonement gives no place for divine mercy, which she describes as "a matter of foregoing at least some of what is owed."[24] If God allows nothing to go unpunished by pouring out the full measure of his wrath on Christ, and thereby on God himself, penal substitutionary atonement shows "only that God has borne the punishment, not that God has agreed to forego any part of the punishment."[25]

Stump dismisses the following rejoinders to her criticism of penal substitutionary: (1) if penal substitutionary atonement says God's mercy is that humans are not required to suffer punishment, she observes that God still has not "agreed to forego any part of the punishment"; (2) if penal substitutionary atonement says God could not overlook sin due to his justice, and so punished Jesus instead, thereby acting mercifully toward humans, she maintains this is actually a "denial" of divine justice, since God punishes a "perfectly innocent person instead"; (3) if penal substitutionary atonement says Christ paid the full penalty of sin, the claim falls short since "everlasting damnation" is the full penalty for sin, and Christ, "no matter what sort of agony" he experienced, did not suffer everlasting damnation; (4) if penal substitutionary atonement says Christ voluntarily suffered punishment, it follows that his volunteerism does not constitute punishment since, following Immanuel Kant, "it is not possible for something to be both voluntary and a punishment"; and (5) if penal substitutionary atonement says Christ paid the full penalty of sin, it falls short since God would unjustly demand some people pay the penalty of eternal condemnation again.[26]

How then might one respond to Stump?[27] First, Stump wrongly defines divine mercy as foregoing punishment. Scripturally, divine mercy is offered

---

23. Leon Morris, *The Apostolic Preaching of the Cross*, 3rd ed. (Grand Rapids: Eerdmans, 1965), 213.
24. Eleonore Stump, *Atonement* (Oxford: Oxford University Press, 2018), 77.
25. Stump, *Atonement*, 77.
26. Stump, *Atonement*, 77–78.
27. For a fuller critique, see Craig's assessment of Stump in Craig, *Atonement and the Death of Christ*, 162–72.

within and through God's full punishment as demonstrated in OT theology, which Paul then uses as paradigm for understanding God's work in Christ (see Hab. 1:1–2:4; Rom. 1:16–3:25). It is within and through Christ's substitution that God provides mercy to believers. Second, with respect to God unjustly punishing an innocent Jesus, as noted above, God imputes humanity's sin to Jesus and thereby legally punishes one who is innocent. Third, to suggest the eternal Son's death at the hand of his Father is not equal to a human's "everlasting damnation" is to discount the unique value of the Son's identity and to presume we can quantify his pain at the cross, which we simply cannot do (Question 40). Fourth, if one volunteers to take the punishment of someone else, it does not follow that their punishment ceases to be punishment. It intensifies the punishment, given their innocence. Fifth, the penalty people eternally pay is ultimately the punishment for rejecting the one whom God punished in their place; therefore, they are not being condemned "again." As John declares, "Whoever believes in the Son has eternal life; whoever does not obey the Son shall not see life, but the wrath of God remains on him" (John 3:36).

Summary

Opponents of penal substitutionary atonement criticize the view on moral, logical, scriptural, and theological grounds. One common thread in this multidimensional criticism is an apparent uneasiness, even embarrassment, with the wrath of God.[28] This is modeled in the way N. T. Wright often caricatures penal substitutionary atonement: he paints its proponents as equivalent to those who have twisted the cross into a horrific symbol on par with misuses by Constantine and even the Ku Klux Klan whose burning of crosses strikes fear in the hearts of those who see them.[29] Wright prefaces his criticism of penal substitutionary proponents with the following:

> The Ku Klux Klan burns crosses, claiming to bring the light of the Christian gospel into dark places. The fact that such nonsense is a scandalous denial of the early Christian meaning of the cross doesn't make it any better. It isn't just those outside the Christian faith who have found the cross a symbol of fear. Many inside the church too have shrunk back from one particular interpretation that, in some form or other, has dominated much Western Christianity over the last half millennium. Once recent hymn put it like this: And

---

28. Michael C. McCarthy, "Divine Wrath and Human Anger: Embarrassment Ancient and New," *Theological Studies* 70 (2009): 845–74.

29. N. T. Wright, *The Day the Revolution Began: Reconsidering the Meaning of Jesus's Crucifixion* (New York: HarperOne, 2016), 38. For a similar caricature of penal substitutionary atonement, see Mark Stenberg, *51% Christian: Finding Faith after Certainty* (Minneapolis: Fortress, 2015), 63–64.

on the cross, when Jesus died, The Wrath of God was satisfied—(This makes it sound like hunger that is satisfied by a good meal).[30]

Here is the caricature of the penal substitutionary atonement that Wright employs. He writes:

1. All humans sinned, causing God to be angry and to want to kill them, to burn them forever in "hell."

2. Jesus somehow got in the way and took the punishment instead (it helped, it seems, that he was innocent—oh, and that he was God's own Son too).

3. We are in the clear after all, heading for "heaven" instead (provided, of course, we believe it).[31]

This caricaturized syllogism hardly serves as a fair representation of penal substitutionary atonement. Concerns that the wrath of God might be weaponized or misrepresented is not a sufficient reason to cease thinking seriously about Scripture's sobering and real presentation of divine punishment that either Jesus endures or those who reject him endure.

REFLECTION QUESTIONS

1. Are there aspects of penal substitutionary atonement you find concerning or confusing?

2. What "hope" does one find in penal substitutionary atonement that might be lacking in other atonement views?

3. What is the scriptural basis for penal substitutionary atonement?

4. How does the OT inform the NT's presentation of atonement?

5. How have you perhaps misunderstood penal substitutionary atonement?

---

30. Wright, *The Day the Revolution Began*, 38.
31. Wright, *The Day the Revolution Began*, 38.

Did Jesus Suffer Spiritual Death on the Cross?

But one of the soldiers pierced his side with a spear, and at once there came out blood and water.

~John 19:34

The immediate flow of water and blood extracted by a soldier's spear confirmed Jesus's physical death, as did his subsequent burial. What a Roman spear could not detect is the extent of Jesus's death. Did Jesus die "spiritually" on the cross, as some suggest?

The most well-known proponents of the "Jesus died spiritually" (JDS) view include controversial figures such as E. W. Kenyon and so-called Word of Faith leaders, such as Kenneth E. Hagin and Kenneth Copeland. William Atkinson, who offers one of the best critiques of this position, and to whom I am indebted for much of what is discussed here, summarizes their position as follows: "Kenyon, Hagin, and Copeland employ a relatively small number of biblical texts to agree that to state that Jesus 'died spiritually' is to aver that Jesus was separated from God, participated in a sinful, satanic nature, and became Satan's prey."[1] Many JDS proponents assert that without Jesus's spiritual death "atonement is impossible."[2]

Many discussions of atonement theory do not directly engage this view, as its proponents are neither theologians nor biblical scholars. However, given the popularity and influence of those who advocate the view, it deserves

---

1. Kenneth W. Atkinson, *The 'Spiritual Death' of Jesus: A Pentecostal Investigation*, Global Pentecostal and Charismatic Studies 1 (Leiden: Brill, 2009), 252. I am helped a great deal in this chapter by Atkinson's excellent work.
2. Atkinson, *The 'Spiritual Death' of Jesus*, 253.

inclusion here. What follows is an examination of the biblical texts and arguments that JDS proponents often put forward. We need to understand the implications for the doctrine of atonement in answering the question, "Did Jesus suffer spiritual death on the cross?"

Jesus's Separation from God?

One of the three main claims in the JDS view is that Jesus, in his death, was separated from God for three days. Proponents claim the separation began either in Gethsemane or at the cross, continued during Jesus's death, and ended just prior to his physical resurrection. They explain the separation in spatial and relational terms. Spatially, the perception is that God literally abandoned Jesus at the cross and sent him away to hell.[3] Relationally, the perception is that God "turned his back" on Jesus at this moment.[4] JDS proponents are not always precise with their language here, even as they wrestle with the Trinitarian implications of their assertions.[5]

As Atkinson explains, while describing Copeland's teaching, JDS proposes momentary separation within the Godhead and the momentary severance of Jesus's divinity from his humanity. Copeland suggests the "very inside of God hanging on that cross is severed from Him" and that Jesus is "separated from His God. And in that moment He's a mortal man—capable of failure and death!"[6] For scriptural support of Jesus's separation from God, as they understand it, JDS proponents often point to Jesus's cry of dereliction—"'Eli, Eli, lema sabacthani?' that is, 'My God, my God, why have you forsaken me?'" (Matt. 27:46)—which is sometimes read through the lens of 2 Corinthians 5:21: "For our sake he made him to be sin who knew no sin, so that in him we might become the righteousness of God."

However, neither these scriptural texts nor Christian tradition support the notion that the Son was separated from the Father in this way. Jesus's cry of dereliction finds its inner logic from the theology of the psalms of lament, wherein lamenters simultaneously vocalize a protest of their pain (given God's prior promise to the righteous), petition God's deliverance, and trust

---

3. Atkinson, *The 'Spiritual Death' of Jesus*, 150.
4. Atkinson, *The 'Spiritual Death' of Jesus*, 149. See also E. W. Kenyon, *The Father and His Family* (Lynnwood, WA: Kenyon's Gospel Publishing Society, 1998), 126.
5. Atkinson summarizes the nature of the separation within the JDS view, noting, "First, it can be taken to indicate that the human Jesus was separated from undifferentiated God. Secondly, in trinitarian terms, it can be understood as a statement that the Son was separated from the Father. Thirdly, the concept can be taken to represent both the first two ideas, albeit perhaps paradoxically. Neither Kenyon, Hagin nor Copeland deliberately clarifies which of these three he favours" (Atkinson, *The 'Spiritual Death' of Jesus*, 150–51).
6. Kenneth Copeland Ministries, "What Happened from the Cross to the Throne – Part 2," accessed August 30, 2024, https://blog.kcm.org/what-happened-from-the-cross-to-the-throne-part-2/.

in that deliverance through their cries.[7] They do not, however, believe God has ultimately abandoned them. Sustained cries to God—even cries such as "Why have you abandoned me?"—indicate they believe God is still near enough to hear them. Additionally, from the perspective of Christian tradition, Thomas H. McCall rightly observes that the Father abandoned his Son to death but not relationally, with its disastrous Trinitarian implications. As McCall observes in his analysis of Jesus's cry, "If we understand the doctrine of the Trinity properly, we will be in a position to see that saying 'the Trinity is broken' amounts to saying 'God does not exist.' Such a view is utterly antithetical to the Christian faith."[8]

With respect to JDS's use of 2 Corinthians 5:21 to support the notion of separation, two points are in order. First, it is exegetically suspect to interpret Matthew 27:46 (Mark 15:34) through a verse extracted from Paul's contextual argument. Paul has Jesus's death in view; however, he is not directly commenting upon the cry of dereliction or its christological implications. Second, the phrase "he became sin," does not suggest Jesus became a *sinner*, as some JDS proponents seem to conclude. Jesus did not become a sinner in the sense that he himself sinned. Both Paul and the wider NT clearly assert Jesus's sinlessness.[9] Rather, as Mark Seifrid observes in his analysis of 2 Corinthians 5:21, borrowing from Michael Cameron, "Christ thus became the 'sinless sinner.'"[10]

Jesus's Sinful and Satanic Nature?

Kenyon bluntly states, "He (i.e., Jesus) became one with Satan when He became sin" and "The sin-nature itself was laid upon Him, until He became all that spiritual death had made man."[11] Although Kenyon and others do not clearly define how they understand *nature*, Atkinson concludes that their uses of the term refer to all that someone is "inwardly."[12] For Kenyon, Jesus was not "'counted' as one of the fallen human race, but that He became, intrinsically,

---

7. For a full discussion of the relationship between the theology of the psalms of lament and Jesus's cry of dereliction in Matt. 27:46 and Mark 15:34, see Channing L. Crisler, *A Synoptic Christology of Lament: The Lord Who Answered and the Lord Who Cried* (Lanham, MD: Lexington, 2023), 131–43, 201–11.

8. Thomas H. McCall, *Forsaken: The Trinity and the Cross, and Why It Matters* (Downers Grove, IL: IVP Academic, 2012), 44.

9. See, e.g., Matt. 27:24; Luke 1:35; John 8:29; 1 Peter 1:18–19; 2:22; 1 John 3:5; Heb. 4:15. For a discussion of Christ's sinlessness, or impeccability, see Oliver D. Crisp, *God Incarnate: Explorations in Christology* (London: T&T Clark, 2009), 122–36.

10. Mark A. Seifrid, *The Second Letter to the Corinthians*, Pillar New Testament Commentary (Grand Rapids: Eerdmans, 2014), 262. See also Michael Cameron, *Christ Meets Me Everywhere: Augustine's Early Figurative Exegesis* (New York: Oxford University Press, 2012), 143, 145.

11. Atkinson, *The 'Spiritual Death' of Jesus*, 192. See also E. W. Kenyon, *Identification: A Romance in Redemption* (Los Angeles: E. W. Kenyon, 1941), 21.

12. Atkinson, *The 'Spiritual Death' of Jesus*, 187, 189.

what humans had become, without committing actual sin."[13] Similarly, Copeland suggests, "Man is a partaker of satanic nature due to the fall; Jesus bore that nature."[14]

The biblical texts they marshal for this especially unusual position include a misreading of 2 Corinthians 5:21, which I discussed above, and a strained reading of Numbers 21:8 via John's statement: "And as Moses lifted up the serpent in the wilderness, so must the Son of Man be lifted up" (John 3:14). Copeland asserts that the serpent on Moses's pole, and thereby Jesus on the cross, is nothing less than "the sign of Satan was hanging on the cross."[15] Copeland tethers his reading of John 3:14 to his reading of 2 Corinthians 5:21, wherein he asserts that Jesus was spiritually made sin, to assert "Jesus became sin and died spiritually. The worm and the serpent union and harmony with the nature of the Adversary."[16]

In assessing this aspect of JDS teaching, it is noteworthy that neither the biblical text nor the Christian tradition ever asserts that Jesus took on a "satanic nature" in his crucifixion and death. The typological connection John makes between the serpent on Moses's staff and Jesus on the cross has nothing to do with Satan; John draws a parallel between the salvation God provided from his wrath for the wilderness generation and the salvation he provides for an entire world under his wrath. He provided a symbol of salvation atop Moses's staff, which the Israelites could look to and be delivered from his wrath in the wilderness. He provides his Son on the cross that the world can look to by faith and be delivered from his eternal wrath.

However, if one follows the logic of Copeland's exegesis, John would be instructing his readers to look to a crucified Satan for salvation. Such exegesis betrays a lack of understanding and/or care for the inspired writer's original intent. This exegetical hubris is on display in the way Copeland explains the divine origin of his interpretation: "I said, 'Why in the world do You have to put that snake up there, the sign of Satan? Why don't you put a lamb on the pole?' The Lord said, *Because it was the sign of Satan that was hanging on the cross!*"[17] Such a claim implies that to understand the atonement, sound biblical interpretation and two thousand years of Christian tradition can be exchanged for what the interpreter or preacher claims is a direct word from God.

---

13. Atkinson, *The 'Spiritual Death' of Jesus*, 192.
14. Kenneth Copeland, *The Force of Righteousness* (Fort Worth: Kenneth Copeland Publications), 24. See also Atkinson, *The 'Spiritual Death' of Jesus*, 194.
15. Atkinson, *The 'Spiritual Death' of Jesus*, 206.
16. Atkinson, *The 'Spiritual Death' of Jesus*, 206.
17. Kenneth Copeland Ministries, "What Happened from the Cross to the Throne – Part 2," accessed August 30, 2024, https://blog.kcm.org/what-happened-from-the-cross-to-the-throne-part-2/.

Jesus as "Satan's Prey" on the Cross?

The JDS position claims Jesus necessarily and temporarily suffered defeat at the hands of Satan. For Jesus to reverse the legal "satanic dominion" that held sway over humanity since Adam's fall, "Christ had to come under Satan's mastery in his substitutionary atoning work."[18] In this view, Jesus suffered in hell for three days. Proponents here suggest that since Adam died spiritually and came under Satan's dominion, Jesus had to endure a similar experience to undo it. In describing Satan's work in Jesus's death, Copeland asserts, "He (i.e., Satan) murdered Jesus of Nazareth and took Him into hell."[19]

The scriptural texts purported to support the notion that Jesus's atoning work included becoming "Satan's prey" are, not surprisingly, Ephesians 4:8 and 1 Peter 3:19. JDS proponents take these references to Jesus's descent and create an entire theological narrative about what transpired on Holy Saturday, which we will discuss in Question 28. However, little of what they claim can be substantiated by clear scriptural teaching and does not agree with wider Christian tradition.

Summary

JDS claims are out of line with sound exegesis, underrepresented within the Christian tradition, and logically questionable. While we need to understand as best we can the full extent of Jesus's death, including what occurred on Holy Saturday, such concerns do not justify the many outlandish claims of JDS proponents. The JDS position is essentially heterodoxy with no legitimate grounding in biblical exegesis, the orthodox history of interpretation, and the larger orthodox Christian tradition. It is telling that some JDS proponents, such as Kenneth Copeland, have appealed to personal revelation from God as the basis for their understanding of Jesus's death and its atoning value. Scripture warns against those who would take their theological stand on such an "insight" (see Col. 2:18).

REFLECTION QUESTIONS

1. How have you generally viewed the Word of Faith movement?

2. Why is it problematic to assert that Jesus became sinful and satanic?

3. How have JDS proponents mishandled the passages to which they appeal?

---

18. Atkinson, *The 'Spiritual Death' of Jesus*, 221.
19. Atkinson, *The 'Spiritual Death' of Jesus*, 223.

4. What is problematic about a view of atonement that has no representation within the Christian tradition?

5. How would you respond to a JDS proponent?

Did Jesus Descend into Hell and Make Atonement There?

In saying, "He ascended," what does it mean but that he had also descended into the lower parts of the earth?
~Ephesians 4:9 RSV

Some regard Paul's description of Jesus's descent "into the lower parts of the earth" as a reference to the incarnation or Jesus's burial, while others take it as a reference to his descent to the dead or hell.[1] This experience of Christ will occupy our attention here. No current interpretive consensus exists regarding the so-called *descensus ad inferos* ("descent to hell"). To be sure, the notion Jesus descended into hell has enjoyed wide acceptance in most eras of Christian history. As Augustine quipped, "Who, therefore, but an infidel will deny that Christ was in hell?"[2] However, it has fallen on hard times since the Reformation. Martin Bucer (1491–1551), who may have been one of the first prominent voices to deny the doctrine, argued that Christ's descent simply referred to his burial.[3] More recently, as William Lane Craig observes, "Modern critics, however, generally dismiss any role whatsoever for the devil in one's atonement theory. Since Satan is in modern thinking a mythological figure,

---

1. As Matt Emerson asserts, until the Reformation, "descended into hell" (*ad inferna*) and "descended to the dead" (*ad inferos*) were synonymous. See Matthew Y. Emerson, *'He Descended to the Dead': An Evangelical Theology of Holy Saturday* (Downers Grove, IL: IVP Academic, 2019), 4.

2. Augustine, *Epistulae* 164 as cited in Justin W. Bass, *The Battle for the Keys: Revelation 1:18 and Christ's Descent into the Underworld* (Eugene, OR: Wipf and Stock, 2014), 1.

3. Bass, *The Battle for the Keys*, 18.

obviously we cannot have been freed from bondage to him."[4] Some evangelical theologians, who certainly do not regard Satan as mythical, likewise argue against the descent.[5]

Of course, our interest involves more than whether Christ descended to hell. The question is, Did Jesus descend to hell *and* make atonement there? Nevertheless, since these questions are interwoven, we will move in three ways: (1) scriptural evidence of a descent, (2) descent within the Christian tradition, and (3) the relationship between descent and atonement.

Scriptural Evidence of Jesus in Hell

Among the scriptural texts often discussed here, Ephesians 4:9 and 1 Peter 3:19 stand out.[6] The former stands out due to the phrase, "he descended into the lower parts of the earth." Clinton Arnold identifies four possible referents: (1) Jesus's descent to hell, (2) Jesus's incarnation, (3) Jesus's burial after his death, or (4) the arrival of the Spirit at Pentecost.[7] While the wider context of Ephesians 4:9 contains references to both the unity and renewal of the Spirit, the immediate context explicitly stresses Christ's ascent, descent, and dispersion of gifts, according to Paul's reading of Psalm 68:18 (Eph. 4:7–10).[8] Consequently, the most unlikely referent of our phrase is the arrival of the Spirit. With respect to choices 2 and 3, it is noteworthy that Paul had available to him the phrase "to/into the earth" (*eis tēn gēn*) if he wanted to refer to Jesus's incarnation or burial (see Rev. 13:13).[9] Instead, he chose "into the lower parts of the earth" (*eis ta katōtera merē tēs gēs*). Paul contrasts Jesus's descent to the "lower parts of the earth" in Ephesians 4:9 with his ultimate ascent "above all the heavens" in Ephesians 4:10. It follows then that Paul has in mind more than a heaven-and-earth dichotomy. He specifically contrasts "above" heaven and "below" the earth.[10] Within his Greco-Roman and Jewish milieu,

---

4. William Lane Craig, *Atonement and the Death of Christ: An Exegetical, Historical, and Philosophical Exploration* (Waco, TX: Baylor University Press, 2020), 111.
5. See, e.g., Wayne Grudem, "He Did Not Descend into Hell: A Plea for Following Scripture Instead of the Apostle's Creed," *Journal of the Evangelical Theological Society* 32 (1991): 103–13.
6. However, as Bass explains, Acts 2:27, 31, and Rom. 10:7 may be the "strongest passages to be reckoned with if one believes that the doctrine of Christ's descent is not taught in the NT," adding, "It is very difficult to read these passages in any other way" (Bass, *The Battle for the Keys*, 77).
7. Clinton E. Arnold, *Ephesians*, Zondervan Exegetical Commentary on the New Testament (Grand Rapids: Zondervan Academic, 2010), 253.
8. See references to "Spirit" in Eph. 4:3, 23.
9. On this point, see Arnold, *Ephesians*, 253.
10. In his exegesis of Eph. 4:9, as part of his denial of the descent to hell, Wayne Grudem does not include the contrast that Paul makes with "above all the heavens" in 4:10. He is content to focus on the ascent/descent language in 4:9 without fully considering how Paul qualifies these movements and their accompanying spatial dimensions (see Grudem, "He Did Not Descend into Hell," 108).

"below" the earth would be understood "as referring to Hades, Tartarus, or the Abyss."[11] Therefore, the best of the four options listed above appears to be a reference to Christ's descent to hell.[12]

First Peter 3:19 usually garners even more attention in this discussion, though the teaching of Jesus's descent does not hinge upon it.[13] Peter's hymnic description includes, "For Christ also suffered once for sins, the righteous for the unrighteous, that he might bring us to God, being put to death in the flesh but made alive in the spirit, in which he went and proclaimed to the spirits in prison" (1 Peter 3:18–19).[14] Several questions swirl around 1 Peter 3:18–22, including Jesus's precise movement and the referent of the "prison" to which Jesus went to preach.[15] Peter does not describe Jesus's movement as downward in the way Paul does in Ephesians 4:9.[16] Nevertheless, he specifies a movement to a "prison" for disobedient spirits likely associated with the Noahic era's enigmatic reference to the encounter between the "sons of God" and the "daughters of man" (see Gen. 6:1–4).[17] Peter locates Jesus as preaching "in the prison" to which God sentenced these disobedient spirits. The only possible referents for this prison are hell or "an incarcerating place for fallen angels or demons."[18] The difference between a place of incarceration and hell is not necessarily great. Whatever the precise location, Peter and first-century contemporaries would place it "in the lowest depths of the underworld."[19]

Although much more can be said about 1 Peter 3:19, two points are in order.[20] First, whatever Jesus's movement, whatever the timing (Holy Saturday or

---

11. Arnold, *Ephesians*, 253.
12. Cf. Rom. 10:7 and the descent of Christ "to the abyss," which either refers to the reality of Christ's death and burial or to hell.
13. Bass writes, "The doctrine of the Descensus arose independently of 1 Peter 3:18–22" (Bass, *The Battle for the Keys*, 85).
14. On the hymnic nature of 1 Peter 3:18–22, see Matthew E. Gordley, *New Testament Christological Hymns: Exploring Texts, Contexts, and Significance* (Downers Grove, IL: IVP Academic, 2018), 196–200. Regarding the translation of the phrase, Matt Emerson points to four other temporal uses of the phrase in 1 Peter 1:6; 2:12; 3:16; 4:4 (Emerson, '*He Descended to the Dead*,' 61).
15. See the summary of six interpretive issues related to 1 Peter 3:19 in Ben Witherington III, *Letters and Homilies for Hellenized Christians: A Socio-Rhetorical Commentary on 1–2 Peter* (Downers Grove, IL: IVP Academic, 2008), 183.
16. Darian Lockett interprets Jesus's movement in 1 Peter 3:19 in relation to the movement "into heaven" in 3:22 so that Peter describes him only ascending not descending. See Darian R. Lockett, *Letters for the Church: Reading James, 1–2 Peter, 1–3 John, and Jude as Canon* (Downers Grove, IL: IVP Academic, 2021), 82.
17. Other suggested referents for the imprisoned spirits include souls of people who lived before Christ's coming or godless people in Noah's day (see Bass, *The Battle for the Keys*, 86).
18. Witherington, *Letters and Homilies*, 184. For possible references to this place of incarceration, see 2 Peter 2:4; Rev. 18:2; 20:7.
19. Bass, *The Battle for the Keys*, 92.
20. The most detailed analysis of 1 Peter 3:19 remains R. T. France, "Exegesis in Practice: Two Examples," in *New Testament Interpretation: Essays on Principles and Methods*, ed. I. H.

post-Resurrection ascent), and whatever his bodily form (soul, disembodied Logos, incarnate), Peter asserts he went to the underworld/hell. Second, Peter also asserts that he preached a message, which we will return to below.

Descent Within the Christian Tradition

How ancient and widespread is the belief in Christ's descent to hell within the Christian tradition? Neither the Nicene Creed (AD 381) nor the earliest version of the Apostles' Creed (ca. AD 400) explicitly state that Christ descended to hell.[21] Rather, they both refer to his burial. However, the eighth-century version of the Apostles' Creed includes the line, "He descended to hell."[22] Does the later version reflect or distort earlier Christian belief?

Part of the answer depends on how one understands the thought of Rufinus (AD 345–411), a monk whose commentary on the Apostles' Creed preserves the earliest known Latin text of the creed.[23] Although Rufinus asserts that the creed represents the doctrine the apostles agreed upon before taking the gospel throughout the world, it is likely one of many early Christian creeds that "agreed in content, but not in exact wording."[24] Of course, differences in wording exist between Rufinus's version of the creed and its later version, including his reference to "he was buried" in the former, but "he was buried and descended to hell" in the latter. [25]

The crux of the matter is whether "burial" and "descent to hell" are synonymous in early Christian thought. Some have concluded that Rufinus's deletion of a "descent" reference indicates that early Christians did not believe Jesus descended to hell, and therefore the line should be deleted from later versions of the Apostles' Creed.[26] Others, however, have noted that Rufinus's deletion does not imply his rejection of the descent. To the contrary, a contextual reading of his commentary on the Apostles' Creed indicates just the opposite. Burial and descent are one and the same for him. Moreover, as J. N. D. Kelly noted some time ago, early Eastern symbols depicting Christ's descent

---

Marshall (Grand Rapids: Eerdmans, 1977), 252–81. Additionally, one must also consider how 1 Peter 4:6 factors into the conversation.

21. See Donald Fairbairn and Ryan M. Reeves, *The Story of Creeds and Confessions: Tracing the Development of the Christian Faith* (Grand Rapids: Baker Academic, 2019), 117.
22. Fairbairn and Reeves, *The Story of Creeds and Confessions*, 117.
23. See Jeffrey L. Hamm, "*Descendit*: Delete or Declare? A Defense against the Neo-Deletionists," *Westminster Theological Journal* 78 (2016): 94.
24. Fairbairn and Reeves, *The Story of Creeds and Confessions*, 20.
25. See Fairbairn and Reeves, *The Story of Creeds and Confessions*, 20.
26. E.g., Grudem concludes, "My own judgment is that there would be all gain and no loss if it were dropped from the Creed once for all" (Grudem, "He Did Not Descend into Hell," 113). In fairness, Grudem reaches this conclusion based upon his understanding, or perhaps misunderstanding, of Rufinus's position, his exegesis of key texts, and his historical reconstruction of what early Christians believed. For Grudem's misunderstanding of Rufinus, see Hamm, "*Descendit*: Delete or Declare?" 93–116.

likely influenced Western Christians.[27] In their summation of the matter, while acknowledging that the descent "clause made its way into the Apostles' Creed relatively late," Fairbairn and Reeves conclude it had "a long pedigree and widespread affirmation earlier."[28] Moreover, they assert, "We cannot justly argue that the church's early faith did not include Christ's descent into hell."[29]

Descent and Atonement

We have spent most of our time assessing the factuality of Jesus's descent to hell. Although readers are welcome to draw their own conclusion on the matter, I am convinced by both the biblical text and Christian tradition that Jesus did descend to hell. Nevertheless, what matters most here is the relationship between said descent and atonement. Four points stand out in this regard.

First, Jesus's descent did not contribute to the efficacy of his penal substitutionary death. In other words, Jesus did not descend to endure more divine punishment in place of sinners. Scripture simply does not identify this as the purpose of his descent.

Second, the descent did not contribute to the way in which Jesus's death and resurrection freed sinners from the power of sin, death, and Satan. His presence in hell is neither a divine ruse played out on Satan or legal ransom. Scripture also does not identify this as the purpose of his descent.

Third, Jesus did not descend to provide a postmortem opportunity for salvation to unbelievers.[30] Such an interpretation simply does not correspond with the wider and consistent soteriology of the NT. Finally, based on 1 Peter 3:18–22, Jesus arrived in hell to proclaim his victory over and vindication before sin, death, and Satan. The descent then does not continue his humiliation from the cross. Rather, as Matt Emerson remarks, it is the "starting point for Christ's exaltation."[31]

Summary

Although Jesus's descent should neither be overlooked in the biblical text nor deleted from the Apostles' Creed, it also should not be interpreted as a part of his atoning work. That work is "finished on Good Friday."[32] Instead, the descent provides Jesus the opportunity to proclaim the atoning achievement of his death. Of course, we do not have access to the content of that unique homily; however, if it was anything like Jesus's preaching ministry that

---

27. See J. N. D. Kelly, *Early Christian Doctrines*, rev. ed. (New York: HarperOne, 1978), 379.
28. Fairbairn and Reeves, *The Story of Creeds and Confessions*, 121.
29. Fairbairn and Reeves, *The Story of Creeds and Confessions*, 121.
30. See, e.g., Gavin D'Costa, "The Descent into Hell as a Solution for the Problem of the Fate of Unevangelized Non-Christians: Balthasar's Hell, the Limbo of the Fathers and Purgatory," *International Journal of Systematic Theology* 11 (2009): 146–71.
31. Emerson, *'He Descended to the Dead,'* 166–67.
32. Emerson, *'He Descended to the Dead,'* 168.

we find in the Gospels, it follows that the power of his words and the efficacy of his deed complemented and informed one another. In this case, the deed was obedience to the Father to the point of death on a cross. The word would be the announcement that, from that death, sinners were reconciled to God and thereby rescued from the power of sin, death, and Satan himself. To put it another way, Jesus's announcement of victory in hell constituted the first "Christopository" sermon that underscored the benefits of his atoning death (Questions 3 and 4).

REFLECTION QUESTIONS

1. What have you heard in church or in conversations about Jesus's descent to hell?

2. How do you think Peter, Paul, and the other apostles viewed Jesus's "descent" based on the NT references that we have?

3. Why would you include or exclude Jesus's descent in conversations about his atoning work?

4. What is the danger of excluding Jesus's descent from our thoughts about atonement and/or wider Christian theology?

5. If the NT writers believed in Jesus's descent, why do you think they say so little about it?

What Role Does Jesus's Resurrection Play in Atonement?

And if Christ has not been raised, your faith is futile and you are still in your sins.

~1 Corinthians 15:17

Paul needed the patience of Job when it came to the Corinthians. They entangled themselves in factionalism, fornication, and lawsuits (see 1 Cor. 1:10–17; 5:1–5; 6:1–8). However, nothing may have unsettled Paul more than the claim by some that they did not believe in the resurrection of believers (1 Cor. 15:13). In teasing out the implications of this claim, Paul draws a direct line from the unreality of resurrection to the unreality of a risen Jesus to the reality of an empty faith and the absence of forgiveness. More positively, Paul assumes a connection between the risen Jesus and forgiveness. To put it more broadly, Paul links the atoning value of Jesus's death with his resurrection.

But what role does resurrection play in atonement?[1] Surprisingly, some discussions of atonement either wrestle with this question indirectly or not at all. As Adam Johnson maintains in assessing this lacuna in Anselm, "One of the more unfortunate events in the history of the doctrine of the atonement was Anselm's failure to sufficiently develop the role of the resurrection within his construal of Christ's satisfying work" (Question 13).[2] Nevertheless, both

---

1. Although I do not necessarily agree with all of his conclusions, David Moffitt attempts to bring more attention to the role of Jesus's resurrection and exaltation in the NT's view of atonement. See David M. Moffitt, *Rethinking the Atonement: New Perspectives on Jesus's Death, Resurrection, and Ascension* (Grand Rapids: Baker Academic, 2022).
2. Adam J. Johnson, *Atonement: A Guide for the Perplexed*, Guides for the Perplexed (London: Bloomsbury T&T Clark, 2015), 130.

Scripture and the Christian tradition identify a link between atonement and Jesus's resurrection, namely, *intercession.*

Prior to his death and resurrection, Jesus signaled that his unique person, his work on the cross, and his heavenly installment positioned him as the intercessor par excellence. Israel's Scriptures bore witness to interceding prophets, priests with their intercessory sacrifices, and kings who stood in the breach between YHWH and the nation in times of rebellion and rest.[3] Yet Jesus outdid all his predecessors. His resurrection not only confirmed the superiority of his earthly intercessory work but also established him as the eternal and heavenly intercessor.

A Risen Jesus *Promises* His Atoning Work

Even before his heavenly intercession began, Jesus taught and demonstrated the promise of his unmatched intercessory status. In Matthew, Jesus declares, "All things have been handed over to me by my Father, and no one knows the Son except the Father, and no one knows the Father except the Son and anyone to whom the Son chooses to reveal him" (Matt. 11:27). In Mark, Jesus explains to the befuddled disciples, "To you has been given the secret of the kingdom of God, but for those outside everything is in parables" (Mark 4:11). In Luke, Jesus exhorts Peter, "Simon, Simon, behold, Satan demanded to have you, that he might sift you like wheat, but I have prayed for you that your faith may not fail. And when you have turned again, strengthen your brothers" (Luke 22:31–32). In John, Jesus summarily declares, "I am the way, and the truth, and the life. No one comes to the Father except through me" (John 14:6). In short, with respect to atonement, the knowledge, faith, and access that defines reconciliation with God runs only and directly through Jesus. Jesus then must be both crucified *and* risen to provide such intercession, which he promised beforehand.

Jesus continued that promissory announcement through his apostles who bore witness to his resurrection and his heavenly exaltation. In Acts, those who preach the word about Jesus urge their listeners to call upon him for salvation, which of course requires him to be alive (see Acts 2:21; 9:14; 22:16; Rom. 10:12). Jesus must be risen to proclaim the benefits of his atoning death and to call sinners to share in those benefits. As the risen and exalted one, Jesus continues his promissory work, which is all in accordance with Israel's Scriptures. As Peter warns in one of his sermons, Jesus is the prophet whom Moses foresaw: "And it shall be that every soul who does not listen to that prophet shall be destroyed from the people" (Acts 3:23; cf. Deut. 18:15).

---

3.   See Michael Widmer, *Standing in the Breach: An Old Testament Theology and Spirituality of Intercessory Prayer*, Siphrut 13 (Winona Lake, IN: Eisenbrauns, 2015).

A Risen Jesus *Affirms* an Acceptable Atonement

In his sermon at Pentecost, Peter hears Jesus's voice in Psalm 16. He specifically detects Jesus addressing his Father to explain why he was raised from the dead: "For you will not abandon my soul to Hades, or let your Holy One see corruption" (Acts 2:27; cf. Ps. 16:10). Luke also refers to Jesus as "the righteous one" in his two-volume work (see Luke 23:47; Acts 3:14; 22:14). These two christological titles sum up why the Father raised his Son from the dead, namely, because he is uniquely holy and righteous. His holiness and righteousness meant that God could not allow him to rot in death. Therefore, the Father raised him from the dead, which means he accepts both his Son and his atoning work. A risen Jesus affirms that he is in fact the propitiation, expiation, and ransom that God accepts.

A Risen Jesus *Mediates* His Atoning Work

Besides promising his atoning work, Jesus also performs that work. To be sure, the NT makes clear that Jesus died "once for all" (Heb. 7:27; cf. Rom. 6:10; Heb. 9:12; 10:10; 1 Peter 3:18). Therefore, by "perform" I do not mean that Jesus continues to die or suffer an atoning death but rather that he mediates the benefits of that work on behalf of believers as he intercedes for them before his Father.

Hebrews provides one of the more comprehensive discussions regarding the efficacy of Jesus's interceding work based upon his person, work, and risen status. In this ancient homily, as the writer attempts to prevent afflicted Christians from apostasy, he appeals to intercessors from Israel's past who typified the defining work that Christ accomplishes. For example, although angels mediated the Mosaic law to Israel, and disobedience to it sometimes incurred swift penalties, Jesus mediates God's final saving word/work, and disobedience to it incurs an eternal penalty (Heb. 1:1–2:18). Moreover, by sharing in "flesh and blood," Jesus nullified Satan's tyrannical use of death and became a faithful priest to propitiate the sins of the people (Heb. 2:14–18). Nullifying Satan's power over death and propitiating sin go hand in hand. The former does not occur without the latter, in keeping with the writer's Passover allusion, wherein deliverance from Egypt required a sacrifice on behalf of Israel whereby they would not face the same judgment as their Egyptian oppressors.[4]

---

4. This is where Moffit's exegesis of the Passover allusion in Heb. 2:14–18 falls short. Moffit separates Israel's God from the death of the firstborn in Egypt by attributing that plague to the devil based on the reference to a "destroyer" in Exod. 12:23. In this way, Moffit can find in Heb. 2:14–18 an inclusive focus on Jesus's defeat of the devil and mitigate the propitiation of divine wrath through the Passover lamb/Jesus. Moffitt ignores the beginning of Exod. 12:23 in which YHWH allows/disallows the destroyer to strike the firstborn based upon whether the blood of the sacrificial animal was displayed (see Moffit, *Rethinking the Atonement*, 9–27).

With respect to the high priest typology in Hebrews, every element of the Levitical system typifies what the crucified and risen Jesus eternally accomplishes. He is the better high priest based on his divinity ("your throne, O God," Heb. 1:8), sinlessness, and mysterious priestly origin according to the order of Melchizedek (see Heb. 5:10; 6:20–7:27). Jesus presents his atoning work in the heavenly temple of God rather than in its earthly copy (see Heb. 9:1–14). He himself, rather than an animal, is the sacrifice (see Rom. 8:31–34; Heb. 10:11–15). As the *risen crucified one* in the very presence of God, Jesus is able to save continuously and eternally those who come to God through him because he is always living to intercede for them (Heb. 7:25). This means that Jesus "pleads" the believers' cause before God with respect to the need for forgiveness, a right standing, inheritance of promised blessing, deliverance from enemies, and vindication.[5] Jesus's intercession is successful because of his unique relationship to the Father, his obedience unto death, and his risen state.

A Risen Jesus *Reigns* Through His Atoning Work

The NT insists that Jesus is the risen King of kings who rules over the cosmos at God's right hand.[6] What, though, links his reign as Lord to his atoning work grounded in the cross and continued in his intercession? The opening epistolary section of Revelation helps in this regard. John writes, "John to the seven churches that are in Asia: Grace to you and peace from him who is and who was and who is to come, and from the seven spirits who are before his throne, and from Jesus Christ the faithful witness, the firstborn of the dead, and the ruler of kings on earth" (Rev. 1:4–5).

This christological snapshot of Jesus's work attributes his rule over earthly kingdoms to both his resurrection and his ability to free his people from sin, death, and Satan "by his blood." The latter qualifier evokes the sacrificial efficacy of his death. Subsequent references to Jesus's blood specify the atoning value of his death in at least two interrelated ways: (1) Jesus's death cleanses his people from sin (Rev. 7:14; 19:13), and (2) participation in this cleansing includes them in his victory over Satan, which is also accomplished through his death/blood (Rev. 12:11). In short, for John to say that Jesus, by his "blood," "purchased" people for God is to say that Jesus's death cleanses from sin, removes sin's accompanying judgment, and frees sinners from Satan so they now belong to Jesus.

---

5.   Donald Guthrie states, "The function of our high priest is to plead our cause" (Donald Guthrie, *Hebrews*, Tyndale New Testament Commentaries [Grand Rapids: Eerdmans, 1983], 167).

6.   See, e.g., Matt. 26:64; Mark 14:62; Luke 22:69; Acts 2:34; 7:55–56; Rom. 8:34; Eph. 1:20; Col. 3:1; 1 Tim. 6:15; Heb. 1:3; Rev. 5:1.

The latter dimension of this atoning work brings us back to the epistolary opening, where John continues his description of Jesus by noting he made believers a "kingdom, priests to his God and Father" (Rev. 1:6). The risen Jesus builds his kingdom from those whom he cleansed and those whom he freed from sin so they can serve him (Rev. 4:1–5:14; 21:22–27). Jesus then reigns as king who builds his kingdom of worshipers through his atoning work.

Atonement, Resurrection, and the Christian Tradition

Although Scripture clearly links atonement to Jesus's resurrection, the Christian tradition has comparatively lagged. The tradition is not entirely silent on the issue; however, resurrection is not a prominent feature in the major theories/views of atonement. Two exceptions stand out.

John Calvin ties the advantages secured through Christ's death to his resurrection in at least three ways. First, a risen Jesus stands before God so that one's righteousness before him is "renewed and restored" (*Inst.* 2.16). In reflecting on Romans 4:25, Calvin finds in Paul the belief that by Christ's death "sin was taken away" and by his resurrection "righteousness was renewed and restored." He then asks rhetorical questions that underscore the point: "For how could he by dying have freed us from death, if he had yielded to its power? How could he have obtained the victory for us if he had fallen in the contest?" (*Inst.* 2.16.13). Second, a risen Jesus becomes the basis of hope for a new life and its "efficacious cause" (*Inst.* 2.16). This is not to downplay the significance of Christ's death but to make the point that death and resurrection inform and assume one another. Calvin writes, "Not that faith founded merely on death is vacillating, but that the divine power by which he maintains our faith is most conspicuous in his resurrection" (*Inst.* 2.16.13).[7] It is in Jesus's resurrection that he "became the resurrection and the life" (*Inst.* 2.16.13). Third, a risen Jesus "assures us of our own resurrection" (*Inst.* 2.16.13).

T. F. Torrance provides another exception regarding the atonement-resurrection link. Among other things, Torrance argues that atonement without resurrection would not qualify as true reconciliation between the sinner and God.[8] That is because, without Christ's resurrection, the goal of atonement—"communion with the life of God"—ultimately falls short.[9] Torrance explains, "In summary, the resurrection means that the divine act of reconciliation reaches its completion and end and that apart from the resurrection,

---

7. Calvin goes on to note, "Let us remember, therefore, that when death only is mentioned, everything peculiar to the resurrection is at the same time included, and that there is a like synecdoche in the term resurrection, as often as it is used apart from death, everything peculiar to death being included" (*Inst.* 2.16.13).

8. See Paul D. Molnar, "Resurrection and Atonement in the Theology of Thomas F. Torrance," in *The T&T Clark Companion to Atonement*, ed. Adam J. Johnson (London: T&T Clark, 2017), 64.

9. T. F. Torrance, *Space, Time and Resurrection* (Edinburgh: T&T Clark, 1998), 67.

reconciliation would prove a hollow fiasco, for separation between humanity and God would have remained in force."[10] For Torrance, only a crucified *and* risen Christ overcomes that separation, because in his risen state Jesus continues the sinner's justification; in his risen state there is "actual redemption" of the entire person now and eschatologically; and in his risen state the goal of atonement is reached, which is a peaceful union with God in Christ.[11]

Summary

The latter discussion of Calvin and Torrance is not a full endorsement of their views; however, they are to be commended for carefully thinking about the connection between Christ's atoning work at the cross and his resurrection. In short, the connection can be summed up as "intercession." As the crucified *and* risen one, Jesus brings believers into the benefits of his person and atoning work at the cross, by which he mediates our acceptance before God.

REFLECTION QUESTIONS

1. Why might resurrection be undervalued in atonement discussions?

2. Why should the mention of Jesus's death assume his resurrection and vice versa?

3. What are some of the ways that Scripture links Jesus's atonement to his resurrection?

4. How is John Calvin an exception to the neglect of the resurrection-atonement link?

5. How is T. F. Torrance an exception to the neglect of the resurrection-atonement link?

---

10. T. F. Torrance, *Atonement: The Person and Work of Christ* (Downers Grove, IL: IVP Academic, 2009), 228–29.
11. Molnar, "Resurrection and Atonement," 60–66.

What Is the Relationship Between Christ's Atoning Work and the Requirement to Fulfill the Law?

> *For Christ is the end of the law for righteousness to everyone who believes.*
>
> ~Romans 10:4

Paul's assertion that Christ is the "end" (*telos*) of the Mosaic law has caused not a little consternation among interpreters. Does Paul mean to say that Christ was the "goal" to whom the law directed Israel? Or does Paul see Christ as the cessation of the law in the sense that one is no longer obligated to obey it? To be sure, contextually, Paul's statement forms part of his wider argument that Israel's unbelief in Jesus the Messiah does not signal that God's prior promise to the nation has failed, with all the implications that such a failure would have for believing Jews and Gentiles alike (see Rom. 9:6–9).[1] Nevertheless, such a bold statement reflects a coherent, not contingent, disposition toward the law.[2] Moreover, it raises a larger question for us, namely, what is the relationship between Christ's atoning work and the requirement to fulfill the law?

A whole bevy of related questions lie just beneath the surface here. What does the Mosaic law require of humanity? In what sense did Jesus's death

---

1. See my discussion on Rom. 9:6–9 and 10:4 in Channing L. Crisler, *An Intertextual Commentary on Romans: Volume 3 (Rom 9:1–11:36)* (Eugene, OR: Pickwick, 2022), 46–53, 143–46.
2. Moo refers to Rom. 10:4 as "one of the most famous of all of Paul's theological 'slogans'" (Douglas J. Moo, *The Epistle to the Romans*, New International Commentary on the New Testament, 2nd ed. [Grand Rapids: Eerdmans, 2018], 654).

fulfill the requirements of the law? Are believers in Christ required to obey the law? In answering these questions, we can formulate a more comprehensive answer to our overarching question.

Atonement and the Law's Demand on Humanity

YHWH gave his law to ancient Israel and not to the wider ancient Near East world. However, the OT and the NT signal the Mosaic law embodied God's righteous demands for all humanity. For example, in the theology of the Psalms, the distinction between human beings is predicated upon the righteous who delight in God's instruction (Torah) and the unrighteous who do not (see Ps. 1). Their eschatological fates rest upon this distinction: "For the LORD knows the way of the righteous, but the way of the wicked will perish" (Ps. 1:6). Although non-Israelites lacked access to the Mosaic law, its demands are imprinted on the created order and the human conscience. If the "heavens declare his righteousness," as the psalmist asserts, it follows that the created order points to a Creator who acts justly and demands the same of his creatures (Ps. 97:6).[3]

Matters are even clearer in the NT, where writers sharpen the scope of the law's requirements to include all human beings. Paul makes this explicit by noting that Gentiles occasionally keep the law's requirements even though they do not possess the law "by nature" in the way that Jews do (Rom. 2:14). In such instances, they adhere to the "work of the law written on their hearts" (Rom. 2:15). While making no distinction between Jew and Gentile, John defines sin for all as "lawlessness" (1 John 3:4).

Whether one has the law written on stone or in one's conscience, God demands that Jews and Gentiles obey him. Their disobedience incurs various consequences and penalties, but above all it results in death. This is a righteous requirement, with fatal consequences, that, according to Paul, humanity is well aware of (Rom. 1:31).

In short, both the Adamic and Israelite narratives feature the divine demand of obedience, the reward of life for obedience, and the fatal penalty for disobedience (see Gen. 2:16–17; Deut. 30:15–20). Therefore, atonement for sin must address the law's demand for obedience along with its promise of life for obedience and death for disobedience.

Atonement and Jesus's Fulfillment of the Law

"Do not think that I came to abolish *the Law or the Prophets*; I have not come to abolish them but to *fulfill* them" (Matt. 5:17, italics added). On the

---

3. As Geoffrey Grogan observes in his analysis of Ps. 97, "The natural phenomenon reminds us of Sinai, and the law-giving there was a major revelation of Yahweh's nature and character. His reign is based on his moral qualities, his righteousness and justice, and so his foes cannot stand against him" (Geoffrey W. Grogan, *Psalms*, The Two Horizons Old Testament Commentary [Grand Rapids: Eerdmans, 2008], 166).

one hand, Jesus's assertion means he came to the earth to complete, or fulfill, the redemption God promised through him in both the Law and the Prophets. On the other hand, as the immediate context indicates, Jesus draws attention to how he fulfills the law in the sense that his teaching interprets the commands in a complete way (see Matt. 5:21–48). This includes both the full disclosure of what God required in commands such as "You shall not commit adultery" and how such demands are both exacerbated by Jesus's teaching and carried out in him.

Neither the Sermon on the Mount nor any other teaching should be read apart from Matthew's Immanuel Christology. As Jesus fulfills the law by clarifying its demand, there is an assumption that his presence also plays a key role in how his disciples follow his teaching. That role includes what the law requires with respect to obedience, penalties for disobedience, and the means of atonement. If this messianic Immanuel saves from sin, as the opening frame of this gospel asserts, it follows that he must carry out the atoning work demanded by the law, though Matthew largely assumes, rather than precisely articulates, that atoning work (see Matt. 1:18–25).

Overt references to the link between atonement and Jesus's fulfillment of the law can be found elsewhere in the NT. For example, after the jarring lament by the "I" in Romans 7:7–25, Paul assures those who are in Christ that they are no longer under God's just condemnation for their slavery to sin, and he grounds that assurance in Christ's fulfillment of the law (Rom. 8:1–4).[4] God condemned sin "in the flesh" of the crucified Jesus to fulfill two requirements of the law: (1) death for transgression of the law and (2) obedience to the law (Rom. 8:3–4). Paul makes a similar point in Galatians while drawing from the blessing and curse language embedded in the Mosaic law (Gal. 3:10–14). Jesus redeemed those whom God placed under a fatal curse for their disobedience to the law. Such redemption required that Jesus experience this curse in place of sinners so they might inherit the Abrahamic blessing of justification, which is marked by the gift of the Spirit (Gal. 3:13–14; cf. 2 Cor. 5:20–21).

Besides fulfilling what the law requires with respect to the moral demands it places on individuals, Jesus's atoning work also fulfills priestly requirements with respect to the time, place, and nature of the atoning sacrifice that God prescribes. However, Jesus fulfills these requirements in such a way that it shows the Mosaic law is only the introduction to a better hope (Heb. 7:19). The writer of Hebrews discusses at least seven ways that Jesus's priestly work outpaces his priestly predecessors and thereby fulfills what the law requires: (1) Jesus can sympathize with the temptations that sinners face but without the guilt of sin that plagues them; (2) Jesus comes from the priestly order of

---

4. On reading Rom. 7:7–25 as lament in the vein of OT lamenters, see Channing L. Crisler, "The 'I' Who Laments: Echoes of Old Testament Lament Language in Romans 7:7–25 and the Identity of the ἐγώ," *Catholic Biblical Quarterly* 82 (2020): 64–83.

Melchizedek, which is superior to the Levitical order and unites the offices of king and priest; (3) God established and secured Jesus's priesthood with an unchangeable oath; (4) the risen Jesus enjoys an eternal, living priesthood; (5) Jesus mediates a better and new covenant; (6) Jesus's own blood, not an animal's blood, inaugurates the covenant; and (7) Jesus carries out his eternal priestly work in the heavenly temple before God himself rather than in an earthly temple in the Holy of Holies at the ark of the covenant.[5]

Atonement, Believers, and the Law

If, then, the crucified and risen Jesus fulfills, or completes, the demands of the Mosaic law in his atoning work, what is the believer's and the church's relationship to the law? This has been a nagging question since the patristic era, through the Middle Ages and the Reformation, and up to today.[6] Three salient points emerge from Scripture.

First, the law always leads believers to a knowledge of sin rather than justification and life before God. As Paul writes in Romans 3:20, "For by the works of the law no human being will be justified in his sight, since through the law comes knowledge of sin" (cf. Ps. 143:2; Gal. 2:16). The law lacks the power to "give life" (Gal. 3:21; cf. Rom. 7:10).

Second, in always leading believers to a knowledge of sin, the law always brings to believers' remembrance of the atoning work of Christ on their behalf. The law's unattainable demand, which is ultimately obedience from the heart, always "teaches" believers to find their right standing before God in the crucified and risen Christ (see Gal. 3:19–29; Phil. 3:7–11).

Third, Christ's work and presence in the life of believers and in the church fulfills the essence of what the law demands, namely, love from the heart for God and others. As Paul concludes, "Therefore love is the fulfilling of the law" (Rom 13:10).

Summary

Divine commands and the Mosaic law loom large over the biblical canon. Even prior to God's transmission of the law to Moses at Sinai, a divine command directed to human beings is heard as early as Eden (Gen. 2:16–17; Rom. 5:12–14). At the close of the canon, John gives a Deuteronomic-like warning not to add to or subtract from his apocalypse (see Deut. 4:2; Rev. 22:18). God's demands then are woven into the biblical narrative. It is definitive of who he is as our Creator and who Jesus is as our Lord. All of God's creatures are obligated to obey him.

---

5. See Gen. 14:17–24; Ps. 110:1–4; Jer. 31:31–34; Heb. 4:14–16; 5:1–10; 6:19–10:31.
6. See, e.g., Werner Elert, *Law and Gospel,* trans. Edward H. Schroeder (Eugene, OR: Wipf and Stock, 2007).

But a problem arises here. No one obeys him from the heart as he demands, whether those demands are imprinted on stone, the created order, or the human conscience (see Rom. 3:10–18). Sin is in fact lawlessness, and lawlessness is sin (1 John 3:4). Moreover, even believers who are empowered by the Spirit to obey God do so imperfectly, as evidenced by the existence of the NT letters themselves.[7]

It follows that believers and unbelievers alike need the linkage between Jesus's atoning work and God's demand to obey him/the law. A succinct way to define the linkage is by describing Jesus as the one who "fulfills" the law for those who trust in him. He fulfills it in the sense of teaching his disciples the full meaning of the law. He fulfills it in the sense that he was obedient to the law from the heart in the way that God demands. He fulfills it in the sense that, although without sin, he takes upon himself the legal obligation that transgressors of the divine command must pay the penalty of death. Even more, he dies a kind of death that matches and even outpaces the egregiousness of sin against God (see Questions 16 and 17).

REFLECTION QUESTIONS

1. What kinds of demands does God make of humanity?

2. Why is external obedience to the Mosaic law, or even one's conscience, insufficient for fulfilling the law?

3. How does Jesus fulfill the law for believers in his teaching and life?

4. How does Jesus fulfill the law in his death?

5. What are some ways that Christians might misunderstand Jesus's fulfillment of the law?

---

7. All NT letters address in some shape or fashion the sin of believing communities. It follows that sin was an ongoing problem among believers. Moreover, prayer instructions in the NT, which urge confession, indicate sin is an ongoing problem for believers (see, e.g., Matt. 6:12; Luke 11:4; James 5:16; 1 John 1:9).

How Did Jesus's Death Make Atonement for Old Testament Believers?

Your father Abraham rejoiced that he would see my day. He saw it and was glad.

~John 8:56

During his earthly ministry of the first-century era, Jesus primarily interacted with people in Galilee, Samaria, and Judea. Nevertheless, Jesus's teaching anticipates that believers in and beyond that time and place would share in the benefits of his atoning work (see Matt. 20:28; Mark 10:45; John 12:32). He therefore charges his apostles to go and make disciples of all nations (Matt. 28:16–20; Acts 1:7–8). But what about those who preceded the apostles, reaching as far back as Abraham himself? Or even those from the primeval narrative, such as Adam, Eve, and Abel? While Abraham somehow rejoiced to see Jesus's day, how did Jesus's death make atonement for those who might be called OT believers? In answering this question, we must consider both the typological and ontological presence of Christ in Israel's history.

Christ's Typological Presence in OT Atonement

In an ancient homily that reflects on the connection between Passover and Jesus's death, Melito of Sardis (AD 190) observes, "Nothing, beloved, is spoken or made without an analogy and a sketch; for everything which is made and spoken has its analogy, what is spoken an analogy, what is made a prototype, so that whatever is made may be perceived through the prototype and whatever is spoken clarified by the illustration."[1] Prototypes enhance

---

1. Melito of Sardis, *On Pascha: With the Fragments of Melito and Other Material Related to the Quartodecimans*, trans. Alistair C. Stewart (Yonkers: St. Vladimir's Seminary Press, 2016), 60.

our understanding of what they precede. Even before Melito, the NT writers found tremendous explanatory power in an approach to the OT that is often referred to as "typology."[2] Typology, in its simplest form, consists of an OT *type*, such as a person, place, or event that anticipates its NT *antitype*, or fulfillment, in the person and work of Jesus. What characterizes the relationship between type and antitype is the escalation that occurs in the latter. Jesus's person and work broadens the scope of the OT type that preceded him.[3] Much of NT typology revolves around the work of atonement, and this typological connection helps to explain the relationship between Jesus's death and OT believers. Three points are in order here.

First, as we have discussed already, the OT establishes the parameters and patterns of atonement (Question 24). God chose a specific people, place, time, and means to facilitate his reconciliation with Israel. The Levites performed a variety of duties within the tabernacle/temple at divinely prescribed moments and with divinely approved sacrifices. The Day of Atonement, to reiterate, provides one of the most important typological links between the OT sacrificial system and Jesus's sacrificial work. The typological elements of that day outline and clarify key components of Jesus's work. In short, Jesus is both the eternal high priest and the sacrifice whose enthronement as Lord facilitates his perpetual mediating work and status in the very presence of God.

Second, the OT offices of prophet, priest, and king typify the atoning work accomplished by Jesus as prophet, priest, and king. The OT prophets routinely announced Israel's sin and impending judgment, but not without the hope of salvation. The latter would require a sacrifice for the forgiveness of sin, which required a priest. Moreover, the hope of salvation required a ruler, a kingly figure whom God would send and thereby save his people. Israel's reconciliation required the work of all three offices, as seen in texts such as Psalm 110, where a prophetic promise by YHWH to his anointed king and priest results in deliverance from enemies and inheritance of divine blessing.[4] Jesus unites all three offices by announcing his atoning work in the vein of a prophet, a work that he accomplishes as the priest par excellence and the promised Davidic king who delivers his people from the enemies of sin, death, and Satan.

---

2. For a classic work on typology, see Leonard Goppelt, *Typos: The Typological Interpretation of the Old Testament in the New Testament*, trans. Donald H. Madvig (Grand Rapids: Eerdmans, 1982). For recent works on typology, see Mitchell L. Chase, *40 Questions About Typology and Allegory* (Grand Rapids: Kregel Academic, 2020) and James M. Hamilton, *Typology: Understanding the Bible's Promise-Shaped Patterns* (Grand Rapids: Zondervan Academic, 2022).
3. "Broadens" in the sense of both the number of people impacted by Christ's atoning work and the eternal—rather than temporary—nature of his work.
4. See the use of Ps. 110 in Matt. 22:44; 26:64; Mark 12:36; 14:6; Luke 20:42; 22:69; Acts 2:34; Rom. 8:34; 11:29; 1 Cor. 15:25; Eph. 1:20; Heb. 1:3, 13; 5:6; 6:20; 7:3, 11, 17, 21; 8:1; 10:12.

Third, OT believers participated in Christ's atoning work through their participation in the types that anticipated him. Those who believed prophetic warnings, trusted in the forgiveness that God provided through the sacrificial system, and looked for deliverance from enemies through the kingly figures whom God sent participated in the atoning work that Christ would accomplish as prophet, priest, and king. Some even realized their trust in the types God provided anticipated something greater to come. For example, the writer of Hebrews attributes Moses's refusal to be called a "son of Pharaoh's daughter" to his consideration of the "reproach of Christ," which he found more valuable "than the treasures of Egypt" (Heb. 11:24, 26). Moses was looking ahead to the greater reward, namely, Christ. Peter asserts that the very "Spirit of Christ" worked through the OT prophets; as they carried out their prophetic duties they were looking for the person of Christ and his "sufferings" and "glories" (1 Peter 1:10–12).

Christ's Ontological Presence in OT Atonement

In the gospel of John, Jesus explains unbelief in the signs he performs by appealing to portions of Isaiah 6 and 53 (John 12:37–40; cf. Isa. 6:1; 53:1). Isaiah anticipated later unbelief in the signs that would reveal Jesus's person and atoning work. In fact, Jesus goes as far as to say Isaiah "saw his glory" (John 12:41). Jesus's claim that Isaiah saw him signals that Jesus was not only typologically present in Israel's history but also ontologically present. It follows that Jesus was present with Israel in the typological moments that anticipated his atoning work. His presence is not necessarily "pre-incarnational," as some have described it. The NT writers do not pontificate on what "form" Jesus took in his presence with ancient Israel. Instead, they simply assume Jesus's presence in the same way the OT writers assumed YHWH's presence. Multiple NT examples bear this out.

Jude locates Jesus at Israel's deliverance from Egyptian bondage: "Now I want to remind you, although you once fully knew it, that Jesus, who saved a people out of the land of Egypt, afterward destroyed those who did not believe" (Jude 1:5). He not only places Jesus in Egypt but also credits him with destroying unfaithful Israelites in the wilderness (see Num. 14:29–37). Along the same lines, Paul places Jesus in the wilderness as the one who supplied water to Israel from a rock ("And the rock was Christ"), the one who slew the idolatrous rebels of Israel in the wilderness, and the one who silenced murmuring through destruction (1 Cor. 10:1–11; cf. Num. 14:16; 21:5; 26:62).

Jesus's real, or ontological, presence at these events is significant for this discussion because they are events related to atonement. Deliverance from Egypt is more than a pattern for the deliverance that Christ accomplishes in his atoning work. Jesus was present at these seminal moments in Israel's history; therefore, their belief or unbelief in what YHWH did is at the same time belief or unbelief in what Christ did.

Although the NT writers do not make the same overt connections between the ontological presence of Jesus at events such as Yom Kippur, it stands to reason that Jesus was there when the priests made atoning sacrifices both at the mercy seat and in the scapegoat. To borrow from John's Logos Christology, if the Word was with God in the beginning, he was also present at all subsequent moments of God's work, including the atoning work carried out within Israel (John 1:1–5). Therefore, when OT believers participated in this Levitical work by faith, they also participated in Christ's work by faith. They participated not only typologically but also ontologically.

Christ's Proleptic Work in OT Atonement

Even with these typological and ontological connections between OT believers and Christ, participation in the benefits of the atoning work are ultimately predicated upon what unfolds at Golgotha. Without the actual death of Christ, ancient Israel's typological and even ontological participation in him by faith is superfluous. The death and resurrection of Jesus, along with the atoning benefits that emanate from it, are proleptically (i.e., bring future judgment into the present) applied to OT believers who participate in the sacrificial system and trust in the prophetic and kingly figures whom God sends for their instruction and deliverance.

If Jesus is the Lamb who "was slain before the foundation of the world," as John describes him, it follows that God applied the atoning work of Christ to OT believers as far back as Abel, Enoch, and Noah (Rev. 13:8),[5] though they could not necessarily see a crucified and risen Christ. Chronologically speaking, at least from the human perspective characterized by space and time, such an event had not taken place. Nevertheless, in his sovereign and eternal purposes, God willed that OT believers would share in the benefits of Christ's atoning work. He even foreshadowed/typified it through various figures, places, customs, and events in ancient Israelite history. What they experienced in these types before the incarnation functioned as a kind of proleptic experience of what was eternally willed but temporally established in the first-century death and resurrection of Jesus.

Summary

Complexity characterizes the participation of OT believers in the atoning work of Christ. There is not one single answer to our question but a nexus of answers. Their share in Christ is grounded in the eternal will of God, which he expressed typologically throughout Israel's history. From Adam and the garden to Solomon and the temple, so many figures, locations, customs, and

---

5.   Abel, Enoch, and Noah are appropriate examples given the fact that the writer of Hebrews begins his explanation of the painful experience of justification by faith with these three prominent figures in the primeval narrative (Gen. 4:1–16; 5:21–24; 6:9; see Heb. 11:4–7).

events pointed to a greater, cosmic atoning work. Even more, God did more for Israel than foreshadow the atoning work of Christ. He promised it through his prophets.

For those who participated in these types and clung to these prophetic promises by faith, God reconciled himself to them through Christ, who was never an entirely distant figure. As noted above, the NT writers placed him with Israel at seminal moments such as the exodus and the wilderness wanderings. Why then could he not be present in some way at Yom Kippur and other atoning activities at the tabernacle/temple?

The typological and even ontological presence of Jesus in Israel's history, along with the eternal and sovereign will of Israel's God, facilitated a proleptic experience of this defining atoning sacrifice. While the sacrifice needed to take place within real space and time, its benefits are not confined to space and time. Because Jesus is the same "yesterday, today, and forever," it follows that those who trust in the divine promise of his work could experience its benefits both before and after his incarnation.

REFLECTION QUESTIONS

1. What are some of the explanations you have heard regarding the eternal condition of those who lived before the incarnation?

2. How do the NT writers link Jesus to the OT typologically?

3. Why is it incorrect to say that OT figures were reconciled to God through their obedience to the law?

4. What are some ways that OT figures, events, and the like inform our understanding of God's atoning work in Christ?

5. If someone asked you how Jesus's death atoned for the sins of OT believers, how would you respond?

PART 5

The Implications
of Christ's Atoning Work

Questions About Christ's
Atoning Work and the Identity of God

How Is the Triune God Involved in Christ's Atoning Work?

And when he came up out of the water, immediately he saw the heavens being torn open and the Spirit descending on him like a dove. And a voice came from heaven, "You are my beloved Son; with you I am well pleased."

~Mark 1:10–11

Father, Son, and Spirit are present at Jesus's baptism. This inaugural moment in Jesus's ministry indicates that the work of atonement is the work of the triune God. Nothing reveals the character of the triune God like the atonement. Father, Son, and Spirit work in a way that simultaneously accentuates their relational unity and distinctiveness in reconciling fallen humanity. The three persons of the Trinity eternally share in the life of one another (*perichoresis*), and the atonement amplifies that relationship.[1] Scripture provides a portrait of how all three members of the Trinity are involved with one another in this endeavor. It is a portrait that reflects God's will, the wonder of his triunity, and the intensity of his love.

The Triune God Eternally Willed Christ's Atoning Work

Jesus's death was never God's plan B. Although the eternal relationship between Father, Son, and Spirit needed no other participants, God chose for

---

1. Alister McGrath defines *perichoresis* as "The basic notion is that all three persons of the Trinity mutually share in the life of the others, so that none is isolated or detached from the actions of the others" (Alister E. McGrath, *Christian Theology: An Introduction*, 2nd ed. [Oxford: Blackwell, 1994], 574).

those made in his image to experience his love.[2] Unfortunately, the events described in Genesis 3 plunged humanity into sin, death, and separation from him (Gen. 3:24; Rom. 5:12–14). These events also placed atonement at the center of God's work in Scripture. From the promise that one born of a woman would crush the serpent's head to the vision of a new heaven and earth, God works to reconcile human beings to himself so they can find eternal life in him (Gen. 3:15; Rev. 22:1–4). However, the triune God does not *react* to humanity's fall. Atonement is his eternal will.

Scripture indicates the Father willed his Son's death before he founded the world. Peter describes Jesus Christ as a Lamb who "was foreknown before the foundation of the world" (1 Peter 1:20).[3] This description indicates that "God knew the complete program of redemption before the foundation of the world."[4] Similarly, John describes the Son as the "*Lamb slain from the foundation of the world*" (Rev. 13:8 NKJV).[5] In other words, the Father *eternally* willed the sacrificial death of his Son.

If the triune God willed Christ's atoning death eternally, it follows that his foreknowledge of the fall did not deter him from creating human beings. To the contrary, he wanted to share his love with them. This does not necessarily require a view wherein the Father willed (decreed) the fall because he predestined the Son to death (*supralapsarianism*). Nor does it require the view that God logically decrees creation and permits the fall prior to decreeing redemption (*infralapsarianism*). Herein lies one of the mysteries of the atonement that we will return to in Question 40.

The Triunity of God Makes Atonement Possible

The triunity of God makes discussing the atonement challenging, but it is also makes atonement possible.[6] The triune God relates to himself in a way that he can deal with sin.[7] God is one; therefore, the atonement accords perfectly with the will of all three persons of the Trinity. The Father willed the death of his Son. The Son willed to be sacrificed by his Father. The Spirit

---

2. See Augustine, *De Doctrina Christiana*, 1.5.
3. Some translations describe Jesus as one "chosen," rather than "foreknown," before the foundation of the world. The differences arise from the sense that προγινώσκω bears in this context. For other NT passages that point to the eternal plan of redemption, see e.g., Rom 8:28–30; Eph 2:8–10.
4. Karen H. Jobes, *1 Peter*, Baker Exegetical Commentary on the New Testament (Grand Rapids: Baker Academic, 2005), 119.
5. Italics added to all Bible citations in this chapter.
6. As John Bainbridge Webster explains, "The bedrock of soteriology is the doctrine of the Trinity" (John Bainbridge Webster, "'It Was the Will of the Lord to Bruise Him': Soteriology in Theological Perspective," in *Soteriology in Theological Perspective*, eds. Ivor J. Davidson and Murray A. Rae [Burlington, VT: Ashgate, 2011], 18).
7. See Adam J. Johnson, *Atonement: A Guide for the Perplexed*, Guides for the Perplexed (London: Bloomsbury T&T Clark, 2015), 82.

willed to enable the sacrifice. Within this intratrinitarian life, there exists a relational and functional distinction between the three persons.[8] The Father is the Father based on his relationship with the Son. The Son is the Son based on his eternal generation from the Father. To put it another way, "Because Father, Son, and Spirit are God, everything that is true of the Father is true of the Son and the Spirit *except* for their particular relationships."[9] These relationships are not broken in Christ's death, though some make this suggestion.[10] A fissure in these relationships would mean that the triune God ceases to exist.

Scripture discusses the atoning work of Christ by highlighting the work carried out by each person of the Trinity. We should not infer from these distinctions that the Father, Son, and Spirit divided this work among themselves. The three persons of the Trinity are involved in the distinctive work of each person so that "the works of God are indivisible."[11] Such interrelated involvement makes atonement possible. Moreover, in this unified and distinctive work of the triune God, the divine attributes displayed in Christ's atonement are not opposed to one another. The triune God is not "composite" but "altogether simple" (*divine simplicity*). It follows that the love of God revealed in the death of Christ is not opposed to his wrath or vice versa.[12] Instead, God fiercely loves the sinner in his righteous wrath to the point that he offers his Son as an atoning sacrifice.

The Father Sends, Gives, and Vindicates His Son

Scripture often describes the Father's atoning action through the motif of *sending* the Son. The Father lovingly *sent* his Son to save sinners from sin, death, Satan, and eternal judgment. He sent the Son so that, through his work, sinners might be reconciled to the Father and flourish as his children through a knowledge of him and his Son (John 3:16–17; 10:10; 17:3).[13] Jesus frames his identity and ministry as the Son *sent* by the Father (John 20:21).

---

8. Thomas H. McCall explains, "The three divine persons are genuinely distinct; the Father is really distinct from the Son and Spirit—he does not merely appear to be distinct but really is so within the intratrinitarian life. But what makes divine persons distinct from one another is only the relationships that hold between the three persons" (Thomas H. McCall, *Forsaken: The Trinity and the Cross, and Why It Matters* [Downers Grove, IL: IVP Academic, 2012], 33).
9. Beth Felker Jones, *Practicing Christian Doctrine: An Introduction to Thinking and Living Theologically* (Grand Rapids: Baker Academic, 2014), 69.
10. See, e.g., Jürgen Moltmann, *The Crucified God: The Cross of Christ as the Foundation and Criticism of Christian Theology* (1972; repr., Minneapolis: Fortress, 1993), 152.
11. Jones explains, "An ancient rule governing trinitarian speech helps us talk about God's oneness: the works of God are indivisible. This rule recognizes that God's unity is such that any work that God does is the work of all three persons of the Trinity" (Jones, *Practicing Christian Doctrine*, 71).
12. Aquinas, *Summa Theologiae*, 1.3.7.
13. Adam Johnson stresses that God's atoning work is both "from" and "for" something (Johnson, *Atonement*, 38–43).

The Father also *gives* the Son, or *hands him over*, to death. John's well-known statement exemplifies this motif: "For God so loved the world, that he gave his only Son, that whoever believes in him should not perish but have eternal life" (John 3:16). John quantifies the Father's love for sinners in the sense that he "gave what was most dear to him."[14] Paul describes this giving as a "handing over" in the sense that the Father handed over his Son to death like an enemy handed over to judgment.[15] As Paul expresses it rhetorically, "What then shall we say to these things? If God is for us, who can be against us? He who did not spare his own Son but *gave him up* for us all, how will he not also with him graciously give us all things?" (Rom. 8:31–32).

The Father's work does not end with *sending* and *giving* the Son. He also vindicates his Son by raising him from the dead. The resurrection affirms the Son's relationship to the Father and the Son's work in the Father's name. As Peter declares at Pentecost, "For you will not abandon my soul to Hades, or let your Holy One see corruption" (Acts 2:27; Ps. 16:10).

The Obedient Son Gives Himself over to Death

The Father sends, hands over, and vindicates the obedient Son. While the Father hands the Son over to death, the Son also hands himself over. As Paul explains: "I have been crucified with Christ. It is no longer I who live, but Christ who lives in me. And the life I now live in the flesh I live by faith in the Son of God, who loved me and gave himself for me" (Gal. 2:20). Jesus describes his self-giving as a ransom. It is a price paid through death that frees those enslaved to sin, Satan, and death (Mark 10:45). The biblical witness neither states nor implies that the Father had to convince the Son to give his life. He is a thoroughly willing participant. Even in anticipating the gravity of this work on the night of his arrest, the Son shows his willingness to die an incomprehensibly painful death by praying, "Abba, Father, all things are possible for you. Remove this cup from me. Yet not what I will, but what you will" (Mark 14:36).[16] While some interpreters have detected here an incongruity between the wills of the Father and of the Son, the opposite is true. Jesus's prayer reflects the degree to which he felt the sting of his impending death, the degree to which he was tempted to acquiesce, and the degree to which he

---

14. Leon Morris, *The Gospel according to John*, New International Commentary on the New Testament (Grand Rapids: Eerdmans, 1995), 204.

15. This is clear in Romans where Paul describes God "handing over" (παραδίδωμι, Rom. 1:24, 26, 28) idolatrous creatures to judgment while also "handing over" (παραδίδωμι, Rom. 4:25; 8:32) his Son to death.

16. As William Lane observes, "Fully conscious that his mission entailed submission to the horror of the holy wrath of God against human sin and rebellion, the will of Jesus clasped the transcendentally lofty and sacred will of God" (William L. Lane, *The Gospel according to Mark*, New International Commentary on the New Testament [Grand Rapids: Eerdmans, 1974], 518–19).

was resolved to do his Father's will. Some mystery remains in all of this that we will discuss further in Question 40.[17]

The words of Jesus from the cross also reflect the Son's trust and obedience. His cry, "My God, my God, why have you forsaken me?" signals the Father's genuine abandonment of the Son (Ps. 22:1; Matt. 27:46). Denial of abandonment altogether drifts toward Docetism, which argues that the Son is "a purely divine being who only had the 'appearance' of being human."[18] To say that the Father only abandoned the Son in his humanity is to drift toward Nestorianism, which is the "radical separation of the two natures of Jesus so that there were virtually two persons, two Christs."[19] This is not abandonment with respect to the eternal relations of the Father and the Son as if a break within the Trinity occurred at the moment of Jesus's death, by which the triune God would cease to exist. The Father abandoned his Son to death. He left him to die. Nevertheless, the eternal Son did not experience a break in his relationship with the Father. The Son entrusted himself to the Father: "Father, into your hands I commit my spirit" (Luke 23:46; Ps 31:5). Jesus's combined laments from Psalms 22 and 31 reflect his trust in the Father despite being abandoned to enemies and to death. The Son's dying words reveal the grand truth that the plan orchestrated by the Father, who abandoned him to death, did not break their filial bond.[20]

The Spirit Leads, Fills, and Vindicates the Son in His Atoning Work

In his inaugural sermon, Jesus reads from Isaiah 61: "The Spirit of the Lord is upon me" (Luke 4:18; Isa. 61:1). The statement is indicative of the NT's wider description that underscores the Spirit's presence with Jesus from his conception to his resurrection. The Spirit comes upon Mary, resulting in the conception of the Son (Luke 1:35), and the Spirit comes upon the Son at the Jordan River, inaugurating his mission (Matt. 3:16; Mark 1:10; Luke 3:22). The Spirit *leads* the Son, *fills* him, and even *thrusts* him into the wilderness where he is tempted by Satan (Matt. 4:1; Mark 1:12; Luke 4:1). The Spirit's presence throughout Jesus's ministry implies his presence in the event of the cross. The

---

17. As J. I. Packer insists, "How strong was his temptation to say 'amen' after 'take away this cup from me,' rather than go on to 'nevertheless not what I will, but what thou wilt' (14:36 KJV), we shall never know" (Packer, *Knowing God* [Downers Grove, IL: InterVarsity Press, 1993], 192).

18. Alister E. McGrath, *Christian Theology: An Introduction*, 2nd ed. (Oxford: Blackwell, 1994), 568.

19. James Leo Garrett Jr., *Systematic Theology: Biblical, Historical, and Evangelical*, 2nd ed. (North Richland Hills, TX: Bibal, 2000), 616. As Beth Felker Jones describes it, "Nestorian Christology looks at Jesus's actions and tries to sort out which nature is responsible for each" (Jones, *Practicing Christian Doctrine*, 130).

20. Thomas H. McCall lays out what should be affirmed and avoided in discussions on Jesus's cry of dereliction (McCall, *Forsaken*, 42–47).

Spirit continually "mediated to Jesus the presence of the Father."[21] The Spirit's mediating work did not insulate the Son from suffering. To the contrary, the Spirit mediated an experience of the Father comprised of "death, forsakenness, judgment, and expulsion."[22] However, the same Spirit mediated the Father's vindication of the Son by raising him from the dead. Paul describes the Spirit as the one "who raised Jesus from the dead" (Rom. 8:11), though, of course, not to the exclusion of the Father (1 Cor. 6:14).

Summary

The Father, Son, and Spirit willed the atonement. The work can be carried out because of the triunity of God. The Father sends his Son, hands him over to death, and vindicates him through the resurrection. The Son willingly participates in this work by handing himself over to death and trusting in the Father who abandons him to death. The Spirit leads, fills, and vindicates the crucified Son by raising him from the dead in accordance with the Father's faithfulness to the Son and the Son's trust in the Father. Though we talk about these actions separately, the three persons of the Trinity do not work in isolation from each another. This triune God is involved in Christ's atoning work in a way that reflects relational unity, distinctiveness, and unfailing love for sinners.

REFLECTION QUESTIONS

1. Why should we reject the notion that Christ's atoning work was plan B?

2. What is problematic about believing a "break" occurred within the Trinity at Jesus's death?

3. How does the triunity of God make atonement possible?

4. What does the Father's abandonment of the Son reveal about the relationship between them?

5. How does the Spirit participate in the Father's giving and vindicating his Son?

---

21. Johnson, *Atonement*, 82.
22. Johnson, *Atonement*, 82.

What Does Christ's Atoning Work Reveal About God's Character?

And I heard every creature in heaven and on earth and under the earth and in the sea, all that is in them, saying, "To him who sits on the throne and to the Lamb be blessing and honor and glory and might forever and ever!"

~Revelation 5:13

In John's glimpse of eternal worship, he witnesses the praise of both "the one who sits on the throne" and "the Lamb." The latter description occurs repeatedly in Revelation as a christological title that keeps before the reader's eyes the centrality of Jesus's sacrificial death.[1] This death is central to understanding the character of Jesus and the one who sits on the throne and receives worship forever. In short, Christ's atoning work reveals the character of God that in turn elicits eternal praise. But what, specifically, does Christ's atoning work reveal about God's character?

Before answering this question, two stipulations are in order. First, in consideration of the doctrine of divine simplicity, the triune God does not consist of parts. Therefore, although we will discuss here a "plurality of divine attributes," it does not follow that God consists of different characteristics that he slips in and out of.[2] When Scripture highlights one attribute of God, or when it indicates that a particular divine action reveals a particular attribute, it does not cancel other attributes. As Steven J. Duby notes, "In his boundless

---

1. "Lamb" (*arnion*) as a reference to Jesus occurs twenty-eight times in Revelation.
2. On the relationship between divine simplicity and the "plurality of divine attributes" ascribed to God in Scripture, see Steven J. Duby, *Divine Simplicity: A Dogmatic Account*, T&T Clark Studies in Systematic Theology 30 (London: T&T Clark, 2015), 179–234.

perfection, each of God's attributes is really identical with his essence, and each of the divine persons is really identical with the divine essence subsisting in a certain manner."[3] Second, what follows is not an exhaustive description of what Jesus's death reveals about God's character, because an exhaustive description is simply out of everyone's theological reach. Jesus's atoning work in fact has a mysterious element that includes what his death reveals about God (Question 40).

The Revelation of God's Holiness in Atonement

God is set apart from what he creates prior to and following the rebellion at Eden. Prior to that rebellion, God welcomed those made in his image into his holy presence. He gave Adam and Eve dominion over his very good creation (Gen. 1:27–29). However, the first couple forfeited access to God's holy presence, and thereby share in his rule, by exchanging trust in God's word with trust in the serpent's word. Their expulsion from the garden marks the first of many instances in which God separates himself from that which is unholy.

Among these instances, the holiness that God requires of Israel stands out. He inundates the nation with expressions of his holiness and commands: "For I am the LORD your God. Consecrate yourselves therefore, and be holy, for I am holy" (Lev. 11:44a).[4] Among the expressions of God's holiness in ancient Israel, nothing matches the sacrificial system established through the Levites. If Israel's holy God were to remain in the nation's presence to provide deliverance, provision, protection, and guidance in their relationship, perpetual atonement would need to be made on their behalf (see Deut. 23:14). Therefore, God provided acceptable agents, sacrifices, times, and places to make such atonement. The Day of Atonement (Yom Kippur) is the quintessential expression of the atonement that God provides that granted Israel the access they needed into God's holy presence (Question 24).

The OT expression of holiness in atonement takes on cosmic and eternal dimensions through the person and work of Jesus Christ. The arrival of the eternal Son in the flesh emphatically reveals what it means to call God "holy" and the degree to which he wants his creatures to share in his holiness and to be holy. Jesus is both the eternal Son of God and man who lives an entirely holy life in keeping with all the acceptable parameters established in the law and the Levitical system that prefigured him (see Mark 1:24; 4:34; John 6:69; Acts 2:27; 13:35). Therefore, he is the acceptable priest, sacrifice, and mercy seat throughout all the ages, whose person and work alone provide access into God's holy presence. Even more, it is through the atoning work of the

---

3. Duby, *Divine Simplicity*, 235.
4. See also Lev. 11:45; 19:2; 20:26; 21:8; 23:20; 1 Sam. 2:2; 6:20; Pss. 22:3; 71:22; 77:13; Isa. 6:3; 1 Peter 1:16; Rev. 4:8.

crucified and risen Christ that believers receive the Holy Spirit whose work renews and ultimately raises saints, or "holy ones," from the dead (see Rom. 8:11; 2 Cor. 4:16). After all, God neither allows his Holy One nor the saints who share in Christ's holiness to undergo decay (Ps. 16:10; Acts 2:27).

Overall, the prefigured and actualized death of Christ implies the value of God's holy presence. Its value can be estimated by what is both required and willingly offered in order to bring sinners back into the presence of a holy God, namely, the death of the eternal Son.

The Revelation of God's Love in Atonement

Both inside and outside of the church, one of the most common descriptions of God is that he is loving. An oft-cited verse in this regard is "God is love" (1 John 4:8). Of course, believers and unbelievers alike often disregard the wider context of John's statement. The immediately following verses specifically qualify God's love according to the incarnation and atoning work of Christ. John in fact ties divine love to the defining purpose and outcome of Christ's death: "In this is love, not that we have loved God but that he loved us and sent his Son to be the propitiation [*hilasmos*] for our sins" (1 John 4:10; cf. 2:1–2). While *hilasmos* has fallen on hard times for various interpretive reasons since the mid-twentieth century, the wider Septuagintal and NT use of this word group conveys two interrelated actions. Jesus's sacrifice both *expiates* sin (i.e., cleanses the sinner) and thereby also *propitiates* God's righteous wrath for sin (i.e., it satisfies divine wrath). If Jesus's sacrifice did not cleanse and satisfy, it neither aligns with its OT precursors nor adequately addresses human rebellion against God's holy and righteous character. Humans would then be left in the proverbial lurch and deprived of a genuine experience of divine love.

In this way, rather than distorting God's love as some suggest or insinuate, the expiating and propitiating quality of Christ's death defines God's love. In fact, one cannot define or understand God's love apart from Christ, who is the propitiation for sinners. God loves people so much that he hands his eternal Son over to death to cleanse them from sin and thereby satisfy his own righteous indignation against them. To say that "God is love" while ignoring or downplaying Christ's atoning death is to eclipse and/or distort his love entirely. To put it another way, one can never truly know God's love apart from the atoning work of Christ. Acceptance of a crucified and risen Christ by faith is the true embrace and experience of God's love.[5]

The Revelation of God's Faithfulness in Atonement

The dynamics of God's faithfulness are simple. God makes a promise and then he completes it, or fulfills it, which consequently demonstrates his

---

5. The NT writers repeatedly tie God's love to Jesus's death (see, e.g., John 3:16; Rom. 5:6–8; 8:31–34).

faithfulness. All of God's promises, and thereby the ultimate demonstration of his faithfulness, are fulfilled in Christ's person and work, which are defined by his death and resurrection. As Paul remarks, "For all the promises of God find their Yes in him [i.e., Christ]. That is why it is through him that we utter our Amen to God for his glory" (2 Cor. 1:20). It follows that Christ's atoning work somehow fulfills all prior promises and thereby reveals God's faithfulness.

How does Christ's atoning work fulfill the promise that one born of a woman would crush the Serpent's head (Gen. 3:15)? His death provides the sacrifice that God requires for the cleansing of sin and the satisfaction of wrath, which places believers on his side so that in the crucified and risen Christ he delivers them from the serpent whom he defeats, disarms, and crushes.

How does Christ's atoning work fulfill the promise of land, glory, and cosmic blessing through Abraham's seed (Gen. 12:1–3)? In his death and resurrection, Christ provides believers with the blessing of redemption from sin, death, Satan, and eternal condemnation. The redemptive blessing encompasses both the promise of cosmic-wide glory through preaching the gospel to the ends of the earth and the promise of land, which is the inheritance of the entire world in the crucified and risen Christ (see Matt. 24:14; Rom. 4:13; 1 Cor. 3:21–23).

How does Christ's atoning work fulfill the promise of an eternal king (2 Sam 7:10–14)? Christ's eternal reign, though planned before the foundation of the world, is revealed and rooted in his death, where Christ endures the divine penalty for sin in place of and on behalf of believers so that the power of sin and Satan can no longer wield the penalty and power of death against them (see John 12:27–33; Heb. 2:14–18; 1 John 3:8). Moreover, his resurrection vindicates the efficacy of his death and establishes his eternal reign as the prophetic and priestly king par excellence. Simply put, the crucified One reigns as the risen One to fulfill what God promised to David.

How does Christ's atoning work fulfill the promise of a new covenant (Jer. 31:31–34)? As Jesus explains at the last meal with his disciples, his body and blood fulfill the eternal sacrificial requirements of God, whereby sin is expiated and propitiated. Jesus then serves as the reason for and the mediator of a new relationship, or covenant, between sinners and God. Moreover, the gift of the Holy Spirit, given after the exaltation of the crucified one, is the assurance of God's faithfulness to the promise fulfilled in the gospel, including what is yet to be experienced by believers (see John 7:39; 2 Cor. 1:22; Eph. 1:13–14).

Overall, then, the question is not so much "How does Jesus's death fulfill God's prior promises and thereby reveal his faithfulness?" The question is, "How can God be faithful to any of his promises apart from the death of Christ?" Although people are not faithful to God, he remains faithful in Christ, because he cannot deny his own faithful character (2 Tim. 2:13). He promised much in Israel's Scriptures, and he completed it all in the atoning work of his Son.

The Revelation of God's Righteousness in Atonement

The crux text here is once again, not surprisingly, Romans 3:21–26. Paul explicitly states that God's "righteousness" (*dikaiosynē*) is revealed in the proclamation of Jesus's death and resurrection (Rom. 3:21; cf. Rom. 1:16–17; 2 Cor. 5:21; Phil. 3:7–11). He sums up the revelation of that righteousness against the backdrop of God who "had passed over former sins" and the juxtaposition of God being both "just" and the "the justifier of the one who has faith in Jesus" (Rom 3:25–26). The phrase "had passed over former sins" signals that God had not brought the full weight of his judgment on sinners until he did so in the crucified Christ. This act fully revealed God's righteousness in two overlapping ways: (1) he fully and righteously judged sin/sinners in the death of his Son, and (2) he fully and righteously makes believers right with him in the crucified and risen Son.

Summary

Simply put, the death of Christ says so much about the character of God. Every word about God is in a sense a cruciformed word, because every divine attribute finds its meaning and expression in a crucified and risen Jesus. It is not possible to understand, or responsibly discuss, God's holiness, love, faithfulness, righteousness, and the rest apart from the death of Christ. The reason that John, through the Spirit, sees eternal worship directed to both the One who sits on the throne and the Lamb is the perichoretic (intertwining/interpenetrating) character of God, which is only explained in the death of the Son. As John concludes at the end of his prologue, "No one has ever seen God; the only God, who is at the Father's side, he has made him known" (John 1:18). And the center of that explanation is cross-shaped.

REFLECTION QUESTIONS

1. What do you think of when you hear about God's attributes such as holiness, love, righteousness, and faithfulness?

2. Why should our thoughts about God's character be "cross-shaped"?

3. What other attributes of God does Scripture discuss?

4. How are those other attributes defined by Jesus's death?

5. What do nonbelievers think about God's character that Jesus's death challenges or corrects?

What Does Christ's Atoning Work Reveal About God's Care for the Church?

Husbands, love your wives, as Christ loved the church and gave himself up for her.

~Ephesians 5:25

While admonishing husbands in Ephesus to love their wives, Paul appeals to the way Christ demonstrated his love for the church through his death. He specifies that Christ "gave himself up," or "handed himself over," for the church, which complements how he expresses elsewhere that God "handed over" his Son (see Rom. 4:25; 8:31; Gal. 2:19–20). The Father and Son in harmony, as testified to by the Spirit, emphatically demonstrate their love for the church in the death of the Son. To be sure, as John famously expresses it, the cross measures the extent of God's cosmic care: "For God so loved the world, that he gave his only Son, that whoever believes in him should not perish but have eternal life" (John 3:16; cf. Rom. 5:8). Although John identifies the "world" as the recipient of God's love, the link between Christ's atoning work and the church presents a unique dynamic of divine care.

Both the Old and the New Testaments testify that God cares for his people. He chooses, calls, guides, provides, delivers, protects, and renews them so they can share in who he is. He demonstrates this care in various ways, such as through supplying believers' physical needs, protecting them from harm, guiding them in the mission that he gives them, cultivating love for others through the Holy Spirit whom he gives, and more. However, Christ's atoning work defines all aspects of God's care for the church in three interrelated ways: (1) atonement is the earthly assurance of God's care; (2) atonement is the eschatological guarantee of God's care; and (3) the church's spiritual gifts are the consequence of atonement.

Atonement as the Earthly Assurance of God's Care

One term often associated with Martin Luther's theology is *Anfechtung*, which, though difficult to translate from German to English, bears the sense of "assault" or "agonizing struggle," at least in the way Luther uses it.[1] Luther faced a variety of afflictions that sparked extensive reflection upon the seeming incongruity between God's promised love, on the one hand, and his seeming absence, on the other. Relief in these scenarios came by way of the cross, as Luther explains in a letter to his dying father: "I commend you to Him who loves you more than you love yourself. He has proved his love in taking your sins upon himself and paying for them with his blood, as he tells you by the gospel."[2] In the face of death, which could be interpreted as God's judgment rather than his care, Luther encourages his father to look at the proof of God's love in the death of Christ. It provides a kind of assurance.

The assurance needed by Luther's father reflects a need of all Christians since the days of the nascent church. Agonizing struggle defines the experience of Jesus's disciples just as he promised, "In the world you will have tribulation" (John 16:33b; cf. Matt. 5:11; 10:17–20; 24:9–10; Mark 13:9–11; Luke 21:12). Assurance in tribulation comes in a variety of forms, including Scripture, God's people, and, of course, the Spirit (cf. Rom. 8:15; 15:4; 2 Cor. 1:3–7). However, whatever form that assurance takes is grounded in, animated by, and connected to Christ's atoning work. As Paul reminded the Christians in Rome, although their afflictions made it appear as if God has abandoned them like sheep to the slaughter, God did not spare his Son but "handed him over" for them (Rom. 8:31–35). Therefore, God was emphatically "for them" and nothing could separate them from God's love, of which he assured them in the crucified and risen Christ (Rom. 8:36–39) (Question 35). Paul argues from "the greater" (God reconciling himself to sinners through Christ) "to the lesser" (God graciously giving what is needed in the face of ongoing affliction). The revelation of God's eternal care in the atoning work of Christ provides assurance of his care in everyday life. As Paul explains, "He who did not spare his own Son but gave him up for us all, how will he not also with him graciously give us all things?" (Rom. 8:32).[3]

---

1. See Alister E. McGrath, *Luther's Theology of the Cross: Martin Luther's Theological Breakthrough* (Oxford: Blackwell, 1990), 170.
2. Martin Luther, *Letters of Spiritual Counsel*, trans. Theodore G. Tappert (Vancouver: Regent College, 2003), 32.
3. Autobiographical fragments in Paul's letters provide examples of the link between God's care during earthly affliction and his eternal gift in Christ (see, e.g., 2 Cor. 1:8–11; 12:6–10; Phil. 2:25–30).

Atonement as the Eschatological Assurance of God's Care

While believers need assurance of God's care in everyday life, they also need assurance as they look toward the "day of the Lord" (Question 38). Despite attempts to mitigate the importance of the Final Judgment in some expressions of Christian theology, Scripture discusses the moment at length. As Fleming Rutledge observes, "Whatever our cultural biases may be, it is incontrovertible that the imagery of condemnation at the bar of judgment pervades the Bible."[4] One can speak about God's wrath for sin without being guilty of blanket and silly caricatures such as N. T. Wright's inflammatory suggestion that those who sing "And on the cross, when Jesus died, the wrath of God was satisfied" inevitably give the impression that God is a "bloodthirsty tyrant."[5] The NT writers do not frighten their audiences by depicting God as a tyrant; however, they also do not gloss over what lies ahead, namely, inevitable final judgment. As the writer of Hebrews plainly states, "And just as it is appointed for man to die once, and after that comes judgment" (Heb. 9:27).

Given this inevitability, assurance for God's care on the last day is a necessity. It is not an anachronistic imposition on the NT to suggest that early Christians had a concern about the last day.[6] Such concern is reflected in Romans 5:9–10: "Since, therefore, we have now been justified by his blood, much more shall we be saved by him from the wrath of God. For if while we were enemies we were reconciled to God by the death of his Son, much more, now that we are reconciled, shall we be saved by his life." The prepositional phrase "by the death of his Son" summarizes the assurance to the Christians in Rome that God will care for them and express his love to them on the last day. God's atoning work in Christ provides the assurance they need for their inevitable appearance before him in judgment. It is an assurance for all who confess that "Jesus is Lord" and believe that "God raised him from the dead" (Rom. 10:9).

The Spirit and Gifts as the Consequence of Atonement

The Holy Spirit testifies to and actualizes God's care for the church. Due to Christ's atoning work, the church received both the Spirit and spiritual gifts so that God's people might *share in* and *share with* others the benefits of the atonement. John makes this connection with descriptions of the Spirit, such as, "Now this he said about the Spirit, whom those who believed in him were

---

4. Fleming Rutledge, *The Crucifixion: Understanding the Death of Jesus Christ* (Grand Rapids: Eerdmans, 2015), 313. Rutledge offers a biting critique of the present culture's disdain for "judgment" language of any kind: "In our present culture, 'judgmental' has become one of the worst things that can be said about a person. We seem to have lost the ability to understand 'judgment' as having any positive connotation" (pp. 312–13).
5. N. T. Wright, *The Day the Revolution Began: Reconsidering the Meaning of Jesus's Crucifixion* (New York: HarperOne, 2016), 38–39.
6. See, e.g., Acts 10:42; Rom. 2:1–16; 14:10–12; 2 Cor. 5:10; 2 Tim. 4:1; 1 Peter 4:17–19; Rev. 20:11–15.

to receive, for as yet the Spirit had not been given, because Jesus was not yet glorified" (John 7:39).[7] The latter phrase, "not yet glorified," is Johannine shorthand for glorification that proceeds from Christ's death.[8] One result of Jesus's atoning work in the glory of his death and resurrection is the gift of the Spirit who indwells the earth and believers "on his behalf and in his name."[9]

The Spirit bears witness to believers about their status before God, which is rooted in Christ's atoning work. As Paul asserts, "For you did not receive the spirit of slavery to fall back into fear, but you have received the Spirit of adoption as sons, by whom we cry, 'Abba! Father!'" (Rom. 8:15). With the same divine vocative in Galatians, Paul draws a direct line between the incarnate Christ's atoning death, adoption, and the lament of the Spirit: "But when the fullness of time had come, God sent forth his Son, born of woman, born under the law, to redeem those under the law, so that we might receive adoption as sons. And because you are sons, God has sent the Spirit of his Son into our hearts, crying, 'Abba! Father!'" (Gal. 4:4–6).

The link between God's care, Christ's atoning work, and the gift of the Spirit is also characterized by spiritual gifts. These gifts build up the body of Christ toward its completion and fullness (see 1 Cor. 14:26; Eph. 4:11–16) in bearing the image of Christ presently and eschatology.[10] At the same time, the Spirit's presence and the gifts he gives in Christ help the body carry out its commission to the world (Matt. 28:16–20; Acts 1:7–8).

The gifts are not additions to Christ's atoning work but rather divinely empowered expressions of it. Those expressions are most evident in the love those within the body of Christ have for one another (see 1 Cor. 13:1–13). At the same time, love for one another in the church as an expression of Christ's atoning work is a key element of disciple making. As Jesus tells his disciples, "By this all people will know that you are my disciples, if you have love for one another" (John 13:35). This testimony of love, however, is only effective

---

7. The exact location of this OT citation is uncertain. Possibilities include Isa. 43:19 or Ezek. 47:1–12. See the discussion in Leon Morris, *The Gospel According to John*, rev. ed., The New International Commentary on the New Testament (Grand Rapids: Eerdmans, 1995), 375–76.

8. See, e.g., John 8:54; 11:4; 12:16, 23, 28; 17:1; 21:19. As Jörg Frey observes in his reflection on John's motif of glory, "Those who believe in Jesus through the word of the witnesses (17.20), i.e., not least the readers of the Gospel (19.35; 20.31), are to perceive Jesus's δόξα — the glory of the crucified one" (Jörg Frey, *The Glory of the Crucified One: Christology and Theology in the Gospel of John* [Waco, TX: Baylor University Press, 2018], 237).

9. As Christopher R. J. Holmes maintains, "Jesus's ascended presence is as intensive as his earthly presence because of the Spirit's testimony and indwelling on Christ's behalf and in his name" (Christopher R. J. Holmes, "The Atonement and the Holy Spirit," in *The T&T Clark Companion to Atonement*, ed. Adam J. Johnson [London: Bloomsbury T&T Clark, 2017], 92).

10. On completion in the church as bearing the image of Jesus in the church, see Rom. 8:28–30; Eph. 4:11–16.

inasmuch as loving disciples preach the gospel. Here the Spirit likewise shows his care for the church by empowering its proclamation of Jesus's atoning work in the gospel.[11]

Summary

Although Christ is the propitiation for the sins "of the whole world," it is the community of believers who ultimately experience the benefits of his atoning work (1 John 2:1–2). That atoning work defines the church's perception of how God cares for his people. He roots present and eschatological assurance of his care in the cross at Golgotha with all the benefits that flow from it. Likewise, the Spirit's presence and gifts are indissolubly linked to Jesus's atoning work. The glorification of the crucified one results in the arrival of the Spirit who works to conform those in the body to the image of the suffering and glorified One.

REFLECTION QUESTIONS

1. Why do people need assurance that God cares for them in everyday life?

2. How is God's care for the church defined by Christ's atoning work for it?

3. What is the relationship between Christ's atoning work and the work of the Spirit?

4. What are your perceptions of the last day, and how should the atoning work of Christ inform those perceptions?

5. How does the church find assurance of God's care for it on the last day?

---

11. See the link between the Spirit and preaching Christ's atoning work in Acts 4:8–12 and 2 Cor. 3:4–18.

Questions About Christ's Atoning Work and the Christian Experience

How Does Christ's Atoning Work Inform the Suffering of Christians?

For as we share abundantly in Christ's sufferings, so through Christ we share abundantly in comfort too.

~2 Corinthians 1:5

Paul assures the Corinthians that both the sufferings of Christ and the comfort of Christ are in abundant supply. With all the transparency it can muster, the NT informs believers that suffering will define their Christian experience. While not devoid of joy and hope, suffering nonetheless marks the believer and the church. Jesus makes this clear: "Then they will deliver you up to the tribulation and put you to death, and you will be hated by all the nations for my name's sake" (Matt. 24:9). Paul also makes this clear: "Indeed, all who desire to live a godly life in Christ will be persecuted" (2 Tim. 3:12; cf. Rom. 8:17; 2 Cor. 1:3–7).

This inevitable suffering described in the NT comes in various forms, including ongoing struggles with sin, ecclesiastical infighting, false teachers, cultural ostracism, seizure of property, Satan, the power of death, and more (see Rom. 7:7–25; 1 Cor. 1:10–17; Heb. 10:32–39; 1 Peter 4:1–6; 1 John 1:5–2:2). To be sure, there is overlap between what believers and nonbelievers suffer. Believers and unbelievers alike live in a world under God's wrath and ruled by Satan, though not outside of God's ultimate power (see Rom. 1:18–32; 2 Cor. 4:1–6; Eph. 2:1–3). However, Christian suffering is unique with respect to how believers experience the power of sin, the reality of their guilt, the work of the tempter, the promise of new creation in which God's righteousness dwells, conformity to Christ's suffering, and sharing in Christ's suffering. This unique experience of suffering has marked all generations of

Christians up to the present day because it is an inherent and defining trait of the Christian life.[1]

What, though, is the relationship between this defining quality of the Christian life and the defining work of Christ's atonement? Scripture draws some links between the two even if they are sometimes underappreciated.[2] We will explore three of these links here: (1) atonement and the clarification of Christian suffering, (2) participation in Christ's atoning suffering, and (3) atonement and the limitation of Christian suffering.

Atonement and the Clarification of Christian Suffering

Paul famously declares in his letter to the Romans, "There is therefore now no condemnation for those who are in Christ Jesus" (Rom. 8:1). Yet, a few paragraphs later, even as Paul maintains the removal of condemnation, his catalog of afflictions includes experiences associated with God's judgment of his people in the OT: "Who shall separate us from the love of Christ? Shall tribulation, or distress, or persecution, or famine, or nakedness, or danger, or sword?" (Rom. 8:35; cf. Deut. 28:48, 53; Isa. 8:22; Jer. 5:12; 11:22; 24:10). Even more, Paul follows his list with a citation from a psalm of lament in which the speaker cries out to God on behalf of the believing community in the face of inexplicable divine rejection: "As it is written, 'For your sake we are being killed all the day long; we are regarded as sheep to be slaughtered'" (Rom. 8:36; Ps. 44:22; see also 2 Cor. 4:7–15). These pieces of Paul's argument indicate his awareness of a seeming incongruity between the promise that those who are in Christ no longer face divine condemnation and the reality of Christian suffering that bears a striking resemblance to divine condemnation.

In response to this seeming incongruity, Paul clarifies that the Christians in Rome are not suffering because of God's condemnation against them. He grounds that clarification in the atoning work of Christ. Paul first makes this clarification toward the beginning of this epistolary section (Rom. 5:1–8:39) where he explains that suffering ultimately leads to hope of God's love rather

---

1. As C. F. D. Moule put it some time ago in reflecting on Christians and non-Christians alike, "Suffering in some measure is the lot of us all" (C. F. D. Moule, *Suffering and Martyrdom in the New Testament* [Cambridge: Cambridge University Press, 1981], 1).

2. Secondary literature offers some treatments. E.g., Bruce L. McCormack offers a brief discussion of atonement and the "problem of human suffering." However, he presupposes that most forms of suffering are unrelated to sin: "Human suffering has many sources, many if not most unrelated to sin. Growth, degeneration, decay, and death are natural to the finite creature in this world that is passing away—and suffering is part of that experience, an ever-present feature of life" (Bruce L. McCormack, "Atonement and Human Suffering," in *Locating Atonement: Explorations in Constructive Dogmatics*, eds. Oliver D. Crisp and Fred Sanders [Grand Rapids: Zondervan Academic, 2015], 206–7). I am presupposing the opposite here. All human suffering has some relationship to human sin, either directly or indirectly. Death is not natural from a scriptural perspective. Rather, "the sting of death is sin" and permanently removed at the parousia (1 Cor. 15:55–56).

than the prospect of his condemnation (Rom. 5:1–5). He then grounds that explanation in the atonement, which he evokes through a reference to Jesus's blood and death: "Since, therefore, we have now been justified by his blood, much more shall we be saved by him from the wrath of God. For if while we were enemies we were reconciled to God by the death of his Son, much more, now that we are reconciled, shall we be saved by his life" (Rom. 5:9–10; cf. 1 Thess. 1:10; Col. 1:21–23). Paul revisits this dynamic toward the end of this epistolary section, where he draws out the implications of God's sovereignty for believers in the face of their suffering (Rom. 8:28–30) and prefaces his catalog of afflictions with an assurance of God's favor, given the atoning work of Christ (Rom. 8:31–34).

Believers' angst regarding what their suffering implies about their standing before God is not an imposition upon Paul's thought energized by the troubled consciences of later Pauline interpreters such as Augustine and Luther.[3] It can reflect the experiences of Christians from the first to the twenty-first centuries. Nevertheless, Christ's atoning work clarifies that, although some reasons can be offered for why Christians suffer, God's condemnation is not one of them.[4] Jesus suffered condemnation in his flesh for believers; therefore, what they suffer in their own flesh is not God's condemnation (see Rom. 8:1–4).

Participation in Christ's Atoning Suffering

In summing up parts of Paul's preaching and ministry, Luke observes the following: "When they had preached the gospel to that city and had made many disciples, they returned to Lystra and to Iconium and to Antioch, strengthening the souls of the disciples, encouraging them to continue in the faith, and saying that through many tribulations we must enter the kingdom of God" (Acts 14:21–22). However, although tribulations are necessary, they are not experienced alone; they are experienced with Christ. Just as the full experience of inheriting the blessings of redemption are experienced with Christ, suffering prior to that inheritance is shared with him. As Paul tells the Romans, "The Spirit himself bears witness with our spirit that we are children of God, and if children, then heirs—heirs of God and fellow heirs with Christ, provided we suffer with him in order that we may also be glorified with him" (Rom. 8:16–17). Many of the NT's descriptions of suffering with Jesus include references to his crucifixion and thereby his atoning work. It follows that those who participate in Christ's sufferings participate in his suffering that brings atonement. What, though, is the nature of this participation

---

3. This claim, and others like it, has been popular in some circles of interpretation since Krister Stendahl's seminal essay: "Paul and the Introspective Conscience of the West," *Harvard Theological Review* 56 (1963): 199–215.

4. The NT points to some instances wherein God disciplines believers, either for correction or maturation, which can include afflictions of some kind; however, divine discipline and divine condemnation are not one and the same (see, e.g., 1 Cor. 11:27–32; Heb. 12:4–11).

in relation to Christ's atoning work? Three salient points emerge from our reading of the NT.

First, to suffer with Christ is to suffer the denial of self-justification, which Christ's atoning work overturns. Those outside Christ justify their actions before people, but God sees them as they are. Jesus rebukes his opponents for such self-justification: "You are those who justify yourselves before men, but God knows your hearts. For what is exalted among men is an abomination in the sight of God" (Luke 16:15; cf. Luke 10:29; 18:9–14). The antithesis of self-justification is suffering with Christ by daily "picking up" the cross upon which he carried out his atoning work (Luke 9:23). Jesus here does not call for mere imitation but the exchange of self-justification, or the attempt to save one's own life, with his gracious work of atonement, which the cross encapsulates (Luke 9:24–27). Participation with the crucified Christ by faith is at the same time to suffer the denial of all attempts at self-justification, the very attempts for which Christ died.

Second, to suffer with Christ is to bear witness to his suffering that atones for sin. Paul describes his apostolic hardships by observing, "We are afflicted in every way, but not crushed; perplexed, but not driven to despair; persecuted, but not forsaken; struck down, but not destroyed; always carrying in the body the death of Jesus, so that the life of Jesus may also be manifested in our bodies" (2 Cor. 4:8–10). In discussing Paul's imagery here, Mark Seifrid observes, "The sufferings of Jesus are reenacted in his apostles, and so is his resurrection."[5] Paul preaches the atoning death of Christ and suffers for that preaching, which in turn complements the preaching itself.

Third, participating in Christ's suffering involves a death to the very things for which Jesus died to take the penalty for sinners' rebellion against God and thereby deliver them from sin, death, Satan, the world, and the divine judgment that these entities are slated to experience. Paul sums up this aspect of suffering with Christ toward the close of Galatians: "But far be it from me to boast except in the cross of our Lord Jesus Christ, by which the world has been crucified to me, and I to the world" (Gal. 6:14). As Tom Schreiner writes:

> It is legitimate to speak of Christians in general here, for surely Paul's experience reflects the experience of all believers. The answer to the problem of humanity is death, but the death of believers is in the cross of Christ, for they have been crucified with him (2:20), so that the passions and desires of the flesh have now been crucified (5:24).[6]

5.   Mark A. Seifrid, *The Second Letter to the Corinthians*, Pillar New Testament Commentary (Grand Rapids: Eerdmans, 2014), 208.

6.   Thomas R. Schreiner, *Galatians*, Zondervan Exegetical Commentary on the New Testament (Grand Rapids: Zondervan Academic, 2010), 379.

Moreover, Paul sometimes points to the suffering and death of Christ as an example that believers must painfully follow. For example, in addressing Christian husbands at Ephesus, Paul exhorts, "Husbands, love your wives, as Christ loved the church and gave himself up for her" (Eph. 5:25).

Atonement and the Limitation of Christian Suffering

Although believers participate in the sufferings of Christ, their suffering does not atone for sin.[7] Only Christ's death has that effect due to the hypostatic union that characterizes his unique person and work. The God-man alone suffers in a way that expiates and propitiates sin. Believers then share in the benefits of his atoning work by faith and suffering (i.e., a faith that suffers). They trust in the atoning value of Christ's work and follow him so that they ultimately suffer because of that trust.

Summary

Suffering defines both Christ and those who live in him by faith. In fact, the eschatological and eternal share in the benefits of Christ's atoning work hinges upon whether one suffers in him by faith (Rom. 8:17; cf. 2 Cor. 4:10; 2 Tim. 2:3). Although specific afflictions can vary among believers, as evidenced in the variety of afflictions faced by the recipients of the NT letters, all afflictions ultimately stem from the interrelationship of sin, death, Satan, and the prospect of final judgment. Of course, God's atoning work in Christ secures forgiveness, gives life, defeats Satan, and justifies believers now and on the last day.

Nevertheless, believers continue to live in unredeemed bodies with partial understanding of God's work in Christ in an evil age ruled by Satan. Consequently, though buoyed by the gospel's promise of God's atoning work in Christ, believers are still afflicted by the very things that Christ overcame on their behalf. What emerges is an experience in which believers must trust in Christ's atoning work, on the one hand, and on the other hand, they must suffer with him in a way that reflects that suffering that Christ underwent in accomplishing that atoning work.

REFLECTION QUESTIONS

1. Why does the suffering of Christians not have the same atoning value as Christ's suffering?

---

7. Some interpreters have misunderstood Paul's view of suffering in this manner. See, e.g., Albert Schweitzer, *The Mysticism of Paul the Apostle* (Baltimore: Johns Hopkins University Press, 1998), 147.

2. What is the difference between the moral exemplar theory of atonement (Question 10) and Christian suffering that mimics the suffering that Christ underwent to atone for sin?

3. How might a Christian's suffering cause them to doubt the atoning value of Christ's suffering?

4. What is the common characteristic of every believer's suffering?

5. If Christ's suffering reconciled believers to God, why do believers still suffer?

Is Christ's Atoning Work Efficacious for All Sins?

If anyone see his brother committing a sin not leading to death, he shall ask, and God will give him life—to those who commit sins that do not lead to death. There is a sin that leads to death; I do not say that one should pray for that.

~1 John 5:16

The focus here is not on the well-worn discussion of *limited* versus *unlimited* atonement (Questions 15, 21, and 22). Rather than focusing upon groups for whom Jesus's atoning work is efficacious, we will focus our attention on the sins for which Jesus died. The question, "Is Christ's atoning work efficacious for all sins?" implies a distinction between sins.[1] Scripture makes such distinctions, so that the adage "sin is sin" may need to be modified. Followers of Christ commit sins both before faith in Christ and afterward, which qualifies as a distinction. Scripture sometimes distinguishes intentional, or "high-handed," sins from unintentional ones (see Num. 5:21; Heb. 10:26). The NT warns about a sin that "leads to death," versus sin that does not (1 John 5:16). We also find a warning regarding the sin that "will not be forgiven" (Matt. 12:31).[2] Moreover, we must consider the relationship between

---

1. In the Roman Catholic tradition, sins are divided according to *venial* and *mortal*. "One commits *venial* sin when, in a less serious matter, he does not observe the standard prescribed by the moral law, or when he disobeys the moral law in a grave matter, but without full knowledge or without complete consent" (*CCC* 1862). Contrastively, "For a sin to be *mortal*, three conditions must together be met: 'Mortal sin is sin whose object is grave matter and which is also committed with full knowledge and deliberate consent'" (*CCC* 1857).
2. See also Mark 3:28–29; Luke 12:10.

Jesus's atoning work and the sins of unbelievers who have never heard a message of forgiveness in Christ.

We will consider these concerns in three movements: (1) atonement for sin prior to and after faith, (2) atonement and the unpardonable sin, and (3) atonement within exclusivism, inclusivism, and pluralism.

Atonement for Sin Prior to and After Faith

"For by a single offering he has perfected for all time those who are being sanctified" (Heb. 10:14). This is a comprehensive statement that indicates Jesus's sacrificial death is eternally efficacious for believers' sins both before and after faith.[3] The perfect tense verb *teteleioken* ("he has perfected") combined with the phrase *eis to dienekes* ("forever") stresses that Jesus's sacrificial death on the cross has an ongoing effect upon those whom God has set apart by faith.[4] The crucified Jesus provides complete atonement in the sense that his work expiates and propitiates all believers' sins, past, present, and future.

However, the comprehensiveness of this atoning work does not justify further acts of sin. Such a disposition betrays either a person's misunderstanding and/or falsification of Christ's atoning work (Matt. 1:18; Rom. 6:1–4; James 2:14–26). In his person and work, Christ both saves *from* and *for*. He saves *from* sin and all that accompanies it (death, Satan, judgment), and he saves *for* a new life in him marked by faith, hope, love, and the fruit of righteousness (1 Cor. 13:1–13; Phil. 1:11). To deny one is to deny the other. Therefore, one should not presume upon Jesus's atoning work for future sins by consciously and intentionally committing more of them.

Nevertheless, sin remains a real problem for believers as they live in bodies that have not yet experienced the full redemption pledged to them through the Spirit (see Rom. 8:9–11, 23–25; 2 Cor. 1:22; Eph. 1:14). The very existence of the NT epistles testifies to the early church's ongoing struggles with sin, as authors routinely address a host of wide-ranging transgressions. Even more, Paul defines the internal life of all believers as a battleground wherein the Holy Spirit is in constant conflict with the flesh (Gal. 5:13–26; cf. Rom. 7:7–25). The latter does not refer to the notion of a materially evil body but rather to a mode of existence dominated by the powers of sin and death that define the present evil age (Rom. 7:7–25; Gal. 1:4).

When this internal battle is momentarily—never consistently nor permanently—won by the flesh, Christ is the believer's advocate who secures forgiveness. As John asserts, "My little children, I am writing these things to you

---

3. Those within a Christian tradition that practices paedobaptism often employ the phrase "postbaptismal sin."

4. As Paul Ellingworth explains, "The perfect tense joins with the following phrase to emphasize the permanent effects of Christ's sacrifice" (Paul Ellingworth, *The Epistle to the Hebrews*, New International Greek Testament Commentary [Grand Rapids: Eerdmans, 1993], 511).

so that you may not sin. But if anyone does sin, we have an advocate with the Father, Jesus Christ the righteous. He is the propitiation for our sins, and not for ours only but also for the sins of the whole world" (1 John 2:1–2). John grounds atonement for believers who sin in the propitiating work of the crucified and risen righteous One. To put it another way, since Jesus is an eternal sacrifice and the high priest whose work is grounded in the cross, he perpetually serves as the source of atonement for believers who sin (Heb. 7:25).

Atonement and the Unpardonable Sin?

Although the psalmist boasts that God casts people's sin "as far as the east is from the west," Jesus still speaks of an "eternal sin" (see Ps. 103:12). The "eternal," or "unpardonable," sin is the blasphemous denial of the Holy Spirit's testimony about the crucified and risen Jesus: "Truly, I say to you, all sins will be forgiven the children of man, and whatever blasphemies they utter, but whoever blasphemes against the Holy Spirit never has forgiveness, but is guilty of an eternal sin" (Mark 3:28–29; cf. Matt. 12:31; Luke 12:10). Therefore, the sins of either denying the Spirit's testimony about Jesus and/or consciously turning from him are unforgiveable. What, though, are the implications of an unforgivable sin for Christ's atoning work? Is there no atonement for the unpardonable sin? If not, what are the implications with respect to the efficaciousness of Christ's atoning work?

Hebrews once again proves helpful. Here, the author addresses an unidentified group of believers who, due to their afflictions, seem poised to consciously turn from Christ in favor of a return to the "ways of the old covenant."[5] As the author accentuates Christ's superiority to the old covenant and all that accompanies it, he makes the following sober announcement: "For if we go on sinning deliberately after receiving the knowledge of the truth, there no longer remains a sacrifice for sins, but a fearful expectation of judgment, and a fury of fire that will consume the adversaries" (Heb. 10:26–27). Given the wider context of the ancient homily, the phrase "a sacrifice no longer remains for sin" assumes that only Christ's sacrifice is efficacious for sin. Therefore, if the recipients are insistent upon turning away from Christ, they simultaneously turn away from the only sacrifice that can atone for their sin.

In this way, the only sin that Jesus's work does not atone for is the sin of ultimately rejecting his atoning work by rejecting him. This does not imply an inherent deficiency in Jesus's atoning work. Rather, it accentuates its value. God forgives all sin except the sin of rejecting the very agency and means by which he reconciles sinners to himself. Therefore, from a biblical-theological perspective, when the psalmist uses the picturesque language of casting our sins as far as the east from the west, readers should assume the

---

5. Karen H. Jobes, *Letters to the Church: A Survey of Hebrews and the General Epistles* (Grand Rapids: Zondervan Academic, 2011), 29.

exception of the unpardonable sin (Ps. 103:12). Interestingly, the psalmist himself qualifies God's forgiveness by noting he is compassionate to those who "fear him" (Ps. 103:13, 17).

Atonement Within Exclusivism, Inclusivism, and Pluralism

What, though, are we to conclude about unbelievers who never hear about the atoning work of Christ? If forgiveness is contingent upon consciously responding to the announcement of his merciful work in Christ, how can they respond if they never hear (Rom. 10:14–15)? It is reasonable to conclude from the historical record that countless people have died without hearing the gospel of Jesus Christ. Is it possible that Jesus's death atones for the sins of those who never heard his name? Answers to this question often occur within a wider debate between exclusivists, inclusivists, and pluralists.[6] As Millard Erickson explains, "Exclusivism is the view that Christianity is true and that only those who overtly subscribe to its beliefs and practices receive salvation."[7] Such a view is largely grounded in readings of NT texts such as Jesus's assertion: "I am the way, and the truth, and the life. No one comes to the Father except through me" (John 14:6; cf. John 11:25; Acts 2:21; 4:12; Rom. 10:14–15; Heb. 10:20). It has also been the dominant position of the Christian church for centuries, even if it has seen an uptick in contemporary criticism.[8]

With respect to how atonement functions within exclusivism, or particularism, much hinges upon what brand of exclusivism is in view. For example, while Karl Barth holds that salvation is only possible through Christ, he envisions "the ultimate eschatological victory of grace over unbelief" so that "all come to faith in Christ."[9] It follows that Christ's atoning work is efficacious for all people regardless of whether they hear the gospel. On the other hand, if an exclusivist requires unbelievers to hear the gospel, or at least denies Barth's quasi-universalism, then Christ's atoning work is not necessarily efficacious for those who have not heard the gospel. It is here that one may have to humbly acknowledge a divine mystery, including the mystery of how Christ's work might atone for those who have never heard about Jesus, especially when universalism, inclusivism, pluralism are not viable options (Question 40).

Of course, inclusivists and pluralists might suggest there is a way beyond the mysterious impasse. Inclusivism finds Christ's atoning work efficacious for those who participate in non-Christian religions and have never heard

---

6. See, e.g., Mara Brecht, "What's the Use of Exclusivism?" *Theological Studies* 73 (2012): 33.

7. Millard J. Erickson, *Introducing Christian Doctrine*, ed. L. Arnold Hustad, 3rd ed. abridged (Grand Rapids: Baker Academic, 2015), 322.

8. Brecht, "What's the Use of Exclusivism," 36–37.

9. Alister E. McGrath, *Christian Theology: An Introduction*, 2nd ed. (Oxford: Blackwell, 1994), 533.

the gospel. Such a group is what Karl Rahner famously called "anonymous Christians."[10] These are individuals who "experienced divine grace," which is grounded in Christ's atoning work, "without even knowing it."[11] By contrast, pluralists regard all religious traditions as equal and sufficient for leading to the same God; therefore, the question of whether Christ's atoning work is efficacious for those who never heard the gospel, or even rejected it, is moot.

Overall, the problem with any form of universalism, inclusivism, and pluralism is that they run contrary to the biblical witness and large swaths of the Christian tradition. If Jesus does not change, then it remains that his exclusivist soteriology remains in place. No one can enter eternal life apart from faith in him (see John 3:36; 14:6; Acts 4:12). Moreover, without such a soteriology, the message of the early church and many portions of the NT become nonsensical.

Summary

Prayer sometimes functions as the clearest indication of what someone believes. When Jesus taught his disciples to pray, he included the ongoing confession of sin, "Give us this day our daily bread" (Matt. 6:11). The prayer instruction signals Jesus's understanding that his followers would sin even after his atoning death and resurrection. It follows that Jesus atones for all sin at any time. However, the assurance of forgiveness through God's atoning work in Christ is not divine carte blanche to sin (see Rom. 6:1–4; Gal. 5:19–21).

The one sin for which Christ does not atone is the unbeliever's rejection of the Spirit's testimony to him. This exception does not undercut the efficacy of Christ's atoning work. Rather, it enhances its value as the adjudicating factor on the day of judgment. That factor even holds true for those who never hear the gospel; however, Scripture does not clearly reveal how God's justice works in this instance. It simply leans into the fact that he is eternally just.

REFLECTION QUESTIONS

1. How does Christ atone for sins committed after a believer's conversion?

2. What are some of the explanations that you have heard regarding the so-called unpardonable sin?

---

10. McGrath, *Christian Theology*, 535; Karl Rahner, "Christianity and the Non-Christian Religions," in *Theological Investigations, Volume 5: Later Writings*, trans. Karl-H. Kruger (London: Darton, Longman and Todd, 1966), 115–34.
11. McGrath, *Christian Theology*, 535.

3. If someone asked you about the eternal destination of those who have never heard the gospel, how would you respond?

4. From a scriptural standpoint, why are inclusivism, universalism, and pluralism problematic?

5. Why does sin remain a problem for believers and how does Christ's atoning work help?

QUESTION 37

Does the Atoning Work of Christ Reconcile People to One Another?

For he himself is our peace, who has made us both one and has broken down in his flesh the dividing wall of hostility.
~Ephesians 2:14

Much of our thinking about Christ's atoning work is vertical in nature. Concerns related to God's reconciliation of himself to sinners understandably dominates the conversation. Scripture places such reconciliation at the heart of its instruction on atonement. Nevertheless, folded into that instruction is a neglected but integral aspect of reconciliation with God, namely, the effect of Christ's atoning work on the enmity that has existed between people since the rift between Adam and Eve which is followed by Cain's murder of Abel (Gen. 4:1–16). Both in my own cultural setting of North America and in many cultures around the globe, enmity between people is especially palatable today. Social media platforms have amplified and accelerated divisions that exist between people with respect to politics, religion, the arts, sexuality, science, and so much more. Given this amplification, there is an acute need to see how vertical conceptions of the atonement are related to horizontal ones.

Caution is prudent here. Expressions of tolerance, inclusion, acceptance, and freedom of expression that violate the biblical parameters of these virtues are seemingly slated to become the cardinal virtues of the twenty-first century. There is a temptation to understand the horizontal dimensions of Christ's atoning work through this prism of newfound virtue. Of course, it is only when biblical texts are ripped from their contexts and read in isolation from Christian orthodoxy that Christ's atoning work becomes a hollow pretense for an equally naïve vision of human reconciliation. Just as the vertical dimension of Christ's atoning work has clear parameters and specific

253

requirements, so too does the horizontal dimension. Therefore, qualification and explanation are necessary for answering the question, "Does the atoning work of Christ reconcile people to one another?"

Reconciliation Within the Body of Christ Alone

True, God-given reconciliation between human beings only exists within the church as it holds to Christ who alone atones for their sin. The actual cessation of enmity between God and sinner through Christ must precede, animate, and facilitate the cessation of enmity between people. Paul's discussion of horizontal reconciliation proceeds along these lines.

In Ephesians 2:11–12, perhaps the key text for this issue, Paul intertwines God's reconciliation to sinners with reconciliation between Jews and Gentiles. The preceding movement of Paul's argument features an abbreviated reference to how God reconciles himself to those who are dead in sin, under Satan's power, and under God's wrath (Eph. 2:1–3). Such individuals were made alive with Christ and saved by grace (Eph. 2:5, 8). Paul then teases out one of the results of this reconciliation between God and people, which is reconciliation between Jew and Gentile:

> For he himself is our peace, who has made us both one and has broken down in his flesh the dividing wall of hostility by abolishing the law of commandments expressed in ordinances, that he might create in himself one new man in place of the two, so making peace, and might reconcile us both to God in one body through the cross, thereby killing the hostility. (Eph. 2:14–16)

Paul does not suggest that Christ merely serves as an example of reconciliation between Jews and Gentiles. The phrases "in his flesh," "through the cross," and "having killed" indicate that Jesus's death produces horizontal reconciliation just as it does vertical reconciliation. However, the horizontal and vertical differ at the point of source and order. The source of reconciliation between human beings is reconciliation with God; therefore, the latter must precede and animate the former.

It follows that the church is the only place on earth where people are truly reconciled to one another. Those reconciled in both senses comprise the spiritual dwelling place of God upon the earth. God constructs that dwelling place on the atoning cornerstone of Christ and the foundation of the prophets and the apostles who announced that atoning work so that Jews and Gentiles alike might be reconciled to God and to one another (Eph. 2:19–22).

Ongoing Hostility Between the Church and the World

Christ's atoning work clearly reconciles believers to one another. However, he does not reconcile believers to unbelievers, though he calls for the former to love the latter. The enmity between an unbelieving world and those who are in Christ has at least two definitive characteristics.

First, unbelievers remain unreconciled to God and therefore the church remains unreconciled to unbelievers. As James summarily insists in his rebuke of an early Christian congregation: "You adulterous people! Do you not know that friendship with the world is enmity with God? Therefore whoever wishes to be a friend of the world makes himself an enemy of God" (James 4:4; see also Rom. 8:7; 1 John 2:15). Clear lines of demarcation remain between the church and the world. Those lines are predicated on more than incongruous morals and values. To be sure, the NT writers admonish those who are in Christ to conduct themselves in a way that reflects wisdom and faith in the gospel (see Eph. 5:15). Nevertheless, these writers assume requisite faith in Jesus and his atoning work. It follows that what ultimately separates the world from the body of Christ is the former's lack of faith in the crucified and risen Christ. Unbelievers remain in their sin, so they remain guilty and under divine condemnation (see Rom. 1:18–32; Eph. 5:6; Col. 3:6; Rev. 19:15). This separation often results in open hostilities by the world against the church; however, such open hostility must not move in the opposite direction, that is, from the church against the world (see John 15:18).

Second, given their condemnation before God, unbelievers remain under Satan's power, from which only the crucified and risen Christ can deliver them; therefore, unbelievers cannot be reconciled to believers, because unbelievers are aligned with the "god of this age" rather than the God who made heaven and earth (see 2 Cor. 4:4). Paul thus warns the Corinthians: "Do not be unequally yoked with unbelievers. For what partnership has righteousness with lawlessness? Or what fellowship has light with darkness? What accord has Christ with Belial? Or what portion does a believer share with an unbeliever?" (2 Cor. 6:14–15; see also 1 Cor. 10:2).

The Ministry of Atonement in Christ

It does not follow that the enmity between believers and unbelievers should result in the former's withdrawal from the world. As Paul clarifies for the Corinthians, "I wrote to you in my letter not to associate with sexually immoral people—not at all meaning the sexually immoral of this world, or the greedy and swindlers, or idolaters, since then you would need to go out of the world" (1 Cor. 5:9–10). Paul commanded withdrawal from those who claimed to be in Christ and yet lived in sexual sin (1 Cor. 5:11–13). Alternatively, engagement with unbelievers is crucial to the loving ministry of reconciliation that Jesus gave to the believing church.

Paul explicitly frames his ministry in terms of proclaiming a "word of reconciliation" between sinners and God that is grounded in Christ's atoning work: "All this is from God, who through Christ reconciled us to himself and gave us the ministry of reconciliation [*diakonian tēs katallagēs*]; that is, in Christ God was reconciling the world to himself, not counting their trespasses against them, and entrusting to us the word of reconciliation [*ton logon tēs katallagēs*]" (2 Cor. 5:18–19). The noun *katallagē*, along with its Latin translation *reconciliatio*, often rendered in English as "reconciliation," is of course the term William Tyndale rendered as "at-one-ment."[1] Paul links his "ministry," or service, of reconciliation to a "word" that reconciles sinners to God, namely, the gospel of the crucified and risen Jesus (see also Rom. 1:16–17; 10:5–15; 1 Cor. 1:18–31; Col. 1:21–23). To be sure, the believing church should reflect God's atoning love in Christ (see John 13:35). However, that reflection cannot eclipse the proclamation of the gospel that Paul refers to here as a "word" that reconciles God to sinners who believe, for that word reveals Christ's atoning work.

Ecclesiastical Mitigation of Proclaiming Christ's Atoning Work

This emphasis upon the proclamation of Christ's atoning work and its soteriological value is lacking among some contemporary reflections on atonement and the church's engagement with the world. One example of this mitigation will have to suffice here.

In his work titled *A Community Called Atonement*, Scot McKnight's frustration with "an old-fashioned atonement theology that does not make a difference" minimizes the church's primary responsibility of proclaiming the saving benefits of Christ's atoning work.[2] McKnight measures the value of a church's atonement theology according to whether it produces loving Christian communities who reflect human-to-human reconciliation through Christ. He operates with the "dialectical assumptions" that the kind of atonement a church preaches shapes that church and the kind of church one has shapes the atonement that it preaches.[3] "Dialectical" refers to a way of thinking about something from perspectives that clash with one another, and in that clash a new way of understanding emerges. With this kind of thinking in tow, McKnight sets out to deconstruct "one-sided theories of atonement," such as penal substitutionary atonement.[4] He does not eschew the latter altogether; however, he aims to "baptize" it into "the larger redemptive grace of God more adequately."[5] For McKnight, this larger picture of atonement features "atoning moments" of which Christ's cross ultimately restores "cracked Eikons [i.e., image bearers] to union with God and communion with others."[6] McKnight explains, "God designed the moments of atonement to deal a deathblow

---

1. Alister McGrath, *Christian Theology: An Introduction*, 2nd ed. (Oxford: Blackwell, 1994), 566.
2. Scot McKnight, *A Community Called Atonement*, Living Theology (Nashville: Abingdon, 2007), 2.
3. McKnight, *A Community Called Atonement*, 5.
4. McKnight, *A Community Called Atonement*, 62.
5. McKnight, *A Community Called Atonement*, 43.
6. McKnight, *A Community Called Atonement*, 62.

to evil and therefore to restore cracked Eikons to be Christ-like Eikons by drawing them into union with God and communion with others."[7] In this all-encompassing understanding of atonement, the church's mission is itself atoning and consists of fellowship "where we are healed with one another," justice "where we are healed with the world," and missional presence and activism "where we engage others to be healed through the story of Jesus."[8]

McKnight's concerns are admirable. It is true that churches should reflect the love of Jesus and that one's view of the atonement can impact how well or poorly we do that. Nevertheless, to borrow from McKnight's golf bag analogy, which he employs to describe the variety of atonement views, his overall argument is a swing and a miss.[9] It "misses" for at least two reasons. First, individual and thereby communal incorporation into Christ does not take place without repentance from sin which is not a point of emphasis in McKnight's work. A conscious turn away from sin toward God's revelation in Christ is required for "incorporation" into him and his people (see Mark 1:14–15; Luke 10:13; 11:32; 15:7, 10; 16:30; Acts 2:38; 8:22). Along these same lines, McKnight does not emphasize the church's responsibility to preach Christ as the apostles did, namely, calling their listeners to believe in the crucified and risen Lord. Second, McKnight burdens the church in its mission, suggesting that atonement is something the church does with God for others.[10] In fairness to McKnight, he acknowledges, "But lest I be accused of something worse than heresy, let me make it clear up front: I do not believe humans atone for others and I do not believe humans can atone for themselves."[11] Nevertheless, by amplifying the church's missional "praxis" as fostering a community of faith that reflects God's atoning work of restoring broken "eikons," McKnight perhaps, and unintentionally, runs the risk of replacing the power of the preached gospel with the power of a loving community.

---

7. McKnight, *A Community Called Atonement*, 78.
8. McKnight, *A Community Called Atonement*, 117. McKnight notes what he perceives as a larger and more encompassing view of atonement mirrors the aims of the so-called New Perspective on Paul. McKnight insists, "The New Perspective, in other words, gives new shape to the story of atonement. It might be easiest to suggest that the Reformation told the story of an individual, soteriological understanding of atonement and the New Perspective wants to tell an *individual, ecclesial,* and *soteriological* story of justification" (McKnight, *A Community Called Atonement*, 91).
9. E.g., In his analysis of Rom. 3:21–26, McKnight explains, "Because the cross figures in most of what follows, I will simply sample this one text as we move onward in our construction of a bag big enough to hold all of the atonement clubs" (McKnight, *A Community Called Atonement*, 64).
10. McKnight explains, "I stand here on the threshold of a doorway that few enter: atonement is something done not only by God for us but also something we do with God for others" (McKnight, *A Community Called Atonement*, 117).
11. McKnight, *A Community Called Atonement*, 119.

Summary

The question we have been wrestling with here illustrates that sometimes order and emphasis matter in doctrine. Reconciliation between human beings in the church and in the world must be preceded by individual reconciliation between God and the sinner. The latter requires repentance, faith, and a cry to Jesus for salvation. Those who are at enmity with God are neither reconciled to him nor incorporated into him and his people apart from hearing the gospel and responding in faith. Moreover, reconciliation through faith in God's work in Christ must remain the point of emphasis for believers who are reconciled to one another. Simply put, horizontal reconciliation is eternally supported through vertical reconciliation.

REFLECTION QUESTIONS

1. Why do you think reconciliation between human beings is sometimes overlooked in discussions on the atonement?

2. What are some key biblical texts that inform our understanding of reconciliation between people?

3. How might an emphasis on reconciliation between humans enhance our understanding of Christ's atoning work?

4. What are the risks in discussing human-to-human reconciliation through Christ?

5. Why does reconciliation between believers and unbelievers in Christ not work?

Questions About Christ's Atoning Work and Eschatology

What Is the Relationship Between Christ's Atoning Work and Final Judgment?

Do not marvel at this, for an hour is coming when all who are in the tombs will hear his voice and come out, those who have done good to the resurrection of life, and those who have done evil to the resurrection of judgment.

~John 5:28–29

Scripture frequently describes the judgment doled out on the last day as an action that God performs based upon the "good" and/or the "bad" things that people did over the duration of their lives.[1] Despite the insistence of some, this "judgment according to works" involves believers and unbelievers alike.[2] This description of judgment seems to stand in tension with texts that assure believers of salvation by grace through faith, such as Paul's assurance to the Ephesians: "For by grace you have been saved through faith. And this is not your own doing; it is the gift of God, not as a result of works, so that no

---

1. See, e.g., Ps. 62:2; Prov. 11:31; 24:12; Matt. 12:36–37; Rom.; 2:6; 1 Cor 3:8; 4:5; 2 Cor 5:10; Col. 3:25; 1 Peter 1:17; Rev. 20:12.
2. Some within the Christian tradition argue that believers will appear at a judgment for rewards but not at final judgment in which God adjudicates on eternal life. See, e.g., Robert N. Wilkin, "Christians Will Be Judged according to Their Works at the Rewards Judgment, but Not at the Final Judgment," in *Four Views on the Role of Works at the Final Judgment*, ed. Alan P. Stanley, Counterpoints: Bible and Theology (Grand Rapids: Zondervan Academic, 2013), 25–50. However, the exegesis promoted by Wilkin strains clear NT teachings that place believers at the final judgment.

one may boast" (Eph. 2:8–9).[3] The frame for this discussion is often the relationship between faith and works.[4] However, I want to ask here an adjacent question that will further inform our understanding of atonement.

Simply put, "What is the relationship between Christ's atoning work and Final Judgment?" To ask it another way, if Christ's atoning work reconciles believers to God, what does a person's final judgment according to their works imply about Christ's work? Is his atoning work insufficient for the believer on the day of judgment? Does his work merely afford believers an opportunity, or even the power, to do the works that God will approve on judgment day? Or are there dimensions of Christ's atoning work that are not diminished by judgment according to works but further defined by and enhanced by it?

The Proleptic Nature of Christ's Atoning Work

We have noted at various points in the preceding questions that the NT writers portray the benefits of Jesus's atoning work in a proleptic manner.[5] *Prolepsis*, that is, bringing the future benefits of Christ's atoning work into the present, here refers not to rhetorical or grammatical features.[6] For example, Wolfhart Pannenberg often described the resurrection of Jesus as a proleptic event. Panneberg, while stating how the incarnate and risen Jesus "mediates the creation of the world and executes God's royal leadership," avers:

> All such statements anticipate something that will be shown to be real before the eyes of all only in the eschatological future, even though it has already happened to Jesus. This *proleptic* (italics added) structure constitutes the inadequateness, the provisionalness of all Christological statements. After all, we derive the words with which we speak of the

---

3. See also John 6:29; Acts 15:10–11; Rom. 3:24; 1 Cor. 1:30–31; Gal. 2:15–16; 2 Tim. 1:9; Titus 3:5.
4. E.g., Alan P. Stanley asks, "So here is the basic tension we have uncovered: the Bible teaches that people are justified by grace through faith in Jesus Christ and yet will be judged according to their works. Are we to conclude, then, that the Bible has created for itself an intolerable impasse? Or should we resort to prioritizing doctrines? In particular, for the believer, what role do works play at judgment?" (Alan P. Stanley, introduction to Stanley, *Four Views on the Role of Works at the Final Judgment*, 16).
5. The English word *prolepsis* is derived from the Greek noun πρόληψις, which can bear the sense of "anticipation" or a "concept acquired beforehand." See *BrillDAG*, s.v. "πρόληψις."
6. Along these lines, prolepsis can refer to the way that "speech sometimes begins before the idea it intends to express is fully formed" (Gilbert Van Belle, "Prolepsis in the Gospel of John," *Novum Testamentum* 43 [2001]: 339). A grammatical instance of prolepsis is when the subject or object of the subordinate clause is anticipated by the subject or object of the main clause. To put it another way, one that matches our theological concern here, grammatical prolepsis refers to the way the subject-object of a sentence's later subordinate clause is brought into the subject-object of the main clause (see, e.g., John 8:54).

eschatological reality that has appeared in Jesus from the experience of a reality that is not yet the reality of the *eschaton* (emphasis in original).[7]

As Ted Peters summarizes Pannenberg on this point, "The Easter resurrection of Jesus is the prolepsis—that is, a concrete anticipation—of a larger reality yet to come in the future, namely, the eschatological kingdom of God (the new creation) in which all the dead will rise."[8]

Similarly, the *risen* crucified One is the "concrete" anticipation of God's favorable judgment toward the believer on the last day. Jesus's resurrection signals that his Father finds pleasure in, or approves of, his atoning work; therefore, those who are in Christ by faith share in that favorable judgment both now and on the last day.[9] Paul's summary statement in Romans 4:25 is instructive on this point, in which he describes Jesus as one "who was delivered up for our trespasses and raised for our justification." The justification that Paul has in view is proleptic in nature, as the next section of the letter indicates (see Rom. 5:6–11). The assurance of a believer's favorable judgment on the last day is the proleptic judgment now received through and with the *risen* crucified one. As Mark Seifrid maintains, "Our justification in Christ carries us forward to meet our justification before God and the world at the final judgment."[10]

The Purpose of the Believer's Works in Life

What then is the point of works in the meanwhile? If the believer's right standing with God in the present time depends entirely upon Christ's atoning work, what is the purpose of a believer's works in this life? Scripture offers multiple answers.

First, works carried out by faith please God because they are both eternally prepared by him and animated by Christ's atoning work.[11] Paul follows his classic statement of salvation by grace through faith, which excludes human boasting, with the explanation, "For we are his workmanship, created

---

7. Wolfhart Pannenberg, *Jesus—God and Man*, 2nd ed. (Philadelphia: Westminster, 1977), 397. See also Pannenberg, *Jesus—God and Man*, 108, 157, 185, 187, 374, and 391.

8. Ted Peters, "In Memoriam: Wolfhart Pannenberg (1928–2014)," *Dialog* 53 (2014): 367.

9. The divine-pleasure language stems from the divine voice at Jesus's baptism, the transfiguration, and the ironic sarcasm of the mockers at Jesus's crucifixion who jeer, in connection with the mockers in Ps. 22:8: "He has trusted in God, let him deliver him now if he wants him; for he said, 'I am the son of God.'" See also Matt. 3:17; 17:5; Mark 1:11; and Luke 3:22.

10. Mark A. Seifrid, *Christ Our Righteousness: Paul's Theology of Justification* (Downers Grove, IL: IVP Academic, 2000), 184.

11. The NT's definitive statement on the relationship between faith and work may come at the end of Paul's admonition to those who are strong and weak in faith: "But the one who doubts if he should eat has been condemned, because it is not from faith; and everything which is not from faith is a sin" (Rom. 14:23).

in Christ Jesus for good works, which God prepared beforehand, that we should walk in them" (Eph. 2:10). Through his atoning work, Christ creates believers who then participate in the very deeds God prepared for them before they were created in Christ and even before the creation of the world (cf. Eph. 1:4). Paul then lays out the referents of these deeds in the subsequent chapters where his admonitions touch on several ethical spheres, including unity within the church, prayer for understanding the depth of God's love in Christ, obtainment of the "perfect" within the body of Christ, the absence of caustic and dishonest speech, abstention from drunkenness, and the like.[12]

Second, good works distinguish authentic saving faith in Christ from inauthentic faith that does not save. Here the classic text is James 2:14–26. James's axiomatic approach to Christ's atoning work undergirds the discussion.[13] A faith that saves is a faith that works, as demonstrated in Abraham who offered Isaac as a sacrifice and in Rahab who hid Joshua's spies from the king of Jericho (James 2:21–26). In short, the purpose of works is to distinguish faith that authentically shares in the benefits of Christ's atoning work, and thereby saves, and a faith that does not. A mixture of inauthentic and authentic believers existed in the earliest church in keeping with Jesus's teaching; therefore, James found it necessary to distinguish the two.[14] A similar necessity exists in the contemporary church.

Third, works bring glory to God and his atoning work in Christ, which can lead others to share in it. Paul sums up this dynamic in his description of Jesus as one "through whom we received grace and apostleship to bring about the obedience of faith *for the sake of his name* among all the nations" (Rom. 1:5, italics added). Grace (*charis*) here is a theological abbreviation for God's gift of justification before him through the atoning death and resurrection of Jesus, whose person and work provides salvation for those who believe. The phrase "obedience of faith," though disputed among Pauline interpreters, most likely refers to "obedience which is faith" and in turn produces works through the indwelling Spirit that are presently and eschatologically pleasing to God.[15] But they are ultimately pleasing in the sense that they demonstrate the efficacy of Christ's atoning work rather than the efficacy of the believer's work, or "allegiance" as some have asserted.[16]

---

12. As Harold W. Hoehner writes, "But what good works did God prepare beforehand? It is the good works or conduct given in chapters 4–6, that proceed from salvation" (Harold W. Hoehner, *Ephesians: An Exegetical Commentary* [Grand Rapids: Baker Academic, 2002], 349).

13. That James assumes Christ's atoning work is clear in James 1:19–21.

14. For Jesus's teaching regarding authentic and inauthentic faith, see Matt. 7:7:21–27; 13:24–43; John 6:26–29.

15. For a discussion of the phrase εἰς ὑπακοὴν πίστεως ("for the obedience of faith") in Rom. 1:5, see Thomas R. Schreiner, *Romans*, Baker Exegetical Commentary on the New Testament, 2nd ed. (Grand Rapids: Baker Academic, 2018), 40.

16. On "allegiance" to Christ, see Matthew W. Bates, *Salvation by Allegiance Alone: Rethinking Faith, Works, and the Gospel of Jesus the King* (Grand Rapids: Baker Academic, 2017).

The Nature of the Believer's Works in Final Judgment

Scripture is filled with imperatives. The biblical writers sometimes boil these hundreds of commands down to the intertwining admonitions of "believe" and "love." This ethical compression emanates from Christ himself, who, when asked what the "works of God" were, answered, "This is the work of God, that you might believe in him whom he has sent" (John 6:29).[17] And in defining the essence of discipleship, Jesus gave a "new" commandment "that you love one another" (John 13:34). In one of his letters, John combines both of Jesus's admonitions: "And this is his commandment, that we believe in the name of his Son Jesus Christ and love one another, just he has commanded us" (1 John 3:23).

To be sure, faith and love must define the believer's life, because adherence to these commands will be the focus of judgment on the last day (see John 12:48). However, there is also an all-encompassing dynamic that defines believers' lives and the judgment they face, namely, life *in Christ*. We should take seriously Paul's self-description to the Galatians: "I have been crucified with Christ. It is no longer I live, but Christ who lives in me" (Gal. 2:20; cf. Phil. 1:21). It follows that the works believers do in their lives are the result of Christ's presence in their lives. Consequently, judgment according to works on the last day is ultimately a judgment of Christ's work in them, which is indissolubly and eternally bound to his atoning work. Seifrid wonderfully sums up this line of thought:

> Our righteousness therefore is not properly ours, but an alien righteousness given us in Christ: "I live, yet no longer I, but Christ lives in me" (Gal. 2:20a). Consequently, there can be no talk of merit in any form. The "work of faith" and the works which faith produces are God's and not our own. They are the new creation which is already present in Christ. Our justification in Christ carries us forward to meet our justification before God and the world at the Final Judgment.[18]

Summary

Neither faith nor works add anything to the efficacy of Christ's atoning work.[19] Instead, faith in the gospel and the indwelling presence of the Spirit are gifts from God whereby one shares in the benefits of Christ's atoning work.

---

17. As Luther expressed it, "The foremost and noblest good work is faith in Christ" (*TAL*: 1:267).
18. Seifrid, *Christ Our Righteousness*, 14.
19. As Seifrid explains in his discussion of Paul's theology of justification, "Obviously, Paul does not suppose that faith adds something to Christ's death. He also speaks of 'justification by Christ's blood' (Rom. 5:9). Nevertheless, it is only through faith that Christ's death is effective as atonement" (Seifrid, *Christ Our Righteousness*, 134).

The works that ensue are an outworking of sharing in the crucified and risen Christ, whose person and work reconcile believers to God now and on the last day. While it is true that God will judge believers according to their works on the last day, those works are a feature of Christ's atoning work on their behalf. To put it another way, our judgment on the last day is a judgment of Christ's atoning work on our behalf who has already received a favorable judgment through his resurrection and enthronement. Therefore, preparation for our judgment according to works always remains abiding by faith in Christ who is our righteousness, sanctification, and eternal intercessor.

REFLECTION QUESTIONS

1. What do you find confusing about the relationship between Christ's work, faith in him, and a person's final judgment according to works?

2. What is the ultimate role of works in the Christian experience?

3. How do believers sometimes misunderstand the role of works?

4. How does Christ himself prepare us for judgment according to works on the last day?

5. If Christ's atoning work is sufficient for a right standing with God, why are we judged according to works on the last day?

How Does Christ's Atoning Work Impact the New Heavens and the New Earth?

No longer will there be anything accursed, but the throne of God and of the Lamb will be in it, and his servants will worship him.

~Revelation 22:3

I am always fascinated by the christological title John most frequently applies to Jesus in his apocalypse: "the Lamb."[1] It reminds us that no matter how ominous the world may seem or how frightening the future may appear, victory and vindication for God's people is securely grounded in Christ's death and resurrection. "Lamb" in fact specifically grounds this assurance for the church in Christ's atoning work. This atoning work looms large over John's entire apocalyptic vision, which reaches its climax in the appearance of a new heaven and a new earth devoid of the "first things" that caused death and tears (see Isa. 25:8; Rev. 7:17; 21:1–8). The combination of the Lamb, new creation, and the absence of suffering implies that the impact of Christ's atoning work is of cosmic proportions. As T. F. Torrance observes, "Just as the whole of creation was affected by man's fall in sin, so here we have in the death of Christ a cosmic reversal on a scale utterly transcending the fall of mankind and the curse of the world."[2]

---

1. John applies the christological title ἀρνίον ("Lamb") to Jesus twenty-eight times. Interestingly, there is a distinct "turn to the Lamb" in Revelation 5, as the title does not occur prior to Revelation 5:6.
2. T. F. Torrance, *Atonement: The Person and Work of Christ* (Downers Grove, IL: IVP Academic, 2009), 196.

How, though, do we quantify and qualify the impact of Christ's atoning work on the promised new creation? On the one hand, the link between the crucified risen One and the new heavens and the new earth remains beyond our grasp as a mystery (Question 40). After all, it has not yet been experienced in a way that anyone can report back to us.[3] On the other hand, Scripture and the Christian tradition shed some light on the issue that helps us appreciate how far-reaching the effects of the cross really are. The little light that we have serves as a catalyst for the hope with which we were saved (Rom. 8:23–25).

It is ultimately the hope of living in a resurrected body within a new heaven and a new earth (see Rom. 8:18–25; 2 Peter 3:10–13; Rev. 21:1–8). Just as an individual's resurrected body has a material link to one's physical body, the new heaven and the new earth have a material link to the earth we currently live in. Moreover, just as the enjoyment of a resurrected body results from Christ's atoning work, the enjoyment of a new heaven and a new earth does as well. The manner of this impact involves a reversal of the cursed material fabric of the universe so that human beings are reconciled to the world in which righteousness will dwell. And that experience of creation is not merely a return to Eden. It is something even better.

The Cursed Material Fabric of the Universe

In considering how God doled out judgment in Eden, one should not overlook the judgment leveled against the earth: "Cursed is the ground because of you" (Gen. 3:17).[4] God folds this judgment of the earth into his judgment of Adam and Eve. Obviously, the earth is distinct from human beings who are created in God's image; therefore, it does not "suffer" judgment in the way Adam and his progeny do. However, the personified motif of an afflicted material creation is threaded into both Testaments.[5] One finds multiple examples in which an afflicted and cursed creation is intertwined with an afflicted humanity.[6]

---

3. There are underlying questions here about the state of those who die before Christ's parousia and/or the participant's conception/experience of time in relation to God. Two viable possibilities exist: (1) believers who die before Christ's return live in an intermediate state wherein they are with Christ but do not yet enjoy resurrected bodies in all of their fullness, or (2) believers immediately inherit resurrected bodies and experience new creation, even if earthly onlookers can only conceive of a period of time between death and such an experience. See the discussion in Douglas J. Moo, *A Theology of Paul and His Letters: The Gift of the New Realm in Christ* (Grand Rapids: Zondervan Academic, 2021), 543; and J. T. Turner, *On the Resurrection of the Dead: A New Metaphysics of Afterlife for Christian Thought* (New York: Routledge, 2019), 183–216.

4. I am informed here by Torrance's expression "reconciliation with the fabric of the universe" (see Torrance, *Atonement*, 198).

5. See, e.g., the deconstruction of the created order poetically described in Jer. 4:23–31.

6. E.g., ancient Israel's rebellion against God in the OT is sometimes described as a "defilement" of the land (see, e.g., Lev. 18:24–25; Deut. 21:23).

Of course, what stands out protologically and eschatologically is the Noahic flood. Humanity's moral corruption passes a threshold that triggers God's cosmic destruction of the them (see Gen. 6:5–7, 11–13; 7:10–12, 17–24). YHWH used a deluge to kill everything that had the breath of life in it (Gen. 7:22–23). In a parallel manner, the NT writers pattern the eschatological destruction of the earth after the Noahic flood (see Matt. 24:37–39). Rather than a deluge of water, Peter envisions a deluge of fire (2 Peter 3:10–11). It does not follow that the eschatological fire results in the total disappearance of the created order.

Between the protological flood of water and the eschatological flood of fire, the cursed material fabric of the universe experiences countless disasters that afflict both the righteous and unrighteous alike. Scripture itself reports famines, earthquakes, and storms at sea (e.g., Gen. 12:10; 26:1; 41:54; Ruth 1:1). Some of these disasters stem from seminal moments in YHWH's dealings with Israel and its enemies (e.g., Isa. 24:4–13). Some are inexplicable (e.g., Ps. 44:9–26). And some are the "birth pangs" of the eschaton inaugurated by the incarnate Christ and his work. As Jesus explains in his little apocalypse, "For nation will rise against nation, and kingdom against kingdom, and there will be famines and earthquakes in various places. All these are but the beginning of the birth pains" (Matt. 24:7–8; cf. Mark 13:8; Luke 21:11). The "birth pains" metaphor perfectly captures the tension between the pain of the righteous in the presently cursed created order and the hope they have of sharing in the new created order.

Atonement and the Hope of New Creation

Hope for the new created order is grounded in Jesus's atoning work as described in Romans 8:18–27. Paul portrays creation, the children of God, and the Holy Spirit as those who cry out to God in concert with one another.[7] The collective aim of their cry is that God would usher in the eschaton, wherein Jesus's return ultimately results in resurrection from the dead. Paul identifies resurrection, or "redemption of the body," as the hope that the Romans were saved in and it is the hope for the which they "groan" (Rom. 8:23–24).[8] This hope also supplies the referent of the "groanings too deep for words" uttered

---

7. Paul unifies these three figures through his use of *stena* (στενα) root words in Rom. 8:22, 23, and 27, respectively. For an in-depth conversation of the lament language that Paul employs here, see Channing L. Crisler, *Reading Romans as Lament: Paul's Use of Old Testament Lament Language in His Most Famous Letter* (Eugene, OR: Pickwick, 2016), 119–31.

8. See also the link between believers groaning/crying out for resurrection of the body in 2 Cor. 5:2 (στενάζομεν). As Seifrid observes in his analysis of 2 Cor. 5:1–10: "Paul's thought is not distant from that of Romans 8:23–27, where he speaks of the Spirit as interceding for us as the interpreter of our groaning in the hope of the 'redemption of the body'" (Mark A. Seifrid, *The Second Letter to the Corinthians*, Pillar New Testament Commentary [Grand Rapids: Eerdmans, 2014], 225–26).

by the Holy Spirit in accordance with the divine will on behalf of believers who do not know what to pray (Rom. 8:26–27). How then does creation fit into these cries for resurrection from the dead? And what is the connection to Christ's atoning work?

Paul prefaces his comments about the cries of God's children and the cries of the Spirit by juxtaposing two grand truths: (1) those who are in Christ are no longer under divine condemnation; and (2) those who are in Christ must suffer with Christ if they are to be glorified with him in the resurrection from the dead (Rom. 8:1–17). Those in Christ must live in a world shaped by a related tension, namely, that God subjected creation to futility and yet gave it the hope of something beyond the judgment of futility (Rom. 8:19–20).

The language in Romans 8:18–22 evokes several interconnected intertextual strands from the OT, as scholars often note.[9] Most notably, it evokes Genesis 3 and Ecclesiastes 1. The former, as referred to above, includes God's curse against the earth as judgment for humanity's rebellion. The writer of Ecclesiastes then interprets that judgment as "futility" in the sense that creation is meaningless and redundant, given the fact that it outlasts human beings who should in fact rule over it (see Eccl. 1:1–11). Paul then personifies creation as a person painfully and hopefully awaiting the full redemption, or resurrection, of the sons of God (Rom. 8:19). The atoning work of Christ grounds the creation's hope of full redemption in the sense that the children of God are already reconciled to God through faith; therefore, how much more certain is their resurrection from the dead that will usher in a new creation. The collateral damage suffered by creation via God's judgment of it and Adam in Eden is undone by the Second Adam, who reconciles sinners to God and thereby creation to him as well.

Better Than Eden

In his provocative and often overlooked little book titled *Deep Comedy*, Peter Leithart identifies a defining difference between Scripture's conception of history and that of its ancient contemporaries.[10] From the perspectives of ancient writers such as Hesiod and Ovid, history is cyclical and thereby a tragedy in the literary sense. History devolves from the heights of a "golden" age to lesser ones and then makes its way back "up," only to repeat the whole process.[11] Contrastively, Scripture depicts history as moving toward a divinely intended goal and thereby is a comedy in the literary sense. Leithart contends:

---

9. See, e.g., Jonathan Moo, "Romans 8.19–22 and Isaiah's Cosmic Covenant," *New Testament Studies* 54 (2008): 74–89.
10. See Peter J. Leithart, *Deep Comedy: Trinity, Tragedy, and Hope in Western Literature* (Moscow, ID: Canon, 2006).
11. Leithart maintains, "In the classical world, in any case, Hesiod's myth was understood as degenerative. Hesiod's basic framework was taken up by Ovid, who tells the story in

> Against the classical nostalgia for a golden age lost and un-
> likely to be revived, the Bible, beginning with the prophets
> of Israel and continuing into the New Testament, holds out
> the promise of a future age of glory, peace, justice, and abun-
> dance. The last state is not worse than the first. In every way,
> the last state is superior to the first, and infinitely superior to
> the painful evils of the ages between first and last.[12]

What I want to underscore here is Leithart's contention that the "last state" is superior to both the current evil age and even Eden itself.

Although John evokes Edenic imagery to articulate his vision of the new heavens and new earth, it does not follow that either he or any other NT writers perceive the experience as a mere return to life before the fall.[13] Instead, there is a marked improvement in the movement from Eden to the new creation. The "improvement," however, is difficult to define. Is new creation better than Eden because so many more people enjoy unmitigated access to God? Is it an improvement in how we experience the divine presence? Is it better in the sense that the potential for death, sin, and temptation are eliminated? Is it better because the experience can never end in crying caused by separation but only in laughter caused by the eternal experience of the Creator himself?

All of this and much more may define the superiority of the last state to the Edenic one. In any case, what is abundantly clear is that the "improvement" stems from Christ's atoning work. His person and work are the guarantee of eternal forgiveness, the eternal defeat of sin, Satan, the eternal removal of death, and the eternal enjoyment of God himself. In that sense, Christ's atoning work makes the new heaven and earth far better than the first because there is no potential of another "fall" nor subsequent condemnation. The crucified and risen Christ has permanently defeated sin, Satan, and death, though believers do not yet experience all the results of that victory (1 Cor 15:50–58).[14] Moreover, Jesus's death provides the requisite atonement for sin by which believers are justified before God and thereby recipients of God's redemptive blessings (Rom 8:1–11).

Summary

We live in a time where signs of a corrupted creation are all around us. Disease, famine, drought, natural disasters, wars, and so many other sorrows plague the planet. Unfortunately, this is nothing new. Every age of history

---

four ages, apparently to bring out the correspondence with four seasons" (Leithart, *Deep Comedy*, 6).

12. Leithart, *Deep Comedy*, 15.
13. See, e.g., the Edenic imagery in Rev. 2:7; 22:2.
14. Of course, this is not to imply that creation in Gen. 1–2 had a fatal flaw or defect.

is marked by these cosmic corruptions to varying degrees and with various human perceptions of them. The hope of God's people, however, is ultimately not in an upward political trend, withdrawal into the fellowship of one another, or even some ill-conceived notion of escapism. Instead, our hope is in the one who makes all things new. That newness is not something that God creates out of divine thin air. Newness in all its features, including a new creation, stems from the atoning work of Christ himself. His reconciliation of sinners to God signals the dawn of a new creation even if it is currently obscured by the shadow of evil (see 2 Cor. 5:17). That promise of a new creation begins within those redeemed by the crucified Christ. As odd as it may seem, new creation and the death of Christ are inseparable. As Paul told the Galatians, "But far be it from me to boast except in the cross of our Lord Jesus Christ, by which the world has been crucified to me, and I to the world. For neither circumcision counts for anything, nor uncircumcision, but a *new creation*" (Gal. 6:14–15, italics added).

REFLECTION QUESTIONS

1. How does Scripture link human sin to the corruption of the created order?

2. How should Christ's atoning work shape our thinking about eternal life with God?

3. What is the connection between Christ's atoning work and the new creation?

4. How could God's "end" in the new creation be better than its "beginning" in Eden?

5. How does Christ's atoning work fulfill the promise in Genesis 1:31?

What Remains Mysterious About Christ's Atoning Work?

For now we see in a mirror dimly, but then face to face. Now I know in part; then I shall know fully, even as I have been fully known.

~1 Corinthians 13:12

I have come to appreciate those who speak humbly about their understanding of God's atoning work in Christ. References to "mystery" or "hiddenness" often indicate such humility. For example, J. I. Packer and Mark Dever note, "If we bear in mind that all the knowledge we can have of the atonement is of a *mystery* about which we can only think and speak by means of models, and which remains a mystery when all is said and done, it will keep us from rationalist pitfalls and thus help our progress considerably (emphasis added).[1] Georges Florovsky suggests, "The *mystery* of the Cross cannot be adequately expressed in terms such as satisfaction, retribution, or ransom" (emphasis added).[2] The much-maligned Anselm of Canterbury admitted to Boso, "Indeed, it is a matter of certain knowledge that, whatever a human

---

1. J. I. Packer and Mark Dever, *In My Place Condemned He Stood: Celebrating the Glory of the Atonement* (Wheaton, IL: Crossway, 2007), 64.
2. Georges Florovsky, "*In Ligno Crucis*: The Church Father's Doctrine of Redemption Interpreted from the Perspective of Eastern Orthodoxy Theology," in *On the Tree of the Cross: Georges Florovsky and the Patristic Doctrine of Atonement*, eds. Matthew Baker, Seraphim Danckaert, and Nicholas Marinides (Jordanville, NY: Holy Trinity Seminary Press, 2016), 144.

being may say on this subject, there remain deeper reasons, as yet *hidden* from us, for a reality of such supreme importance" (emphasis added).[3]

These admissions echo Paul's well-known admission to the Corinthians that their knowledge of God in Christ was partial.[4] Obviously, Paul was not speaking directly about views of the atonement. Nevertheless, his broad reflection on the mystery of God's work in Christ and its implications for the church can include how God reconciled himself to sinners in the crucified and risen Jesus. The reality is that, in this lifetime, even with the sufficiency of the biblical text and extensive reflection on the matter within the Christian tradition, our knowledge of the atonement remains partial, hidden, and mysterious.

Against the backdrop of this admission, the discussion here could go in several directions, including revisiting issues addressed in previous questions, such as competing views of the atonement, its logic, and its implications. Instead, I want to focus on some nagging questions that have not received much attention up to this point. In this regard, we will limit ourselves to three areas that highlight some aspects of the atonement that remain a mystery: (1) the relationship between Jesus's teaching and his atoning work on the cross, (2) the degree of Christ's atoning suffering on the cross, and (3) the nature of the eternal enjoyment of God's atoning work in Christ.

Atoning Teaching and Atoning Death?

I sometimes tell my students that Jesus's teaching is just as salvific as his death and resurrection. It is a bit of hyperbole that can be easily misconstrued. The point of the statement is to draw attention to the theological gap that often exists between the teaching of Jesus and what we normally associate with his saving work at the cross. That gap was not as wide for Jesus's disciples, who certainly found something salvific in his teaching. When would-be disciples of Jesus began to abandon him after his difficult teaching that only those who consume his flesh and blood will live eternally, he turns to the Twelve and asks, "Do you want to go away as well?" (John 6:67). Peter's response underscores the saving nature of Jesus's teaching: "Lord, to whom shall we go? You have the words of eternal life" (John 6:68; cf. Acts 5:20). Peter's response reminds us that Jesus not only laid down his life to reconcile sinners to God; he also taught toward this end.

---

3. Anselm of Canterbury, *The Major Works*, eds. Brian Davies and G. R. Evans (Oxford: Oxford University Press, 2008), 268.

4. As Richard B. Hays maintains in his analysis of 1 Cor. 13:8–13: "We know only in part and act constantly on the basis of incomplete information. We have no choice about that in this time between the times. The force of verses 8–13, however, is to encourage us to have a sense of humility and a sense of humor about even our gravest convictions and activities" (Richard B. Hays, *First Corinthians*, Interpretation: A Bible Commentary for Teaching and Preaching [Louisville: Westminster John Knox, 2011], 233).

Jesus's teaching in the Gospels often has an atoning, or reconciling, motif. In the Synoptic Gospels, Jesus's teaching on the kingdom of God/kingdom of heaven has at its core a message about God's reconciliation of himself to sinners. Jesus introduces and frames his message along these lines: "The time is fulfilled, and the kingdom of God is at hand; repent and believe in the gospel" (Mark 1:15). While Jesus never explicitly defines the kingdom, we can infer from the Synoptic Gospels that it means something like God's rule and reign in the person of Jesus, so that wherever Jesus is, that is where the kingdom is. It follows that to be rightly related to Jesus is to be rightly related to God and thereby enjoy the benefits of his kingdom.

The means of this right relationship to Jesus is faith expressed through obedience to his teaching; however, such faith is not produced by Jesus's listeners out of thin air (see Matt. 7:21–23; John 15:5). That is because Jesus's teaching is not merely informative but transformative, as illustrated through the miracles that often accompany his teaching. Jesus does not just teach about forgiveness; he demonstrates the power to grant it. He does not just teach about the power of the kingdom; he demonstrates its power through the unnatural multiplication of foods, stilling a storm, driving out demons, restoring health, and raising the dead. In short, the combination of Jesus's teaching and the uniqueness of Jesus as teacher reconciles sinners to God.

But here is where the mystery of the relationship between Jesus's atoning teaching and atoning work related to his death is felt. Does his teaching reconcile sinners to God? Or does his death and all that accompanies it reconcile sinners to God? On the one hand, Jesus's warns his disciples, "Not everyone who says to me, 'Lord, Lord,' will enter the kingdom of heaven, but the one who does the will of my Father who is in heaven" (Matt. 7:21). On the other hand, Jesus explains, "Even as the Son of Man came not to be served but to serve, and to give his life as a ransom for many" (Matt. 20:28). Therefore, does Jesus *teach* the way of reconciliation or *provide* it? Yes. The way through the tension is a life of faith with Christ whose atoning words and deeds are indissolubly and mysteriously bound up with one another. Only those instructed by Christ in the faith share in the atoning benefits of his death, and only those who share in the atoning benefits of his death can truly be instructed by him. And that strikes me as mysterious.

The Degree of Christ's Atoning Suffering

The NT bears witness to the profound suffering Christ endured to reconcile sinners to God. The last week of Jesus's life in the respective passion narratives of the Gospels especially bears this out. He suffers *external* opposition at the hands of the authorities, including the Sanhedrin, the high priest, Pilate, Herod Antipas, and an entire Roman military cohort (see Matt. 26:47–27:31; Mark 14:48–15:21; Luke 22:52–23:38; John 18:2–19:24). Jesus suffers *internal* opposition through Judas's betrayal and the disciples' denial of him, which is spearheaded by Peter's famous denial.[5] There is the emotional toll of fore-seeing and then experiencing this rejection, which is compounded by the anticipation and realization of facing God's wrath, physical torture, actual death, and Satan's temptation and torment. The spiritual and mental anguish moves with Jesus from his lament in Gethsemane to his lament at Golgotha, even as he moves toward the later willingly.

In keeping with the significance of dying words in antiquity, Jesus's final words from the cross indicate the degree to which he suffered. The Markan and Matthean laments of dereliction imply an experience of divine abandonment, though not a fissure within the Godhead. The Lukan lament for vindication, "Father, into your hands I commit my spirit" (23:46), given the wider perspective of Psalm 31, which Jesus cites, implies a trust in divine vindication, even as the unchecked affliction at the hands of enemies unfolds and challenges such trust (Luke 23:44). Even John's well-known *tetelestai* ("it is finished" [19:30]) expresses the exhaustive and painful efforts of Jesus to complete God's assigned task of reconciliation to sinners. Moreover, when Jesus entrusts his mother to the beloved disciple, one senses the pain of separation from a loved one (John 19:26).

More could be included from the crucifixion scene and the NT's wider engagement with the pain of Jesus's death. Nevertheless, the point here is that even with these vivid descriptions, we lack complete access to what Jesus experienced in this moment and thereby a full understanding of his pain. What Jesus felt, thought, and underwent in his death remains a mystery. Suffering within the hypostatic union that defines Jesus's person and within the eternal unity of the Trinity remains a mystery.

Eternal Enjoyment of God's Atoning Work in Christ

How can the death of a Jewish carpenter from Nazareth secure eternal reconciliation between human beings and God? The NT provides partial answers. Part of its answer involves the unique personhood of Jesus as the God-man. In his divinity, Jesus has the requisite divine power to effectively deal with sin, death, Satan, and divine wrath. In his humanity, Jesus deals impeccably and effectively with the human dilemma in the place where it unfolds, namely, in the body.[6] The NT's answer also lies outside of the incarnation and even prior to the appearance of the created order itself. As John expresses in his apocalypse, Jesus is the Lamb "slain from the foundation of the world" (Rev. 13:8b NKJV). God planned the sacrificial death of Jesus on

---

5. See, e.g., Matt. 26:14, 25, 33, 35, 37, 40, 47, 58, 69, 73, 75; Mark 14:10, 43; Luke 22:3, 47; John 13:2, 26, 29; 14:22; 18:2, 5.

6. As Paul writes, "For the inability of the law, because it was being weak through the flesh, God, by having sent his son in the likeness of sinful flesh and for sin, he condemned sin *in the flesh*" (Rom. 8:3).

a tree before the earth and its trees existed (see Acts 5:30; 10:39; 13:29; Gal. 3:13; 1 Peter 2:24). In this way, God's atoning work in Christ can be enjoyed for all eternity, because such an experience accords with his eternal purposes.

However, just as we do not have access to the degree of Jesus's pain in death, we do not have access to the eternal joy that springs from that atoning work. Such knowledge presently remains beyond our grasp. Besides, understanding may not be the goal at all. To understand all the mysteries of the atonement is to understand God himself. And creatures, even eternally reconciled ones, are not meant to reach a level of understanding whereby they lord over divine knowledge. We and Adam tried that already. That is not to say that our understanding of the atonement will not be markedly improved in the new heavens and the new earth. Surely it will. Believers shall all have a Thomas-like epiphany upon seeing and even touching Jesus's atoning scars. But what lies ahead is not a better understanding of atonement language, theories, and arguments. What lies ahead is an eternal experience of God's atoning love in Christ, which will forever infuse our hearts, minds, souls, and bodies with an inexhaustible joy.

Summary

The mystery of the atonement is not ultimately defined by the complexities of a theory or view; it is defined by the mystery of Christ who is neither a theory nor a model nor a view. He is a crucified, risen, enthroned, reigning, and returning Lord. If Christ is our righteousness, sanctification, wisdom, and redemption, as Paul tells the Corinthians, then he is surely our reconciliation and atonement (1 Cor. 1:30). Therefore, the lingering mysteries of the atonement cannot ultimately be unraveled through better exegesis, analogies, and theories, as important as those are. Rather, the mystery of the atonement is the mystery of Jesus himself. Only when he is revealed will the full scope of his atoning work be revealed. It is no wonder that when John peered into the heavenly throne room he saw an atoning Lamb receiving the worship due him: "Worthy is the Lamb who was slain, to receive power and wealth and wisdom and might and honor and glory and blessing!" (Rev. 5:12).

REFLECTION QUESTIONS

1. Why are we often uncomfortable with the notion of mystery?

2. How can we talk about the mystery of atonement without using mystery as an excuse not to think hard about God's atoning work in Christ?

3. What is the connection between Jesus's teaching and the atonement?

4. What can we know and not know about the degree of Jesus's suffering at the cross?

5. What do you still find mysterious about God's atoning work in Christ?

Scripture Index

4 0 QUESTIONS SERIES

4 0 QUESTIONS SERIES